Studies in Judaism and Christianity

Exploration of issues in the contemporary dialogue between Christians and Jews

Editors
Lawrence Boadt, C.S.P.
Helga Croner
Leon Klenicki
Kevin A. Lynch, C.S.P.

A CHRISTIAN THEOLOGY OF JUDAISM

by
Clemens Thoma

with a Foreword by
David Flusser

translated and edited by
Helga Croner

A Stimulus Book

Paulist Press ∎ New York ∎ Ramsey

Library of Congress
Catalog Card Number: 80-82252

ISBN: 0-8091-2310-X

Published by Paulist Press
Editorial Office: 1865 Broadway, New York, N.Y. 10023
Business Office: 545 Island Road, Ramsey, N.J. 07446

Printed and bound in the
United States of America

Contents

PART II
JESUS CHRIST AND HIS MESSAGE IN THE CONTEXT OF EARLY AND RABBINIC JUDAISM

PART III
JEWS AND CHRISTIANS
SINCE THE TIME OF CHRIST

PREFACE TO THE ENGLISH EDITION

I am indebted to many Jewish and Christian colleagues and friends for their suggestions, questions and references. I also learned a great deal from Dr. David Flusser, Professor of the New Testament period at the Hebrew University of Jerusalem, whose scholarly work on Christianity is well known. He spontaneously offered to write the Foreword to this book.

Joachim Silbermann of Geneva, who takes considerable personal interest in the work of Jewish-Christian relations, made it possible by his generous financial aid for Jewish studies to be taught at the Catholic Theological Faculty of Lucerne, and so scholarly talks between Christians and Jews can take place.

Helga Croner translated the book from the original German, a laborious and intricate task because Jewish primary literature is not always easy to interpret, and Jewish-Christian problems are involved and difficult to render.

This book is divided into paragraphs, indicated by the symbol #. By comparing the sub-titles given in the Contents with the Synopsis of individual paragraphs, the reader can easily look up details and consult the book for cross-references, a feature employed to make the work suitable as a teaching tool.

Clemens Thoma

Synopsis of Consecutively Numbered Paragraphs

ABBREVIATIONS

CN	Codex Neofiti
Mekh	Mekhilta
Mish	Mishnah
TB	Babylonian Talmud
TJ	Talmud of Jerusalem (Palestinian)
Tanakh	Hebrew Scriptures (Torah, Neviim, Ketubim)

Foreword:
Reflections of a Jew on a
Christian Theology of Judaism

This book by the Swiss scholar of Judaistic and Bible studies, Clemens Thoma, is important and admirably fulfills its task of presenting a broadly conceived Christian theology of Judaism. It is also a well-written and informed survey of Jewish intellectual currents, with particular emphasis on the period of the Second Temple. Such information on the Jewish history of thought from a qualified Christian scholar with immediate access to the Jewish sources and knowledge of the relevant modern learned literature is urgently needed. It is a field not well known to most Christian theologians, not even those who like to pass strict judgment on Judaism. In order to discuss competently Judaism and the Jews, an outsider must be capable of combining theological evaluation with historical understanding. That is accomplished by Thoma, and a Christian reader will gain important new insights into Judaism and Christianity. The book is also a serious contribution to the so-called Christian-Jewish dialogue.

Is Christian-Jewish dialogue, as conducted since the Second World War, helpful to Jews? And how much can it contribute toward banning the dangers of antisemitism, which in the past has brought such sorrow and persecution to Jews? Does not the "dialogue" at times create unexpected friction, of a kind already forgotten and now rediscovered? The partners to the conversation tend to define their own religion over against that of the other, emphasizing and underscoring the advantages of their own. Sometimes the dialogue even produces aggressive outbursts. The Jewish partner may be embarrassed in ways that differ from the past. In

1

ns the Christian speaker was well aware of the Jew as
Christian; he meant to break the Jew's "obduracy" and
Conversations in our days are more gentle. Instead of
common heritage of Judaism and Christianity, one at-
tempts to ... t Christianity as a Jewish stance, or even the only one. A
Jew who does not rise to such Christian bait risks the unarticulated reproach of spiritual blindness.

Jewish-Christian dialogue is definitely not meaningful if new anti-
Jewish resentments are stirred up and old ones repeated. Christians in our
day should not yet consider themselves capable of proclaiming the Christian message without even a trace of antisemitism. Even now, directly and
indirectly, we hear from pulpit-theologians of the establishment churches
that Christianity must be "de-judaized." That is an alarm signal which indicates that, deliberately or not, consciously or sub-consciously, representative Christian intellectuals become spokesmen for a modern "anti-
judaism," and that is not without danger. Such anti-Jewish attitudes will
not simply vanish into thin air but will hit the real, living Jew. Hitler's followers, propagating their myth of blood and soil, mocked conscience, that
"Jewish invention." Only a short while ago, we could read in the words of
a well-known theologian that "blood and soil" was a Jewish invention,
now practiced in the state of Israel.

I used to think that modern pseudo-universalism of Christian "de-ju-
daizing" theologians was an expression of sympathy with left-oriented,
pseudo-socialist universalism. I have now recognized, however, that there
are exaggerating theologians of the conservative right who conceive of
communism as a Jewish atheist conspiracy. Such people do not care for ve-
racity at all; they only wish to impress others with their ideology.

In this complex situation, Jewish-Christian dialogue is definitely necessary. It must lend support to that current within Christianity which considers Christian rootedness in Judaism beneficial and finds a good remedy
to strengthen Christian faith in the rediscovery of Christianity's Jewish
components. That should help to resolve a profound crisis within the
Christian religion. Christianity becomes credible only if it can rid itself of
old and new anti-Jewish resentments and sinks ever deeper roots into its
Jewish heritage. That is why a Christian theology of Judaism is very relevant today, and the present volume fulfills that task. It is to be hoped that
further contributions to this topic will follow, even by the author of this
book.

During the second half of the nineteenth century, a pseudo-Christian antisemitism within, for instance, Christian socialist groups began to open its poisonous blossoms. It consisted of an assortment of traditional rabid anti-Jewish motifs grounded in the old Christian teaching, added to a new version of Jew-hatred that did not refer itself to Christianity. Hitler was under the influence of pseudo-Christian as well as non-Christian antisemitism, which also applies to the Nazi movement in general. Modern "Christian-socialist" antisemitism was, structurally speaking, a pseudomorphosis of non-Christian and anti-Christian antisemitism. It was conditioned by lower middle-class, social resentment and partly by a virulent reaction to Jewish emancipation, containing already certain racist components. Additional motifs, however, go back to Greek-Roman antisemitism of antiquity (for instance, the accusation of Jewish misanthropy and Judaism as a world conspiracy). Such motifs were apparently adopted by the antisemites from the deistic arsenal.

A proper evaluation of the Hitler era must definitely take into consideration that its antisemitic ideology was not Christian. We should not speak of Christian guilt for Auschwitz indiscriminately, even though the "final solution" was facilitated by Christian Jew-hatred which prevailed not only in Eastern Europe where the gas ovens were built. We should also heed the fact that some time before the Second World War anti-Jewish attitudes in Christian guise were already greatly attenuated, while believing Christians tended to allow themselves fewer antisemitic remarks. Yet, diminishing anti-Jewish behavior did not go hand in hand with renewed awareness of the Jewish elements of Christianity. All of this implies that Auschwitz should cause Christians to revise and reconsider their position.

It was necessary to set down the above observations in order to get out of the way unfair exaggerations and accusations. Next to the all too human guilt of cowardice, the most important and justified accusation against the churches during the Hitler period is, I think, that the laity— and quite often church dignitaries as well—did not realize that love of neighbor is at the heart of Christianity, as it is of Judaism. Furthermore, most Christians were hardly aware of the Jewish component of Christianity. Had they known of it, such information might have served as a powerful stimulus to many Christians to defend their Jewish brothers and sisters in a "Christian" and devoted way. At that time, however, the average Christian hardly knew that Jesus, Peter and Paul were Jews. The blame must be placed with the theologians, pastors, and teachers of religion who were ignorant of the Jewish matrix of Christianity. The teachers and guardians of the churches were rather too listless and indolent with regard to Judaism and the Jews. That is why we now urgently need a Christian theology of Judaism.

The concept of a "Christian theology of Judaism" contains two related and often intersecting strands which had better be kept apart. The first question is how to cope theologically with the fact that in New Testament times and right up to our day there exists a non-Christian Jewish religion and a non-Christian Jewry. From the beginning of Christianity, that fact caused an ambivalent relationship to Judaism and the Jews. The continued existence of Jews and their religion seemed to call in question the solidity and truth of the Christian religion. How was it to be interpreted that most of the Jews for whom the new message was intended did not accept it? Paul wrestled with this problem in his Letter to the Romans. It is the only New Testament document seriously concerned with the question and responding in a pro-Jewish manner. Paul emphasizes that the election of Israel by grace cannot be abrogated, not even after the Jews refused to believe in Christ. Paul does not attempt to evaluate that continued existence in theological terms, nor the effects of Israel's election by grace. Paul saw non-Christian Jews in the perspective of a future when all Israel will be saved. In my opinion, such an eschatological view is not sufficient for our time; Christian theologians must try to interpret for our day the existence of non-Christian Israel here and now.

In a passage not usually given sufficient attention, Luke deals with the problem from a different angle. Simeon speaks of the child Jesus in the Temple in the following words: "For my eyes have seen your salvation which you have prepared for all nations; the light to enlighten the Gentiles and give glory to Israel, your people. . . . See, he is destined for the fall and for the rising of many in Israel, destined to be a sign that is rejected . . . so that the secret thought of many may be laid bare" (Luke 2:30–35). These words are very instructive from a historio-theological point of view, but they do not touch upon the fate of that part of Israel which does not believe in Christ. Yet, Simeon's words in Luke's Gospel are much better and more profound than other New Testament passages on Israel, with the exception of the Letter to the Romans.

The vexing problem of non-Christian Israel was usually "solved" like the Gordian knot. Israel was pronounced rejected. That all too often was the "final solution" to Gentile Christians. To them must be applied the terrible words: "I tell you that many will come from east and west to take their places with Abraham and Isaac and Jacob at the feast in the kingdom of heaven; but the sons of the kingdom will be turned out into the dark, where there will be weeping and grinding of teeth" (Matt 8:11–13). After the destruction of the Temple (70 CE) and the overthrow of the Bar-kokhba revolt (135 CE), many people considered the great afflictions visited upon the Jews as punishment from God for Israel's rejection of Christ. They even hoped that the Jewish problem would be solved by the physical extinction of the "sons of the kingdom." Still, that did not happen and Israel continues to live. Clemens Thoma correctly points out that a limited toleration of Jews in the Christian Roman Empire and during the Middle Ages indicates their special theological position, while heretics were threatened with total destruction. Jewish liturgical service was permitted while it was forbidden to the heretics. Yet, this "preference" for Jews did not help mitigate their hard life under Christian supremacy. The Church Fathers already developed an ideology according to which the Jew had to serve as a debased witness to the truth of Christianity. Quite often it was due to this ideology that up to the late nineteenth century residential limitations were imposed upon Jews in Europe. The time-span between the granting of full civil rights—which were not even quite so full—to European Jews and the seizing of power by the National Socialists was no more than a few decades.

The existence of non-Christian Jewry presents a trauma to Christian theologians, even assuming that all of them were ready to consider Jews their true brothers in a theological sense, and disregarding the recent a-Jewish and anti-Jewish wave of Christian theology. The impact of this trauma cannot be compared to the existence of other non-Christian religions, nor to the alarm about numerous defections from Christianity in Christian countries. The Jewish trauma of Christian theology is stronger and deeper than others, which is tragic and grotesque. Disciples of Sigmund Freud might explain it as a phenomenon of the Oedipus complex, an ambivalent, strained relationship with the father. But it should be evident that a neurosis of this kind is unworthy of Christianity's lofty message of love. Such emotions do not appear in relation to other non-Christian religions nor regarding the catastrophic defections from Christianity.

The so-called Jewish legalism is the second problem with which Christian theologians must deal. From the beginning, Gentile Christians and their Jewish opponents viewed it from an oblique angle. The question of Jewish Law would, paradoxically speaking, be more significant had Christianity become a Jewish religion or sect. In that case, the proper interpretation of the Law would be of serious import. One could have asked whether differences existed—and, if so, how great—between the interpretation of the Law by Jesus' disciples and that by rabbinic-pharisaic Jews.

We can infer from the Dead Sea Scrolls that there would have been fewer divergences between Jewish Christians and Rabbinism than there was between the people of Qumran and the Pharisees. But developments went a different way and Christianity became a religion of non-Jews.

It could equally be maintained that non-Jewish Christians did not find it difficult to adhere to Jewish Law. Judaism as well as the Apostolic Church in Jerusalem held quite rightly that non-Jews were under no obligation to keep the Jewish Law in its entirety; the so-called Noahide commandments were quite sufficient. According to Jewish and early Church opinion, such non-Jews would have part in the redemption. Though non-Jews were not obliged to keep the Jewish Law, they were free to observe as much of it as they wished. Paul did not share that opinion because of his particular theology of the Law and because he held that non-Jewish Christians would become a half-Jewish sect if they adopted a partially Jewish way of life. The pious among the other nations were strongly inclined to keep certain Jewish commandments. The Letter to the Galatians indicates how difficult it proved for Paul to dissuade them. Even today, we sometimes hear that a life according to Jewish Law holds great attraction for non-Jews who want to move closer to the Jewish faith.

In order to combat that danger, it required a precise, versatile theology, an effective anthropology and a whole doctrinal system on the nature of sin, faith, and grace, as well as the activation of those aspects of Christology likely to represent Jewish law in a relativizing, negative way. The demonization of the Jewish way of life soon followed, as did the Christian practice to interpret the commandments and prohibitions of Mosaic law in a purely allegorical sense.

As far as I can see, the emotional distaste of Christians for Jews living according to the Law has greatly diminished. It is doubtful, however, that a serious exposition on the Jewish law exists in contemporary Christian theology. The problem is that the New Testament, Paul's Epistles in particular, contains certain ideas on the nature of the Law which, though possessing some grandeur, one-sidedly distort it. Neither Christians nor Jews understand that the Jewish way which regulates the individual's life style by a ramified structure of precepts and prohibitions is by no means unique. Parsism, Hindusim, Buddhism and other religions of the Far East are of the same type, and the Roman religion in its pre-classic stage was probably a law-religion also. Such information at least lifts out of the absolutism of theological conclusions Paul's Christological and anthropological critique of the Jewish Law. I have encountered a great deal of admiration for Hinduism, yet never did I hear that its "legalism" was closely examined.

Paul's negative Christological relativization of the Law does not exert as much influence today as does his anthropological critique. His anthropology of the works of law, of faith, and of grace has become important in defining Christianity among those Christians who never in their life have seen a Jew who lives according to the Law. Actually, those who rail most against Jewish legalism are strongly "legalistic." As a negative category, I would define legalism as follows: It occurs where moral demands are elevated to normative precepts and prohibitions. This legalistic danger is greater in Christianity than in Judaism. The latter does not teach, by the way, that one is justified by the works of the Law. According to Judaism, faith and the works of the Law are not in a state of tension; and if I understand Paul correctly, his justification by faith does not constitute an autonomous anthropology. Its function is to lay bare the meaning of his theology of the cross. Opposition among Christians against "legalism" demonizes the Jewish law and makes the Jewish religious way of life monstrously hostile to God. When a Jew prays or utters a benediction, or when he eats for the glory of God or refrains from taking certain foods, he does not thereby draw away from God. By his faith, his way of life and his activities, he aspires to come closer to him and his will. Many years ago, a scholarly Christian theologian said to me: "The Jews have come closer to Christianity because many of them no longer live according to the Jewish ritual laws." "My dear professor," I replied, "do you really think that a pork chop brings you closer to Christ?" I am quite sure that Paul would have agreed with my rejoinder.

Within the context of a Christian theology of Judaism, we must also discuss the crisis within modern Judaism. That crisis which now affects all religions does not have the same consequences for Judaism as for Christianity. It was brought about in Judaism by the Emancipation and consequent assimilation. In the course of these intellectual and social upheavals of our time Jews lost their faith in God less than did Christians. Much more serious is the often detectible decline of Jewish identity. It becomes manifest when Jews are assimilated into the modern world which differs in nature from their own. When they attempt to find their way among their non-Jewish neighbors, Jews often lose sight of the meaning of religious laws because a religious way of life linked with law is alien to European and American culture. The Jewish "legal" way of life then tends to crumble away. This often happens to modern Jews as it did to Christians during late antiquity and the early Middle Ages. The environment of those times was a European culture free of any ritual ties. Christianity could hold its own among the nations only by declaring itself "free of the Law." It was at that point that Christianity unhesitatingly opted for assimilation, a leap into freedom from the Law.

Jewish love of the Law is often so deeply inbred and ingrained that most Jews would indignantly reject the idea that the law of God could be religiously harmful or, worse, be an impediment to faith in God and aimed against the unity of the world. Even those Jews in our time who no longer live by the Law or are fairly ignorant of its precepts do not take exception to it. They hold that the Law should be reformed and adapted to modern demands and an advanced style of life.

The crisis among Jews also manifests itself in a severe decline in Jewish learning. Even before Jesus' time, Judaism was not only a religion but a complete culture founded upon learning a great variety of material in addition to the Holy Scriptures. In its all-pervasive structuralization of daily life and the postulate to master an immense store of knowledge, Judaism can be likened to classical Chinese culture. It is much more democratic, however, than the Chinese civilization. Even the plainest Jew had to know a great deal, and the scholars' ranks were open to all. There were no Mandarins or dreaded state examinations. To the overwhelming majority of Jews such learnedness no longer applies. That erudition so characteristic of Judaism for two millennia is now limited to certain well-defined groups. This situation must be realized by Christian partners in the Christian-Jewish dialogue. Among many Jewish participants in these talks, knowledge of Judaism is quite poor.

This Jewry which since biblical pre-Christian days has undergone constant and severe changes must now be accepted by Christians as a community that can never be deprived of the gift of chosenness and to which was prophesied a future "happy end" in the Letter to the Romans. Such a conception is, in my opinion, the only permissible one in keeping with the message of Christianity. It is valid even in spite of the different tone which, as already indicated, sounds in the redacted part of the Gospel of Matthew. Even Augustine held that in the end the Jews would be saved, though he was not a great friend of them and must be considered one of the most important architects of the medieval theory that Judaism was degraded. His theology contains a trace of greatness, yet I think that a believing modern Christian can and must go beyond Augustine of Hippo. The idea that Jews were rejected by God—an idea already opposed by Paul— should be thrown out as dangerous ballast. A Christian must, indeed, do just that if he wishes to contribute to the recovery of the Christian faith. Else, for a long time to come, the reproach of a lack of dialogue and of the perpetual failure toward Jews right up to Auschwitz will continue to adhere to Christianity and the Christian.

Christians must refrain from fabricating a Judaism according to their own latest trends. They must accept Jews as being as "orthodox" as the latter understand themselves. Christian theologians of Judaism must accept that, according to Jewish understanding, it was not a religion that was chosen but a group of human beings, not the Jewish religion but Israel. Even Jews who wandered away from their religion and know little about it are part of Israel. Franz Rosenzweig correctly described the difference on this point between Christianity and Judaism. Christian belief "is belief as the content of a testimony. It is belief in something. That is exactly the opposite of the belief of the Jew. His belief is not the content of a testimony, but rather the product of a reproduction. The Jew, engendered a Jew, attests his belief by continuing to procreate the Jewish people. His belief is not in something: he is himself the belief" (*The Star of Redemption,* p. 342). For the same reason, Paul speaks of Israel as the olive tree. He chooses the organic picture of a tree with roots and branches. A Christian theology of Judaism should, then, be concerned not only with the faith of Israel but with the people Israel as a whole and its divine, irrevocable election by grace. I am fully aware that this is not an easy task.

The country is a part of the people Israel, as attested in the Hebrew Scriptures and never contradicted in the New Testament. Realization of Judaism in the land of Israel is quite definitely a part of the structure of Jewish religion, even though some Jews had lost sight of it in the past. Most of them recovered that sight when they witnessed the return to their land of some of the Jewish people and the renewal of the Jewish state. Even before the growth of Zionism, many Christians believed in the return of the Jews to the land of their fathers; they were clearly not the worst of Christians. I know that in former times the Jews' return from exile had no part in the structure of Christian belief. Yet, in view of the existence of the Jewish state and since Christians are no longer compelled to believe that the dispersion of the Jews is a punishment for alleged deicide, nothing stands in the way of theological deliberations on the propriety of contradicting unanimous Old Testament statements, a book holy to Christians and Jews. Theologically speaking, there is no reason for such contradiction. I prefer to think that a positive grappling with the problem of exiled Israel's return to its land should bring about a release of the churches from a medieval struggle. In any case, a Christian theology of Judaism that does not affirm the divinely willed tie between Israel and the Land appears to me impracticable in our day.

Still another aspect of a Christian theology of Judaism must be that the Jewish elements of Christianity should not only be defined. One must inquire into those traits fused with the Christian religion, into their function within Christianity, and how they were changed and adapted. With regard to the Old Testament, some of this work was already done. The so-called deutero-canonical books—which to Protestants are apocryphal but canonical to the Catholic Church—could be representative of the inter-testamental period. These writings were too much neglected by Catholic scholars, to the detriment of theology. There are other witnesses to early Judaism—for instance, the so-called pseudepigrapha, the Dead Sea Scrolls, Philo, Josephus, and other products of Hellenistic Judaism, and finally the rabbinic literature.

Thoma sets the end of early Judaism with the destruction of the Temple in Jerusalem in 70 CE. I think that is too early a date. The conclusion of the Mishna, that is, around the year 200 CE, or maybe even the first generations of *amoraim,* would be preferable. The year 279 CE, when Rabbi Yohanan of Tiberias died, could serve as the final date. Up to that period, Jewish material was often directly taken over by Christian writers and thinkers, without being considered alien. Oral rabbinic tradition, as it developed after the destruction of the Temple in Jerusalem, has also preserved for us that part of Jewish ideas in which Jesus and the apostolic Christians had their roots.

The importance of Jewish material for Christian theology and its problems can, in my opinion, be hardly overrated. I am thinking here of Christian theology, not the history of Christian thought. It is necessary to understand the teaching of one's own religion in order to reactivate it if possible. Many wrong conclusions about Christianity could be avoided, were one to understand out of what faith-stuff it is built. Jewish motifs, then, not only serve as interpretative material but are part of Christianity's own nature. It is indispensable to understand and be informed about Jewish faith not only as a preparatory step toward the origin of Christianity; one must also consider how faith-contents in Judaism developed alongside of Christianity. Anyone who knows his way about in the field will easily perceive that pre-Christian and post-Christian Judaism was a religion not at all as foreign to Christianity as some would have it.

Many principles and ideas are common to both religions. Not only belief in one and the same personal God and in the Old Testament past, but even the mode of religious creative thought bears similarities. The manner of argumentation is often alike, and it should be easy to see that this is not accidental. Christians should, therefore, be actually seized by curiosity to learn how Judaism was carried on and how it developed those beginnings which Christianity, too, adopted in its early days. This holy curiosity should extend to such situations where it is not a question of transfer from Judaism to Christianity, but a mutual parallel development, independent of interaction. A good example would be the theology and tradition about the sacrifice of Isaac (*akedah*). Christianity's gain from post-Christian Judaism is quite evident in this case. The same applies, for instance, to Jewish ideas on faith, on messianism and eschatology, and on Jewish hope for redemption. Pre-Christian and post-Christian Jewish experience could greatly help Christianity to solve a number of questions.

There are situations when Judaism has greater experience than Christianity and its theology rests on surer foundations. Yet, the reverse holds true as well. Judaism can learn a great deal from Christian treatment of common problems. Judaism and Christianity could be likened to two students with similar backgrounds who have been assigned the same tasks. It is quite fitting, then, that these two should not keep from one another their experience and attempts at solutions but should rather help each other. Now an additional reason will become evident for my setting the end of early Judaism at such a late date (about 279 CE). Even though in the early Church anti-Jewish tendencies developed quite soon as we know, the Judaism of antiquity and the early Church before entering the path to medieval developments (before the end of the third century) were closely related regarding many of their religious problems and particularly regarding their manner of thinking.

All of the following can add to the understanding of Christianity's religious development: Jewish traditions that found their way into the New Testament, non-New Testament Jewish material developed within Judaism, and that Jewish intellectual content taken over by the Church in later periods. Such material could lay bare the fundaments of dogmas and help to understand personalities in the light of their origin. An ususual but true picture of Paul, for instance, will emerge when it is understood what he took over from Judaism, directly or through his Christian predecessors, and adapted for his proclamation, and when the Jewish ways with theology are better understood. Pauline tenets will then take on different meaning and direction. All discussion on original sin, for instance, would have looked different had it been known that the Jew Paul hardly considered how and if original sin was inherited. If one is familiar with Jewish metaphorical thinking which finds its application in Paul's writings, it becomes evident that an inherited sin of Adam could not have been on his mind, when at the same time he was convinced that by the cross humanity was freed from original sin. Paul's train of thought becomes even clearer if the rabbinic parallels are not only known but thoroughly understood. Paul's interpretation was additionally modified by our knowledge of the Dead Sea Scrolls. We now know that what was generally accepted as an anthropology typical with Paul was in fact a Christological adaptation of Essenic anthropology, which Paul probably adopted from his Christian predecessors. According to these ideas, man is by nature in the sphere of flesh and sin and incapable of escaping this sphere by his own efforts. Only by the grace of God can the chosen ones be freed, by the gracious gift of the Spirit, that is.

The Qumran texts indicate, then, that those passages where Paul speaks of sin, of the flesh, of the unique grace of God, and of the spirit are actually independent of a theology of original sin. That deduction could have been made even before the finds of Qumran because in Paul's writings the opposition between flesh and spirit does not depend on some doctrine of sin but on the election by grace—in other words, on a particular form of the idea of predestination. Paul's doctrine of God's unique grace furthermore completely refers itself to his theology of the cross, and that is, I think, of immense importance. If his specific anthropology is absolutized and his Christological allusions ignored, Paul's intentions are misunderstood, and the theologian lowers himself to a pre-Christian, Essene stage. The consequences of this realization for the theology of predestination become easily apparent. The Dead Sea Scrolls proved that Erasmus of Rotterdam in his publication *De libero arbitrio* was right, not his Protestant opponents.

The above was but one example to point out that the study of Jewish sources is of greatest relevance to a fresh dogmatic reflection by Christians. We cannot help thinking that by a thorough confrontation of Christian dogmatics with its Jewish components, Christian theology would be plucked out of the Middle Ages and set down in truly modern times. Such a confrontation would also preserve Christian theology from slipping into amorphous modernism. Some Catholic and Protestant theologians have begun this work, but that is not yet enough. I can here only indicate the significance for Christology of profound Jewish knowledge. It had previously been recognized that the tenet of Jesus' atoning death had for a model the Jewish understanding, since the Second Book of Maccabees, of the atoning death of the martyrs. Less well known is the significant influence on Christology of a Jewish theology on the hypostasis of God. Rabbinic

Judaism contains the important idea of the immanence of God. It is called "word," "spirit," "glory," "wisdom," "power"; these terms, at the same time, are designations or attributes of God. All of these terms occur in the New Testament, referring to God as well as to Christ. They not only define Christ as divine resplendence of the Deity but also proclaim the unity between Father and Son because in rabbinic Judaism as well as in the New Testament they characterize God himself. Rabbinic teaching on the immanence of God was borrowed by Hellenistic Judaism and developed in a philosophical manner—note Philo's *logos* and the wisdom concept in the Book of Wisdom. We must assume that the teaching on the hypostases is more at home in rabbinic Judaism than in Hellenistic literature, as implied by rabbinic structure and diversity. That, in turn, would posit hypostatic Christology in rabbinic Judaism rather than in Jewish Hellenism.

Jewish presuppositions for faith in Christ have not yet been sufficiently and creatively enough drawn upon. Much of the nature of this faith in Christ thereby remains unexplained. That is partially due to an overhasty consensus among Jews and Christians, as if Jewish messianic faith was merely this-worldly and political. Such an interpretation is imprecise, applying as it does to certain trends within Judaism only. It is true in one point, though. The political aspect is nearly always of central importance to Jewish messianic faith while in Christianity it was repressed. Yet, it is not completely set aside but takes on a fresh, rather strange life in Christian chiliastic sects. Within a Christian-Jewish context, we must not suppress the fact that Judaism, too, contains supernatural elements within its messianic faith. Such components are found in the words of the Prophets, which were either openly messianic or interpreted as referring to the messiah. Shlomo Pines discovered the original version of Josephus Flavius on Jesus. Josephus closes his account of Jesus with the following words: "They (the disciples) reported that he appeared to them three days after the crucifixion. . . . For the prophets of God had spoken with regard to him of such marvellous things (as these)" ("An Arabic Version of the Testimonium Flavianum and Its Implications," Jerusalem, Israel Academy of Sciences and Humanities, 1971, pp. 36–37). That is significant for an appreciation of the prophetic accounts and a testimony to the superhuman character of the figure of the messiah, in the eyes of some Jews during antiquity.

The lofty ideas and metaphorical typologies of the Christ in the Letter to the Hebrews can also be shown to be Christian adaptations of Jewish, half-mythical messiah notions. We learned of the priestly component from the Dead Sea Scrolls, in which the messiah-priest is the most important messianic figure. We also know from one of the Qumran fragments that they expected Melchizidek who, like the Son of Man, would be the exalted judge at the end of time. He was even called "elohim," God. The idea of the Christ as high priest and expiatory sacrifice in one does not, however, occur in the Scrolls or in other Jewish writings. This new Christian conviction is a fruit of the experience of the cross, but the statements in the Letter to the Hebrews that Christ is greater than Moses, Abraham, and the angels is, again, not a Christian innovation (cf Heb 1:5–14; 3:1–6; 7:4–10). This metaphorical theme occurs in rabbinic Judaism.

Hence the usual conception of the Jewish messianic idea should be at least partially revised; it was quite often less homely than supposed. Such an understanding should also to some extent change Christian theology. If certain of the lofty attributes of Christ were of pre-Christian and non-Christian Jewish origin, they would not be directly related to post-Easter faith. They were added to the picture of Jesus already and served to enrich, in part even to create, that of Christ. Christology became more clearly defined when Christians assigned to the messiah Christ the hypostatic titles of God's immanence. There are even signs that certain Jewish groups partially transferred hypostatic theology to the pre-existent messiah. The very idea of such a messiah is of Jewish pre-Christian origin, as is the Christian dogma of the three functions of Christ as priest, king, and prophet.

Not only historians but theologians should meditate more deeply on the extent of the historical Jesus' own ideas of authority, and whether there exists a bridge between his self-perception and the "post-Easter" faith in Christ. If it were true, as certain pulpit Christians maintain with masochistic, self-destructive rage, that Jesus did not think of himself as someone special or even as rather significant, and that his claims to sovereignty belong to the period after Easter and that of the Church, then, I think, the Christian faith loses all claim to credibility. But it is not the fault of modern theologians and New Testament scholars that there exists a dichotomy between the historical Jesus and the kerygmatic, "post-Easter" Christ. That, strange to say, existed almost from the beginning of Christianity. The dichotomy was heightened by relying too much on the New Testament Epistles and not enough on the Synoptic Gospels. We learn of his message and, somewhat indirectly, of Jesus' great self-confidence mainly from the Synoptic Gospels. Gotthold Ephraim Lessing (1729–1781) said of the Gospels, with some exaggeration but basically quite correctly: "The religion of Christ is contained in them in the clearest and plainest words, but the Christian (religion) so vaguely and ambiguously that there is hard-

ly a single passage with which, as long as the world stands, two people
have associated similar ideas" *(The Religion of Christ,* para. 7–8).

The fundamentally true observation contrasts acutely with the usual
opinion of contemporary New Testament scholars, according to which the
stuff of the Gospels, and even more so the Gospels proper, developed in
the crucible of the post-Easter experience. They are, therefore, said to proclaim not so much the "religion of Christ" but, overwhelmingly, the Christian religion. Unless by allegory and typology certain ideas are read into
the Gospels, it should, I think, be easy to recognize that in their basic material they contain very little that is "post-Easter." Linguistic and stylistic
analyses confirm Lessing's view that the Christological statements of the
Synoptic Gospels are "vague and ambiguous." The reason is that the basic
material was several times revised in its Greek stage. The redactors and
evangelists were Christians of the early Church who wrote and thought in
Greek. They were either Gentile Christians or Christian Greek Jews who
were on the side of the Gentile Christian Church. They knew and interpreted from their own point of view subject matter that originated with the
disciples of Jesus and had been translated into Greek, and they added
many tendentious corrections. As believing Christians, however, they did
not intend to interfere too deeply with the transmitted material. It is that
which causes the impression that the Christology of the Synoptic Gospels
is "vague and ambiguous." For the same reason, unlike the old material in
the Gospels, the redacted Greek revisions cannot be translated back into
Hebrew or Aramaic. (The Greek corrections, by the way, do not only refer
to the area of faith. Their objective quite often was stylistic embellishment
and dramatization.)

Much can be learned about Jesus, his teaching, and his lofty self-perception by inquiring into the first three Gospels by linguistics and literary
criticism, and particularly with the help of Jewish and Hebrew knowledge.
Without a great deal of information about the Judaism of that time, nothing can be achieved. Yet, Jesus' self-understanding will not become fully
clear to us even in that way because the Gospels make it evident that he intended it to become known to a certain extent only. It could also be that
the disciples who transmitted the original Jesus-material did not fully understand his hints. At times they may have kept silent to their Jewish
brothers, for "pastoral" reasons, on the *tremendum* in the person of their
Master. It is quite obvious that the Greek Gospel redactors of the early
Church revised certain passages in which Jesus talked of his high office.
They wanted to make such words "ecclesial." In my estimation, they did

not thereby do too much harm. In comparing thoroughly the three Synoptic Gospels, much of the original material reappears. Many wrong tracks were taken in the research on Jesus, his self-perception and his message, stemming from the fact that the work was done unphilologically and without essential Jewish learning. Many errors also resulted from the conviction, at that time and even nowadays, that it was really pleasing to God to broaden the gulf between the historical Jesus and the Christ of faith. If with the help of Jewish knowledge it were possible to draw a picture, however incomplete, of the self-perception of Jesus, we would find, I am sure, the historical fulcrum of the Christian faith. That would partially bridge the age-old dichotomy between the historical Jesus and the Christ of faith. Considering furthermore how much post-Easter Christology was enriched by Jewish motifs, a new path opens up for the writing of a "Jewish" Christology, from Jesus to Paul. We do not thereby deny originality to the Christian faith in Christ. Even though the material is Jewish, Christology in general differs fundamentally from pre-Christian and post-Christian Jewish faith.

Many modern theologians increasingly attempt to define the message of Jesus over against Judaism. Jesus is said to have taught something quite different, something original, unacceptable to the other Jews. The strong Jewish opposition to Jesus' proclamation is emphasized. To deal with such views is not the task of New Testament scholarship but belongs to modern research of ideology; yet Jewish parallels to the words of Jesus and the manner in which he revised the inherited material clearly refute the above assumptions. Even though he gave his own personal bent to Jewish ideas, selected from among them, purged and reinterpreted them, I cannot honestly find a single word of Jesus that could seriously exasperate a well-intentioned Jew. Even his criticism of the Pharisees cannot on principle be objected to because there are important rabbinic parallels. On his last visit to Jerusalem, Jesus endangered the Sadducean priests by his accusations He thereby inflamed the people who did not like that caste but loved to listen to Jesus and held him in esteem. That confrontation cost Jesus his life.

Does that justify placing Jesus in opposition to the Jews of the time? By his thinking and his message, Jesus proved himself a true son of his people and a representative of its faith and hopes. It would be absurd and somehow malicious to construe an essential antagonism where none existed. That there actually was no such contradiction only someone with Jewish learning can make credible. Consequently, faith in Christ cannot be in earnest unless that form of Jewish faith which stamped Jesus becomes a part of Christian faith and morality. A Christian should perhaps meditate on certain Jewish ideas which are hinted at in the preaching of Jesus and to which he alludes affirmatively; even those which are mere suggestions are in some way part of a theology of Christianity. In any case, it is important for a Christian to be better informed about Judaism. It would, indeed, be a great Christian event, were many people to recognize that Jesus' faithfulness to his Jewish people, his burning compassion for Jewish suffering, and his Jewish hope for Christians belong to the *imitatio Christi.*

Unfortunately, I now have to talk of antisemitism in the New Testament because a Christian theology of Judaism cannot bypass it. Practically everyone these days attempts to prove that there is no anti-Jewishness in the New Testament. I can well understand this apologetic temptation. Yet, we cannot evade the problem if the evil is to be grasped by the roots. There is no other cure. I myself used to be blind to this question, but more intensive research convinced me otherwise. The New Testament contains accusations and theses which at times are hostile toward certain groups of Jews or toward all of them. Some passages even call in doubt the very essence of Jewish faith and Jewish law. If a Christian were to find anywhere such inimical statements about Christianity, would he not call them anti-Christian? I even dare say that many Christians would not hesitate to state openly their more or less pronounced anti-Jewishness if such passages were found anywhere else but in the New Testament. Do not tell me that such statements and ideas are merely inner-Jewish disputes or prophetic scoldings. All of them sound Greek and not Hebrew, that is, they emerged among Gentile Christians, even though one or the other redactor may have been a Christian of Jewish descent. The strained relationship arose, then, when it became evident that Christianity would be the religion of non-Jews. From a Jewish point of view, that tension was fed by centrifugal forces. An eminent Christian theologian and philosopher rightly said to me: "How can we talk of prophetic rebuke if it was directed at and meant for, not the Jews, but the non-Jews?" We are mainly concerned here with such redacted phrases and revisions in the first three Gospels, which express more or less strain in regard to the Jews. They are of Greek conception and a result of the Gentile Christian mentality, as can quite often be proved by their content. They probably hail mostly from the same redactors who inserted in the Synoptic Gospels the "post-Easter" touch-ups. It would be worthwhile to study this question. My personal impression is that the redacted Christological statements, as also the more or less anti-Jewish revisions of the Synoptic Gospels, do not show much depth. In fact, they are rather commonplace. Their creators were mostly pro-Church, and not in a positive sense. They were active several decades after the death of

Jesus and were exponents of stagnation. It usually does not take long for a stormy, creative movement to show the first signs of a letting-up.

It is not merely of scholarly importance to discover additional redactive encrustations in the first three Gospels by a linguistic and stylistic approach and a consideration of the contents. We also obtain thereby a key to the better understanding of the Gospels proper, that is, their very core. That would be impossible without Jewish learning. Such an understanding enables us to set different and better accents. It would free the Gospels in part from "secondary ecclesialism" and make them more immediate. I find it of great importance to Christian relations to Jews to recognize that redactive measures, which often breathe a spirit unfavorable to Judaism, are not "kerygmatic" statements. They are not meant to provoke the faithful to anger about the Jews. They are not even meant to stand in the center of religious deliberations since they are not the product of a creative ardor of faith; they should be seen as distortions rather than faith-declarations. They represent the first, not quite fully developed expression of a beginning anti-Jewish ideology within the Church.

Theological New Testament statements outside of the Synoptic Gospels are apt to treat Judaism rather grudgingly. In that respect I do not know how to help Christians, unless somebody will understand Holy Scripture as the writing-down by man of a divine revelation extraneous to words and persons. I am willing to take this daring step with regard to the Tanakh. May I expect, though, that my Christian friends do the same with regard to the New Testament? May I at least ask whether or not Paul, for instance, was a little unfair to the essence of Judaism in his serious and profound words? Has there ever lived a Jew who assumed that he could be justified by the works of the Law? Is the Law, then, a benign ogre, as Paul would have us believe?

Pauline statements, on the other hand, must not be taken from their context because that stamps them as unnecessarily severe. Paul's criticism of the Law does not stand by itself. It was first of all a didactic measure for the Gentiles, explaining the dangers of "judaizing." Secondly, Paul's presentation of the Law is part of his portrayal of the meta-historical road leading toward the saving and liberating cross. Though Paul's writings are problematical with regard to the Law, his approach toward the Jews is basically and unproblematically positive. Paul would have agreed with the words of Simeon that Jesus was "a light of revelation to the Gentiles, a glory for your people Israel . . . destined for the fall and for the rise of many in Israel, and for a sign that shall be contradicted" (Luke 2:32–34). Paul knows at the same time that Israel's election by grace cannot be abolished.

The Gospel of John is not very productive regarding the Jews. It is not quite clear what are the Evangelist's concrete accusations against Jews and Judaism. Generally speaking, there is in the polemical New Testament sayings against Jews and Judaism too much abstract ideology which has nothing to do with the concrete nature of Judaism. Regarding the already mentioned redacted passages in the first three Gospels, I may be permitted to express myself even more strongly: Too much of it is vulgar, and it is difficult to see how a reconsideration in our time could derive from it a justified criticism of Judaism. What position should be adopted toward statements which in all likelihood do not hit their mark? It must be willed by God that, in a humanistic spirit, Jews and Christians examine not only traditions that separate the two religions but those that are common to both. At the same time, we must not overlook that a number of theologians find in such an approach, with some justification, certain dangers for both religions.

We have come to the end of this foreword to Clemens Thoma's book. I hope with all my heart that it will find its way to many readers. May it help to stimulate thinking and teaching; then it will fulfill its task. It prepares the way for a better and more balanced Christian relationship toward Judaism. This first step was here made by a man whose ideas about Christianity and Judaism should serve as example for a better future. The conditions for such a brighter future are already present; in the area of Christian-Jewish relations the powers of recovery are at work. At the same time, the "mystery of iniquity" (2 Thes 2:7) is at work, and more and more people are forsaking their faith. We, that flock of Jews and Christians, must now prove ourselves "children of the day . . . comforting and edifying one another" (1 Thes 5:4, 11). This new book was written in such a spirit and will assist its readers to walk on the right path.

David Flusser
Hebrew University, Jerusalem

PART I
INTRODUCTION

1.
The Theological Dimension
of Jewish-Christian Relations

I. IMPULSES TO A CHRISTIAN THEOLOGY OF JUDAISM

#1 Some years ago, a Jewish scholar wrote: ". . . we have to go beyond literary criticism and philological knowledge. We have to bring back the theological dimension—with full awareness of (and protection against) the dangers which, in the past, have infested that dimension. We need, in other words, a Jewish theology of Christianity, and a Christian theology of Judaism."[1]

According to Jakob Petuchowski, Christians must develop a theology which is open-minded and fair to Judaism, placing it within the proper context of the Christian message. In the forefront of this work should be Christians who could shape such a theology based on sound knowledge of Judaism and past Jewish-Christian history, a theology which could no longer be the cause of, or furnish an alibi for, clichés about Judaism or disdain and persecution of Jews. Analyses based on philology and literary criticism are simply not enough. What we need is a view extending far beyond the confines of church and canon, a radical involvement with the Christian message which cannot be proclaimed genuinely without referring to, and taking its bearings from, Judaism. Once such a Christian theology of Judaism exists and is being proclaimed, a path would be prepared for the formulation of a Jewish theology of Christianity.

23

#2 A short time before Petuchowski wrote, the Christian biblical scholar Norbert Lohfink said:

> Christian teaching on Judaism must not take its clues from history alone, important and salutary as such information may be. We must speak of the Jews informed by Christian faith, and that will finally not be possible without a yet to be written "tractatus de Iudaeis."[2]

Lohfink's statement is a critical reference to various Christian declarations on and investigations of Judaism in pastoral practice and catechesis which have appeared since the Second World War. Such statements often attack with historical arguments certain New Testament passages that are critical of the Jews. There also exists the opposite approach, namely attempts to suppress or gloss over harsh New Testament texts about the Jews. Lohfink is not thinking of an abstract, dogmatic "tractatus de Iudaeis" but a biblical, explicative and normative one.

The core problem of such a treatise would be the precarious relationship between a theology formulated by believers and the critical approach maintained by scholars of history. Lohfink, together with many other authors, is dismayed to find that so many attempts at Christian-Jewish dialogue, entered with great enthusiasm, have remained rather ineffectual for the very reason that their orientation toward the New Testament is either too polemical or too appeasingly selective.

In the postscript to a new printing of his book on modern Jewish Jesus research, Goesta Lindeskog writes:

> Christian theologians have increasingly come to recognize that they need the cooperation of their Jewish colleagues. Without such joint efforts, we cannot solve the very considerable problems inherent in the development of Christianity and the unfolding of post-Christian Judaism. The co-existence of the two religions must be reasoned out in theological terms.[3]

Before the Second World War, Lindeskog's book was the only history of recent Jewish contributions to Jesus research. In that book he pleaded for Jewish scholars threatened by destruction in Germany. It was his knowledge of the unexpected, continued blossoming forth of Jewish Jesus research after the Second World War that caused Lindeskog to call for a theological study of the co-existence of Judaism and Christianity.

The New Testament scholar Franz Mussner also mentions the annihilation of Jewry during the Second World War, in arguing for an urgent formulation of a Christian theology of Judaism:

> Not only moral and economic restitution toward the Jews is required but a theological one is just as urgent. What I mean is that Christian theologians, exegetes in particular, must ask themselves if the New Testament scriptures were not often interpreted in an anti-Jewish sense and against the original intent of the New Testament writers.[4]

#3 The quoted Jewish and Christian voices were not alone. When the gas ovens of Auschwitz had ceased to smoke, when the Jews, contrary to the expectations of many people, became re-established in Israel, when it began to dawn on many Christians that they, too, bear responsibility in the mechanical destruction of the Jews under National Socialism, and when it became ever clearer how dangerous the situation in the Middle East could become for the peace of the world, only then—and unfortunately much too late—did Christians and Jews begin to reflect on it all and to talk to each other.

From time to time, respected theological periodicals take up the question of recent developments and new means for a continuation of the Jewish-Christian dialogue.[5] Many Jewish and Christian journals steadily add building blocks to a Christian theology of Judaism and a Jewish theology of Christianity.[6] A number of denominations among the Christian churches have made public statements against antisemitism and for solidarity and cooperation with Jews on humane concerns and theological questions.[7] Several monographs and research publications on the topic have also appeared.[8]

#4 The dangers of reverting to murderous antisemitism have not been fully banned, even in the countries of the Western hemisphere. Yet we can feel a little encouraged by the fact that in our day animosity toward Jews no longer wears a Christian mask, nor could it be draped in official or semi-official clerical garb. Certain church statements and the profound involvement of leading theologians and humanists have done away with such possibilities. If these difficult beginnings are not to atrophy, however, we urgently need a theological overview and discussion of all the problems and malformations that have evolved from the Christian-Jewish encounter. That is what will be attempted here, though the author can hope to succeed only up to a point. A considerable part of this book will be devoted to criticism of relevant literature and past events, while at the same time it is intended to provoke critical reactions.

II. The Essentials of a Christian Theology of Judaism

1. Basic Positions

#5 A Christian theology of Judaism deals with Judaism and its relationship to Christianity from a Christian point of view; any judgment can be approximative and tentative only. Such a theology must be aware of the complex character of Judaism, which is not readily categorized, of the dangers of thinking in clichés, and of past apologetic and polemically contorted discussions between Jews and Christians. Rightly perplexed regarding previous wrong attitudes, a theologian should manifest an unequivocal, clearly Christian approach to all aspects of Judaism. Biblical and post-biblical Jewish-Christian history of revelation, jealousy, and dispute, as well as explanatory and binding faith-positions, forms the fabric of such a theology from which insights may be gained and new paths and passageways discovered. There must be loving and integrative strength to make fruitful for our day a very difficult and misinterpreted past.

In pursuing a Christian theology of Judaism, cheap and trivial solutions are inadmissible. It would be quite wrong to emphasize and absolutize Jewish over against Christian positions, unless the former could be fully substantiated by Jewish writings. Even the most fundamental alternatives do not admit of an easy and superficial answer, e.g.: Were Jews after the death of Christ dismissed from the history of revelation or are they now as ever the people of God? Can we accept theologically mutual influence and exchange or must we move into isolation again? Should we aspire to an intra-Christian ecumenical theology with or without the inclusion of Judaism? A Christian theology of Judaism would, of course, be nipped in the bud, were we not to understand the Jews of our time, in one way or another, as people of God, were we not to rate very highly the Jewish character of Christianity and the Christian character of Judaism, and were we not to extend Christian *oekumene* to include Judaism (without a provocative mission to the Jews). Assenting to all this, we must not and cannot arrive at propositions according to which—after all those unfortunate collisions—Christianity and Judaism become established as two unrelated monoliths. Christian faith cannot completely separate them; there are too many and complex interrelationships. A Christian theologian must hope for mutual stimulation and regeneration from within, instead of continued strife and destruction.

#6 Jewish and Jewish-Christian history must be assessed from an open-minded ecumenical point of view. The Zionist Leon Pinsker (1821–1891) said about the rapid growth of Christian antisemitism in the nineteenth century: "To be plundered as a Jew or protected as a Jew is equally shaming, equally painful, for the humanity of a Jew.[9]

Because of the history of anti-Judaism, Christian theologians must take into account heightened Jewish sensibility to ideological insinuations and trite attempts at conversion. We must be aware of the fact that Judaism is no mere appendix to Christianity, that it does not constitute an opponent to Christianity, nor does it consider Christianity a necessary partner. Judaism is self-reliant and autonomous, much more independent from Christianity than the latter could and should be from the former. We must also consider that personal, intellectual alienation between Jews and Christians is much deeper than warranted by the true differences between Judaism and Christianity. The Church quite often, avowedly or not, took her bearings from post-biblical Jewish tradition in her liturgy, in questions of clerical office, in exegesis, and in several unfortunate fanatic movements. Rediscovery and revaluation of all Jewish contributions to the history of thought in Christianity will enrich a Church impoverished by disregard of the Jews. Finally, Christians and Jews—indeed all human beings—will serve the God of Israel "shoulder to shoulder" (Zeph 3:9). A Christian theologian must emphasize that the Christ event does not diminish or destroy a legitimate and autonomous Judaism after Christ.

2. Definitions

#7 A definition of Jewish theology by the Jewish theologian Louis Jacobs may be helpful in arriving at some short formulas for a Christian theology of Judaism:

> Jewish theology is an attempt to think through consistently the implications of the Jewish religion. . . . The theologian must avail himself of the accurate findings of the historian, otherwise his speculations will belong to fantasy. But while the historian asks what has happened in the Jewish past, the theologian asks the more personal question, what in traditional Jewish religion continues to shape my life as a Jew in the here and now? The historian uses his skills to demonstrate what Jews have believed. The theologian is embarked on the more difficult, but, if realized, more relevant, task of discovering what it is that a Jew can believe in the present.[10]

Jewish theology has always consisted of a tenacious struggle to interpret the Jewish past and make it acceptable to a questioning contemporary generation. Topicality and actuality were more strongly emphasized than attempts at systematization (cf. #88, 214).

A Christian theology of Judaism without knowledge and consideration of Jewish theology is unthinkable. It must include and review the Jewish and Jewish-Christian past for Christians who ask questions in our time. Some such brief formulations might read: 1. A Christian theology of Judaism approaches and interprets with radical seriousness Judaism's functions as origin of, contradiction to, and partnership with, the Christian Churches. 2. It is a theology critical of the Church because and to the extent that it wishes to remind the Christian churches of Christianity's Jewish heritage and the Christian elements in Judaism, it must point out that ignorance of these facts has been partly responsible for superficial attitudes, confusion, and errors, today as in the past. 3. It is a Christian theological attempt to explain and re-present the consequences for Christianity resulting from the fact that Jesus Christ, his first disciples and the evangelists were Jews and lived in a Jewish environment. 4. It is an attempt to decipher the existence of Judaism in a Christological sense. 5. It is a Christian theology without antisemitism.[11] 6. It is an attempt to test the Christian message in relation to Jewish tradition.

3. Links to History

#8 All the above short formulations hint at one particular problem in methodology and content, namely the relationship of history to theological judgment. Theology is a normative discipline that takes its bearings from revelation. While its points of reference are historical, it cannot be guided solely by the varying results of the historical sciences. Yet, we must not forget the mischief that theology has wrought and that for which it bears some responsibility. Theology would be lacking in credibility with regard to Judaism, were it to appeal merely to its own norms and retreat to them without reference to historical events. In that case, theology would be nothing but a sterile, anti-Jewish ideology devoid of relation to reality.

All of Jewish and Jewish-Christian history must be taken into consideration. We can no longer theologize on Jews and Judaism as if anti-Judaism never existed in the Church, as if there had never been a Holocaust, as if the state of Israel did not exist, and as if world peace were not threatened in the Middle East. The inclusion of these and other weighty events must, of course, not lead to uncontrolled subjectivism in scholarship. Yet, a theological view of Jewish history should not exclude these dimensions of reality. A parochial attitude, dealing with Jewish suffering solely in order to make better Christians, would be even less justified. The Jews of the past were not merely passive victims of a history shaped by Christians; they also were active agents of religious and secular history.

#9 The demand that a Christian theology of Judaism should not detach itself from an historical framework to hide behind principles calls for some explanation. There exists a "profound and essential asymmetry"[12] between Judaism and Christianity. It partly stems from the fact that Judaism ("the root") reaches deeply into Christian identity, while Christianity adds very little or nothing at all to Jewish self-understanding.

Furthermore Judaism has no binding dogmas or persons and authoritative bodies with unambiguous functions. Jewish ties between peoplehood and religion have no counterpart in Christendom, which consists of faith communities in which ethnic, biological, and social components play no part. Dialectically refined Christian arguments do not encounter an equally equipped opponent or competent institutions, while polemical theology is quite inappropriate.

A great deal of today's so-called Christian-Jewish dialogue is nothing but confused mental gesticulation in an empty room, not much different from medieval disputations, and clearly destined to fail. Modern Christians engaged in dialogue know their own dogmas and their application, but they are ignorant of Jewish history. They should endeavor to learn more about Judaism and beware of too much pathos in dialogue. The very term "dialogue" should be sparingly used.

It is not a question, after all, of developing a harmonious doctrinal unity between Judaism and Christianity, an impossible goal in any case. Despite opposing Christian expectations and aggressive moods, we must reconnoiter and reconsider Christian history, methods, and contents of faith, based on Jewish faith history, Jewish faith statements, and Jewish life in general. That is no easy task and cannot be accomplished by individuals or within one generation.

Jewish history is of immense diversity and peculiarity. Jewish literature is very rich and difficult to interpret. Language barriers must be surmounted and attention paid to a mentality that often appears strange to us. Characteristic customs must be placed within their proper context. To do justice in a theological sense to Judaism in the pre-Christian era, to the Jewish contemporaries and fellow citizens of Jesus, and to Judaism after Christ right up to our time will require the Sisyphean mental exertions of many Christian theologians. New vistas and dimensions of meaning should thereby open up for the Christian churches.

This volume does not claim to propose a final or unique Christian theology of Judaism. It intends merely to indicate in what manner, at what points, and with what prospects we should approach Judaism, setting an example for the way in which the problems could be treated within their historical framework. It would be quite wrong to speak of Jews and Judaism outside of the context of historical events. Such an approach, though possibly affording greater lucidity and better serviceability, would not do justice to the variety within Judaism and would not correspond to the differences, quite often vague and blurred, between Jewish and Christian dogmas and ways of life.

III. The Place of the Hebrew Scriptures in a Christian Theology of Judaism

#10 The Old Testament is for Christians just as much a witness to the revelation of God as is the New. In order to gain an understanding of Christian faith, the two must be taken as one. A Christian who was to relinquish or despise the Hebrew Scriptures would disclaim or abrogate his Christianity. It is, then, quite wrong to maintain that the very term "Old Testament" is "a Christian anti-Judaic interpretation of the Jewish Scriptures."[13] Though it could be said that "old" may easily have a negative connotation, a mere change of terms would not add anything to Jewish-Christian understanding.

#11 A Christian theology of Judaism is not identical with a Christian Old Testament theology or, generally speaking, with Old Testament research based on Christian faith. Yet, the Hebrew Scriptures are indispensable to a Christian theology of Judaism. Two examples may serve to indicate the connections and intricacies of Old Testament scholarship and a Christian understanding of Judaism. Just a few words by theologians Siegfried Herrmann and Martin Noth indicate how differently Judaism can be viewed, even by authors who apparently share the same Christian faith-positions. The final words of a history of Israel by Siegfried Herrmann are:

> It therefore seems appropriate to end this continuous account of the history of Israel in Old Testament times with Alexander of Macedon. The history of Israel did not end here, but a new phase of the struggle for independence and self-determination began. Israel found itself confronted more intensively than before with attacks from the world of the nations,

by whom in the course of its earlier history it had often been considered as an alien. Yet it bore and still bears the destiny of this world in a remarkably concentrated way. It is beyond doubt a theological task to see the reflection of knowledge of the world and of God in the mirror of Israel; now more than ever this has become a question posed to every thinking person. The presuppositions for understanding Israel are contained in the Old Testament and its history.[14]

Herrmann is convinced of the continuity between Old Testament Israel and contemporary Judaism and considers this of theological significance, but, in his view, the Old Testament forms the basis for understanding present-day Jews. His words make it clear that the importance accorded the Hebrew Scriptures may depend on the Christian's faith-position regarding post-biblical and contemporary Jewry.

Far better known are the final remarks in Martin Noth's *History of Israel* which appeared several years ago:

Even in the insurrection of A.D. 66–70, though in a tremendously distorted form, this same Israel had once again appeared fighting for its sanctuary after it had been violated by the Roman procurator. Jerusalem was now the garrison of a Roman legion, and there was no further point in taking up arms for it. A center in the old sense no longer existed. . . . Even Jerusalem had now ceased to be the vital symbol of the "homeland." There was nothing but Diaspora, and even in the motherland life could only be lived as it had been lived hitherto in the Diaspora. Israel thereby ceased to exist and the history of Israel came to an end.[15]

For basic theological reasons, Noth closes his history of Israel with the year 70 CE because in the meaning of the Old Testament or in continuity of what was laid down by it, Judaism's history ended there and then. Yet, we cannot possibly sever the theological connective tissues between Old Testament Israel and the Judaism of post-biblical and contemporary times without mutilating the Christian message.

#12 The first example given above indicates the rank which the Hebrew Scriptures should be accorded in a Christian theology of Judaism. It forms the common basis, the theological and historical root of Judaism and Christianity. This foundation is an indispensable witness for and against Jewish and Christian communities. Theological discussions between the two groups must always take their measure from the Old Testament, in its original meaning, its interpretations, and its effects on Judaism and Christianity. Not only is the primary meaning of the text important for a theological evaluation; Christian theologians must just as eagerly consult its most important interpretations and consequences in post-Old Testament Jewish history. The problems of a Christian theology of Judaism come to a head when we begin to become aware of the ways in which Jews actually carry forward and live the way of the Tanakh—as the Hebrew Scriptures are called by Jews—though in a manner quite different from Christians. Israel must not be reduced to a biblical quantity of the past.

IV. CONCEPTUAL INCOMPATIBILITIES

#13 When talking about Judaism and with Jewry, we must first of all correct a misunderstanding: Christian theological concepts can be compared to or superimposed upon the same or similarly sounding Jewish concepts. This also applies in reverse; Jewish conceptual contents can be applied in a Christian manner.

Ever since Martin Buber set the Jewish *emunah* over against the Christian faith concept *pistis,*[16] many Jewish and Christian authors have taken it for granted that Jewish *emunah* must be distinguished from the Christian expression of faith. *Emunah* is held to be trust, religious experience, confidence. Faith, on the other hand, is said to be supported by binding dogmas and faith-contents. *Emunah* issued from the dynamic, concrete Hebrew way of thinking, while *pistis* derived from typically Greek abstract, static, analytical thought-processes. These two types of faith, it is maintained even today, oppose one another almost irreconcilably; were this incompatibility left aside, contours which should be strongly etched might become blurred.

No doubt, certain Christian-Jewish questions are tied to this conceptual pair, *emunah* and *pistis,* and we will later return to them (see #119). Still, any Christian with even a minimum of theological knowledge must realize that faith also contains trust, confidence in God (*fides quae, fides qua*). In the same way, anyone being but slightly versed in the Talmud and medieval Jewish theology will understand that the Jewish *emunah* at times applies to the content of faith (in the meaning of Buber's *pistis*). Without much hesitation, then, we can speak of Jewish and Christian faith or Jewish and Christian faith communities without committing a serious conceptual sin. It is similar with other alleged contrasts.

Following Moses Mendelssohn (1729–1787), Samson Raphael Hirsch (1808–1888), and Hermann Cohen (1842–1918),[17] it was overemphasized for reasons of apologetics that Judaism is a revelation of law, a religion of reason, a non-dogmatic community, a critique of myths and religions. On the other hand, Christianity was presented as an ideology, a system of dogmas, belief in mysteries, a mystical, romantic religion, etc. (see #204–210). The truth in all of these statements should be found somewhere in between. Only to a limited extent do concepts derived from nineteenth-century apologetics apply to contemporary Judaism and Christianity.

And yet, we must be cautious. Certain terms and ideas do have different origins and contexts in Judaism and Christianity. A Christian theology of Judaism does not operate within any given framework but reaches toward the frontiers. It attempts to solve problems which until this time have been discussed altogether too grudgingly in exegesis, fundamental theology, apologetics, church history, dogmatics, and moral and pastoral theology. A different kind of vagueness and insecurity might well be created, but we can take some consolation from the words of Franz Rosenzweig (1886–1929) who, great Jewish practitioner of dialogue that he was, had to draw close, time and time again, to the precarious frontiers of Jewish thinking:

> One did not become a Jewish thinker within an untroubled circle of Jews. The world of thought did not merely comprise thinking about Judaism. . . . If you wanted to think about Judaism you were dragged, if not spiritually then at least mentally, to the very boundaries of Judaism. Thus one's thinking was determined by the Power that led toward the brink, and the depth of one's views by the extent to which one was carried toward, up to, or even beyond these borders.[18]

PART II
JESUS CHRIST AND HIS MESSAGE
IN THE CONTEXT
OF EARLY AND RABBINIC
JUDAISM

2.
Early Judaism

I. Concepts and Ideologies

#14 There is no agreement about the time span of early Judaism. Some scholars equate it with the intertestamental period. In that case, the final redaction of the Book of Daniel (about 164 BCE) would be the beginning, and the destruction of the Second Temple in Jerusalem (70 CE) the end, of early Judaism. Others assume the era of the Second Temple (about 500 BCE to 70 CE), and others again the end of the Babylonian exile (539/38 BCE) until 70 CE. An intermediate position is taken by those who posit the beginning of early Judaism with Ezra/Nehemiah (about 450 BCE) or with the invasion of Judea by Alexander the Great (332 BCE) and its end in 70 CE.

To make early Judaism co-extensive with the intertestamental period is not justified by the history of religion. The cessation of scriptural inspiration did not occur at a clear point in time and does not coincide with the turn of an epoch. It seems more meaningful to accept as wide a time span for early Judaism as possible. It began when the Judeans on their return from the Babylonian captivity came to consider themselves the sole remnant of responsible representatives of all Israel (cf. #17). The destruction of the Temple in 70 CE is merely an approximate terminal date because early Jewish spirituality survived in later rabbinic Judaism (cf. #80, 83). We assume that early Judaism lasted, then, from approximately the end of the Babylonian exile (539/38 BCE) until about 70 CE.

A Christian theology of Judaism requires very detailed research into

37

early Judaism's religious history. It was in that period that trends, spiritual movements, and debates developed without which neither Jesus nor the early communities, neither the Church Fathers nor traditional rabbinic Judaism can be understood and discussed. Readers of this book, eager for a theological opinion about Judaism, should arm themselves with patience and persistence in preparation for the following extensive section dealing exclusively with the religious history of early Judaism.

#15 The term "late Judaism" (*Spaetjudentum*) was conceived at a time when Christian biblical religious scholarship and exegesis were stamped by apologetics, ignorance of and animosity toward Jews. This era coincides with early Judaism but, ideologically, it also includes rabbinic Judaism. It was because of serious prejudice that Judaism, which had just been declared reborn, should in its first and second phases of development already be termed "late," indicating that it was destined for an early demise. Such bias became even more pronounced in the second half of the nineteenth century. To scholars of a "late-Judaism-theology," it became the very point of reference which served as a dark background for the New Testament Christian communities, the only legitimate continuation of the Old Testament Israel. Judaism of Jesus' time and of the Talmud was completely disregarded. Developments within Judaism since the Babylonian exile were declared to be paralyzing, obscure, ritualized, and under alien influence. Jewish religion was said to have decayed more and more. This in turn resulted in Jewish "obduracy," making it impossible for Jews to accept Jesus as the true messiah. A divine curse against Jews, who were said to have broken the covenant, seemed logical. According to the Jewish scholar Leopold Zunz (1794–1886), Jews were reduced by such theologians to mere "church material."[19] Some of these writers are even now considered proven scholars because—apart from their ideological positions—they did excellent research on Jewish topics.[20] Scholars who placed their research at the service of National Socialism will, one hopes, no longer be considered authoritative. Before and during the Second World War, an opus in eight volumes by a number of authors was published, pleading for "scholarly" reasons for a "Christianity free of Judaism."[21]

In order to avoid even the shadow of a suspicion of anti-Judaism, the term "late Judaism" should be avoided and replaced by the more relevant "early Judaism" (*Fruehjudentum*).[22] In examining that period of Jewish history in which Jesus of Nazareth lived, we must try to be open toward the manifold ways of God. On no account should we devaluate and close the door on Judaism in order to enhance the Christian image.

II. THE EARLY JEWISH IMAGE

#16 In the course of history, various transformations and modifications took place in Jewish self-perception. These will be discussed later (cf. #203–213). Even early Jewish identity was not the immutable collective expression of a constant "transcendental" Jewish spirituality. When, for example, at the time of the Maccabeans and Hasmoneans, the fragile unity of the people disintegrated, vigorous movements affected Jewish bearing and religious attitudes. We must distinguish between early Jewish identity before and after the division into the early Jewish "sects." In sketching a picture of Judaism since the return from Babylonian captivity until the time of the Maccabeans and Hasmoneans—a period of relative unity—we must realize that this can be done only imperfectly and by implication.

#17 Borne on the wings of high expectations and with great plans for restoration, early Jewish groups in the sixth and fifth centuries BCE returned from Babylonia to the land of Israel. Yet their expectations were soon disappointed. Not only did the revelation of the God of Israel "before the eyes of the nations" (cf. Is 52:10; Ez 20:41) fail to manifest itself. The returned people found in their old homeland residents who had escaped the deportations to Assyria and Babylonia. These had been so strongly infected with syncretism and assimilation that unity with them in the spirit of Israel seemed out of the question (cf. Ezra 4:3). The homecomers soon realized that union with the exiles from the former Northern Kingdom, according to the expectations in Ez 37:15–28 could not be achieved.

Out of such hopes and disappointments, the primary identity of early Jews developed more or less by necessity. They considered themselves the only ones left, the only responsible representatives of all Israel, until that far-away day of hope when Israel would be gathered from the corners of the world as a people obedient to God. According to this identification as representatives of all Israel or as that provisional "remnant of Israel," they sacrificed at the dedication of the temple in 515 BCE "twelve he-goats, according to the number of the tribes of Israel, for a sin offering" (Ezra 6:17). Circumstances of the post-exilic era, then, forced upon the early Jews an awareness of the singularity of their election. They were prepared to hold out and bear all the consequences until such times when a revelatory community, encompassing all the tribes of Israel, would be newly constituted.

#18 The Priestly document of the sixth and fifth centuries BCE indicates important consequences of this early Jewish self-image. According to it, the commandments of revelation became the basis for Israel's life among the pagan nations. They are, moreover, the basic laws for the whole cosmos. According to the Priestly creation account, YHWH rested on the seventh day after the creation of the world (Gen 2:2f). The sabbath rest of the Israelites is thereby, as it were, embedded in the order of creation. Similarly in Third Isaiah (56:1–8), observation of the sabbath is an essential factor in determining whether or not one belongs to Israel.

Two other fundamental precepts were given new meaning by the author of the Priestly document, namely circumcision and the prohibition to partake of blood. Where the covenant between God and Noah, father of post-Deluge humankind, is recounted, we read: "But flesh with its life—that is, its blood—you shall not eat" (Gen 9:4). The Jewish custom of butchering is thereby interpreted as a law for all men. All human beings are actually obliged to keep this commandment, yet only the Jews are observing it. In a similar vein in the Priestly section of Gen 17:11, circumcision is mentioned explicitly as a sign of the covenant. Sabbath, dietary rules, and circumcision were the framework which in later times enabled Judaism to survive meaningfully in history. The historic-theological view that in the distant future Israel and the rest of the world were to be restored and renewed was linked by the Priestly document to the commandments of the law. Observing the law had not only inner-Jewish but cosmic meaning and a universal context.

#19 Synagogue and school were two important institutions complementing each other and probably dating back to the experiences and customs of the Babylonian exile. However research does not actually demonstrate the existence of synagogues before the third century BCE.[23] According to Deuteronomy, Jerusalem was the only legitimate place for the cult of YHWH (cf. 12:5). After the destruction of the Temple in Jerusalem by Nebuchadnezzar and the deportation of the Judeans to Babylonia, worship of God under the changed circumstances became an urgent problem. The assemblies of the "elders of Judea" in the houses of Babylonia (cf. Ez 1:1; 8:1) must be broadly viewed as birthplaces of synagogue and school. These two institutions characterize Jewish religious life even in our day. Early Judaism was stamped by the endeavor to develop, alongside the Temple cult, a religious attitude and scholarship within synagogue and school.

#20 The impression could easily arise that early Judaism in post-exilic times was a mere community of cult, law, and faith, that the awareness of being a special people with a religious, political, cultural, and kinship character had been largely lost or forced into the background, that one could speak of a Jewish "church" in early Jewish times, and that in this "church" only a uniform cult, profession of faith, and observation of the laws were of importance. Yet the writings of the era (in particular the Priestly document and the Chronicler's history) indicate that such an interpretation does not do justice to early Judaism. The following terms are frequently used for the tribes of Israel before the Babylonian exile and, by a process of updating, for the early Jewish congregations, communities and assemblies: people of YHWH (*'am YHWH,* Num 17:6); people of Israel (*'am Yisrael,* Neh 7:7); assembly of Israel *(kahal Yisrael,* 2 Chr 6:3); community (*'edah,* Num 27:16f;P); community of Israel (*'adat Yisrael,* Ex 12:6); and others. The semantic history of *kahal* shows that from the Babylonian exile until the time of Jesus it never identified a mere community of cult, law, or belief. Even Josephus Flavius (about 37–100 CE) uses *kahal* to designate an orderly group assembling for a (military) roll call (cf. *Ant.* 5, 93, paraphrasing Joshua 22). The words *'edah* and *'am* are used by biblical authors to characterize the early Jews as people of God or people of Israel. The sabbath and circumcision commandments, prohibition to partake of blood, the cultic and ritual precepts and prohibitions, communal prayer, reading of the Torah and all the other activities (military, organizational, etc.) were unthinkable in early Judaism unless linked to the people of God. They were expressions of life by the people favored by revelation.

III. EARLY JEWISH GROUPS

1. Historical Relationships and Ideas in General

#21 Throughout the history of the Jewish people, the preservation of unity proved extremely difficult and was never fully achieved. Religious and national-social aspects were needed to effect unity.

Religious unity never referred exclusively to unity in doctrine. Different opinions were accepted as more or less a matter of course, even of enrichment. Unity meant primarily a basic attitude toward worship (in particular, acknowledgment of monolatry; cf. #25), certain forms of its expression (like festivals and times of prayer), and a way of life according to divine law (orthopraxis). Expectations of salvation (hopes for the coming world, etc.) also were part of religious unity. After 70 CE, the *halakhah* and discussions concerning its provisions became the nucleus of this struggle for religious unity (cf. #102–108).

Socio-national unity meant mainly keeping together and bracing one-self against the enemies of the Jews and transgressors within one's own ranks. There is no clear distinction, however, between religious and social and national unity within Judaism; it is characteristic that religious and secular, universal and particular aspects and concerns continuously inter-sect and advance toward one another.[24]

#22 The so-called Samaritan schism was the first great crisis in early Jewish efforts at unification. It began around 330 BCE, following the inva-sion of Judea by Alexander the Great (cf. *Ant.* 11, 304–347). At that time the Samaritans, whose ancestors had been in almost constant internal and external opposition to the Judeans, finally separated from the Jews. Since the time of David the inhabitants of Samaria and the Northern Kingdom had never been satisfied with the Temple cult of Jerusalem; Mount Gari-zim always remained their sacred place. Discord was intensified by differ-ent aims and views of salvation history (the dispute on the prophetic canon). After the separation, hostility between Jews and Samaritans be-came ever stronger. A climax was reached when the Hasmonean prince, John Hyrcanus, destroyed the Samaritan Temple on Garizim in 128 BCE. Yet the early Jews did not consider the Samaritan schism a sundering of peoplehood and religious unity, but rather a long overdue shedding of a burden that had hindered religious development.[25] Even at the time of the Maccabeans the Jews felt fully justified to call themselves "people of Isra-el" (1 Macc 13:42).

2. The Period of the Maccabeans and Hasmoneans— A Basis for New Developments

#23 The period of the Maccabeans and Hasmoneans stretches from the accession (175 BCE) of the Seleucid king, Antiochus IV Epiphanes, to the beginning of the reign of Herod I (37 BCE). During that period, the early Jewish groups that existed in New Testament times began to take shape in Palestine, namely: Pharisees, Sadducees, Qumran people, and var-ious apocalyptic movements. These groups also pervaded the Jewish dias-pora. This also was the time when the foundations were laid for the rebel-lion of the Zealots which came into being in the year 6 CE. Apart from the formation of new groups, the development and transformation of many ideas and ideologies also took place, viz., historical theologies, kingdom of God ideas, war ideologies, priestly and national triumphalism, and reflec-tions on suffering, hope and prayer. The period of the Maccabeans and Hasmoneans is of immense importance to Christianity and Judaism be-cause there we find the religio-historical basis for an understanding of the followers and opponents of Jesus. His message becomes clearer when seen in connection with and contrast to theologies of Jewish groups and authorities of the time. This also applies to rabbinic Judaism which became normative for medieval and modern Judaism (cf. #80). If rabbinic Judaism is seen as continuation and correction of early Jewish beginnings by a number of groups, an important key is obtained for explaining its various ways of expression.

#24 The breaking up of early Judaism's unity was the fault mainly of the Seleucid rulers, Antiochus IV in particular, and the collaborating Jewish-Hellenistic forces, especially the high priests Jason (175–172 BCE) Menelaus (172–162 BCE), and Alcimus (162–159 BCE). Among the instigators and reinforcers of divisiveness must be counted the Hasmonean high-priestly rulers, namely Jonathan (152–143 BCE), Simon (143–134 BCE), John Hyrcanus I (134–104 BCE), Aristobulus I (104–103 BCE), Alexander Janneus (103–76 BCE), Hyrcanus II (67, 63–40 BCE), Aristobulus II (67–63 BCE), and Antigonus (40–37 BCE).[26] These rulers and notables wished to consolidate Hellenism with its power politics and religious and cultural-social aspects, superimposing it upon the Jewish peoplehood and religious fabric.[27] It is not clear whether the pagan Seleucids or the Jewish progressivists were first to demand radical Hellenization.[28] The early Jewish groups were a result of the gigantic struggle between Jewish and non-Jewish Hellenizers on the one hand, and traditionalist Jewish anti-Hellenists on the other. In any case, these groups did not grow out of the quarrelsome attitude of Jews.

#25 These early Jewish groups should not be seen in an exclusively negative light, that is, as an expression of Jewish dissension. Opposition to Hellenizers and the resulting intellectual-religious struggle helped traditional Judaism to resist absorption by Hellenistic syncretism. Antiochus IV and his Jewish helpers carried on their Hellenizing politics for social, political, and strategic reasons, which meant harsh suppression of the YHWH religion and casting doubts on its validity altogether.

Hellenism was that world culture and civilization of late antiquity which was characterized by religious and power-political features, chief among them the mutual influence of various local civilizations with predominantly Greek ideas and life styles. Traditional religions were left as undisturbed as possible but interpreted in the Greek mentality and by Greek ideas.[29] The Hellenizers wished to place YHWH on the same level as the Syrian god of heaven (cf. Dan 9:27) and the Greek Zeus (cf. 1 Macc 1:41–64; 2 Macc 6:1f; AgAp 1:113), and this struck the Israelite-Jewish worship of God at a very vulnerable spot. In pre-Davidic times and particularly since the ninth and eighth centuries BCE, the struggle against syncretism, Baalism, theocracy, and polyatry had been the main topic of disputes among the people of God; it also was the actual cause for a separation from the other nations (cf. Jgs 9; Deut; Hos 2:18; 1 Kgs 17–18; etc.). Jewish non-conformism or obstinacy is directly based on exclusivity, singularity, and the fervor for YHWH and his demand for a special, unadulterated cult (monolatry). For that reason, Judaism is a towering sign against cheap, overhasty religious ecumenism. Religious unity must not be confused with a leveling uniformity and surrender of significant foundations of belief.

#26 Shortly before the division of early Judaism into competing and warring factions, about 175–150 BCE, a name came into use which might indicate certain polarizations. The Books of the Maccabees mention the Assideans *(asidaioi)* (1 Macc 2:42; 7:13f; 2 Macc 14:6), which is the Greek transliteration of the Aramaic-Hebrew word *hasidei, hasidim,* and means the devout ones. It is used with regard to the high priests Alcimus (162–159 BCE) and Judas Maccabeus (d. 160 BCE).

Rabbinic literature also refers to "devout" groups of pre-Maccabean and early Maccabean times. They are called the "early devout," the "early sages" or the "men of the great assembly" (Mish Ber 5, 1; Abot 1, 1; TB Ber 26b; Meg 18a; Yom 69b; etc.). They are described as groups of pious and wise men who devoted their life to exposition and actualization of the Scriptures (Midrash and Halakhah) and the consolidation and formulation of Jewish prayer life. Their work followed in the footsteps of the biblical figures Ezra and Nehemiah who lived about 450 BCE.

The "devout" of the Books of the Maccabees are most likely identical with the "learned," "discerning," "those who fall" (as victims of persecution) and "leaders of righteousness" mentioned in the Book of Daniel (11:33f; 12:3). These groups were filled with the expectation of the soon-to-be-established kingdom of God.

There were two differently motivated groups of pious people: the interpreters of Scripture and founders of the liturgy, and those excitedly awaiting the early *eschaton;* we do not know of any polemics between them. They were even called by the same name and formed the immediate matrix for later groups that were more or less mutually exclusive.

3. Group Divisions and Group Intentions

#27 The Pharisees, Sadducees, Essenes, Zealots, Sicarii, Qumran people, and apocalypticists differed from one another and must not be placed on the same level. Even Josephus Flavius who in simplifying manner speaks of the Pharisees, Sadducees, and Essenes as "sects" or "philosophical schools" (*Bellum* 2, 119; *Ant* 18, 11) admits that Judas the Galilean who founded the Zealots gave rise to a "sect of its own" which "in no way resembled the others" (*Bellum* 2, 118). Contemporary research accepts the term "religious parties" as appropriate for all these groups,[30] yet that agrees with historical facts only if linked to the different causes, aims, and theologies.

#28 The Jewish religious parties from the Maccabean-Hasmonean period until 70 CE are best divided according to certain key words: Hellenism (Jewish and non-Jewish), commitment to the religio-political good of the Jewish people, and eschatological reign of God. We must ask where the different groups stood with regard to these basic questions. In order to give as complete a picture as possible of the characteristics and tensions, we will include in the following schematic presentation certain individuals (Philo, Josephus) and family clans (the Tobiads and Oniads).

#29 Relationship to Hellenism:

Enemies of Hellenism	Enoch and Daniel apocalypticists, Qumran people, early Maccabeans, priests of Leontopolis, rebels of the first Jewish war against Rome
Friends of Hellenism	Hellenistic high priests (Jason, Menelaus, Alcimus), Hasmonean high priests, esp. Simon, Aristobulus I, and Alexander Janneus
Politicians of Hellenism	Tobiads and Oniads
Certain Distant and Middle Positions	Pharisees, Sadducees, Philo of Alexandria, Josephus Flavius, possibly the Essenes

The term "politicians of Hellenism" lends itself to misunderstanding; it is meant to refer to respected and powerful families who attempted to strengthen their own positions by exploiting the struggle between friends and foes of Hellenization in Palestine and the fight for the country between the various non-Jewish power-Hellenists (Seleucids and Ptolemies). The Tobiads were supported by the Ptolemies against the Seleucids in the third and second centuries, but they fell on the accession of Antiochus IV. The Oniads were a conservative family of high priests who more or less rejected

Hellenism. They also entered the power struggle between the Ptolemies and Seleucids and were ruined during the reign of Antiochus IV.[31]

The other sub-divisions involve numerous problems also. Considerable differences existed, for example, between the Pharisees and Philo in their attitude toward Hellenism. Philo considered the "development of a synthesis between Greek culture and Jewish piety"[32] a lifelong task. On condition that the Roman power-Hellenists desisted from Jewish pogroms and obligatory emperor cults, he considered co-existence between Judaism and Hellenism possible and desirable. The Pharisees, on the other hand, had no sympathy whatsoever for pagan or Jewish Hellenism, yet they did not stoop to becoming involved in the Hellenistic struggle. There also were the many "Jewish Greek-speaking Palestinians" who lived in Palestine from about 200 BCE to 70 CE. Their world view consisted of an attenuated Hellenism together with an equally qualified traditional Jewish life style.[33] The schema below is merely a rough outline of the main trends among the religious parties, family clans, and certain individuals.

#30 Commitment to the religio-political good of the Jewish people:

Early Jewish establishment	Hasmoneans, Herodians, Sadducees, Pharisees
Those standing apart	Various apocalyptic groups, Essenes, *Am haarez*, Jewish Christians
Separatists	Qumran people, gnosticizing Jewish groups, possibly Leontopolis high priests
Militant anarchists	Rebellious groups of the first Jewish war against Rome

It is important to note that the Essenes are among those standing apart while the Qumran people are called separatists. The latter considered their own group the only true representative of Israel, and all others corrupt and apostatizing. Such exclusivist self-perception is actually known only in the case of the Qumran people, but we must suspect it also of the Leontopolis priests.[34] Contrary to most of the early Qumran research, scholars are now more inclined to differentiate between the Essenes described by Josephus (*Ant* 18, 18–22; *Bellum* 2, 119–160) and Philo (*Quod Omnis Probus Liber Sit* 75–91), and the people of Qumran. The Essenes did not apparently consider themselves separatists, but they had their res ervations with regard to the Jerusalem cult. If gnosticizing Jewish groups existed before 70 CE, they were probably forced to separate from other groups; their identification with Israel was not thereby significantly influenced.

The early Jewish establishment comprises the internal Jewish self-administration as well as groups taking part in national and religious politics. Before the rebellion of 66–73 CE, these were the Sadducees and Pharisees, together with the ruling house in office (Hasmoneans and Herodians) and their followers. In the Sanhedrin and in the ante-chambers of the Jewish and Roman office holders, they could make their influence felt in a limited way.

The rebel groups of the Jewish war were not simply tyrants, robbers, and enemies of the people, as Josephus Flavius describes them with considerable hostility (*Bellum* 1, 10; 2, 411; 7, 4; etc.). As indicated in the schema above, they wanted to take up arms for the good of the people. They wished to free the people from sinners and oppressors, thereby leading it toward eschatological freedom and moral purity, ideals inspired by a messianic outlook. Toward the very end, however, they drove the Jewish people into the catastrophic situation that ended with the conquest of Judea and Jerusalem, the destruction of the Temple, the decimation of the Jewish population, and the exile of many of the survivors.[35]

#31 Expectation of the kingdom of God (*basileia*):

Those expecting an early Coming	Daniel and Enoch apocalypticists, various messianic-esoteric groups, Qumran people, rebels of the first war against Rome, possibly the Leontopolis priests
Those expecting a later Coming	Pharisees, Sadducees, Philo

This differentiation is of great religio-historical and theological importance. Beginning with the Maccabeans, belief in the approaching reign of God became a leading issue that divided the minds of the people, just as in earlier times the demand for an exclusive recognition of YHWH (monoyahwism) had been. In the following periods, nearly all disorders instigated by religious Jews were related to agitated, eschatological expectations or eschatological unrest (cf. #215–219). In the context of religious need during persecution by Seleucid, Hasmonean, and Roman authorities, many apocalypticists and esoterics unofficially joined ranks. They wanted to suffer and withdraw from the world as a community as they eagerly awaited an early Coming.

The Pharisees did not enter history under the sign of an early expectation of the reign of God. They were more concerned with Bible exegesis and reflections on the Wisdom and Halakhic literature, in the service of a quiet life conforming to revelation. They not only wished to reflect on the *eschaton* but on the ways of continued Jewish existence in this world (cf. #124). Occasionally, they also were seized by the fever of an early messiah expectation.[36] The Sadducees followed a line of thought similar to that of the Pharisees, but close cooperation with the Roman occupation forces hindered them from developing a scholarly Bible tradition.

4. Groups and Ideas—Their Particular Influence and Later Development in Judaism and Christianity

#32 The ideas of the various early Jewish groups were not preserved within these groups exclusively, nor were they proclaimed in precisely the same way at all times. Apocalyptic ideas and trends proved particularly dynamic and diffusive, as did messianic expectations and sapiential and law-inspired reflections and life styles. All of these later on formed the spiritual foundations of Christianity and Judaism, which cannot be fully understood without them. While apocalypticism, messianism, and sapiential reflections on law should not be put aside as merely pre-Christian phenomena, it is just as indefensible to assign apocalyptic to Christianity and sapiential thoughts on law to Jewish thought.[37] Such one-sided divisions are too simplistic, smacking of the clichés of former generations of scholars.

a. Apocalyptic, Apocalypticists, Apocalypses

#33 In recent years it used to be almost a matter of good form to begin a scholarly treatise on apocalyptic with a quotation, to explain that everything in this field was really quite vague. The reference was to Gerhard von Rad:

> Whoever uses the term apocalypticism ought to be aware of the fact that we have not yet succeeded in defining it in a satisfactory way.[38]

Just as popular was the lapidary statement by H. D. Betz: "What apocalyptic really is, is a contested question."[39] Unless one presumed to have found the (apocalyptic) stone of wisdom, such introductory remarks were required to cover the subsequent theses, because apocalyptic is an extremely varied, complicated, and often antithetical combination of problems.

#34 Many approaches to apocalyptic research have been attempted that later on proved to be dead ends. The word *apokalypsis* of Ap 1:1 (revelation, disclosure) is of no help in clarifying the phenomenon of apocalyptic generally. The Apocalypse of St. John is only one form of apocalyptic literature. The greatest number of such writings are contained neither in the New Testament nor in the Tanakh but came into being during early and medieval Judaism.[40]

Another error of method consists in attempts to read apocalyptic writings systematically and to distill from the very considerable body of literature certain general characteristics. Although present-day approaches are no longer quite so clumsy because some aspects of the history of religion and tradition are being taken into consideration, apocalyptic *notae* still tend to be made too early in the research process, so that they become mere irrelevant abstractions. J. Lindblom[41] and H. H. Rowley[42] were typical representatives of the schematizing scholar who helped bring about the disqualification of apocalyptic.

Josef Schreiner no longer displays such bias; on the other hand, he inherited from previous scholars a predilection for premature *notae*.[43] Important observations on the history of religion often come in the pages after his presentation of apocalyptic characteristics.

#35 According to Johann M. Schmidt, "the problem of apocalyptic" is that of "method." In a resigned way he states that the heretofore employed

> theological foundations have not proved adequate for a pertinent historical appreciation of Jewish apocalyptic. . . . We must start all over again to examine historical statements and judgments, as well as to explore such results theologically. We had best begin with the history of religion and tradition. Such studies, however, must be enlarged and freed from deficiencies of concrete historical results and general theological conceptions.[44]

Contemporary research should try to proceed along the lines suggested by Schmidt and pay particular attention to the guidance provided by studies in the history of religion and tradition before venturing on to theological (including Christological) speculations.

The hermeneutical forefield of research begins where one's own philosophy is regard to apocalyptic finds expression. Schmidt enumerates the following hermeneutical problems:

> ... the question of the end of Israel, the question of the historical relationship between Israel and Christianity, and finally the question of the world-encompassing historical link between the Israelite-Jewish and the Christian religion.[45]

Indeed, extra-canonical Jewish apocalyptic can only escape an *a priori* disparagement as epigonic prophetism, as pseudo-mysticism, as a phenomenon of paralysis, rampant growth, etc., if the scholarly authors have command of a wide-ranging theology of Israel. Moreover, they should not play off Judaism against Christianity unnecessarily and place Jewish-Christian revelation in unbridgeable opposition to extra-biblical views. A scholar who merely perceives a paralyzed, withered Israel at the time of the Babylonian exile, at the time of Ezra-Nehemiah and at the time of the destruction of the Second Temple in Jerusalem will consider early Jewish apocalyptic as merely a product of decay. He will be incapable of performing solid work in the history of religions.

#36 From the very beginning, apocalyptic was a literary genre as well as a Jewish religious world view (*Weltanschauung*), i.e., an assessment of cosmic, historic, transhistoric and posthistoric facts and ideas. These dual, variously related levels must be taken into account in classifying apocalyptic. The apocalyptic genre arose at a certain period in time and under the influence of particular religious and national afflictions and corresponding reactions. Only a composite view on historical and religious levels can lead to an understanding of individual apocalypses and of apocalyptic in general.

#37 From the outset in the early Jewish period, apocalyptic as *Weltanschauung* contained a religious view of its time and of history. This characteristic remained, if under changed circumstances, in New Testament, rabbinic, medieval, and modern times. Apocalyptic as a view of history was marked by versatility, totality, and a radicalism not previously known to that extent. In the apocalyptic perspective of the inner-Jewish situation and that of the world-power oppressing the Jews, it was inferred that the world was immediately approaching the final revolution of time and the imminent coming of the reign of God (*basileia tou theou;* cf. Dan 2:34f, 44). The ruling world-power was declared unspeakably sinful because of blasphemy and oppression of God's people. Within the Jewish world, the highest Jewish dignitaries to whom Israel's cult was entrusted were also held to be extremely corrupt and hostile to God (cf. Dan 9:24–27). The oppressing world-power's attitude and that of many apostates and lawless men among the people of God presage the collapse of the present era and the coming of a new one. It was necessary to strengthen the loyalty of the few remaining faithful and to motivate them to perseverance. They had to be protected and, if possible, immunized against the all-pervading sinfulness. Conscious of his divinely willed responsibility for Israel, even for the whole world, the apocalypticist proclaimed—with threats, implorations, and encouragements—his universal message of salvation, which pointed toward the end of time.

In contrast to the mighty of this world and to the Jews bargaining with them for power and progress, the apocalypticist was aware of

> the goal, the end of the ages, the consummation of history. Even that portion of history that has not yet happened has been revealed to him. So he already stands even now, proleptically at the end of history; he can survey it entire, and in the light of future events can also understand the past, interpret it, and make it comprehensible as a necessary step toward the established goal of the ages.[46]

Apocalyptic is, then, a committed, impassioned judgment of time and history, with a view to the approaching reign of God which surpasses all times and ages. It is the expression of a view according to which the soon-to-come kingdom of God is the fulcrum and measure of all activity and thought. All events, merits, and aberrations in the past and present must be seen in the light of the kingdom of God and the events indicating and accompanying its coming (cf. #29–32).

#38 Early and later Jewish apocalyptic would be denied full justice, were one to see their characteristics exclusively in the described "vehement eschatologization of the understanding of their own history" or in the "eschatologization of their historical consciousness."[47] Such one-sidedness would imply, for example, that we no longer can draw the line within the Hebrew Scriptures between apocalyptic and non-apocalyptic. It would mean, for instance, that all Isaiah passages speaking of the God of Israel acting in the future (46:10; etc.) be characterized as more or less apocalyptic. Even more decisive is the fact that in early Jewish apocalyptic the near *eschaton* is frequently mentioned while there are few prophecies in the strict sense. One such prophecy occurs in Daniel:

> In the first year of his (Darius') reign, I, Daniel, tried to understand in the Scriptures the counting of the years of which YHWH spoke to the

prophet Jeremiah: That for the ruins of Jerusalem seventy years must be fulfilled (9:2 NAB).

Daniel 9:24–27 interprets the quoted words of Jeremiah (Jer 25:11ff; 29:10–14) as a sign that the death of the Temple desecrator Antiochus IV was to be the beginning of the end of history (cf. Dan 7:25; 8:14; 12:7). The Apocalypse of Enoch also holds that the history of the world was to last seventy periods of years, that is, seventy human generations. A passage in the Ethiopic Enoch,[48] which probably contains an older tradition than the quoted Daniel words, says:

> And when all their sons (the descendants of the fallen angels and the beautiful daughters of men, cf. Gen 6:1–4) kill each other, and when they see the destruction of their beloved ones, bind them for seventy generations under the hills of the earth until the day of their judgment and of their consummation (*syntelesmon*), until the judgment which for all eternity is accomplished (1 Enoch 10, 12: Knibb II, 89).

At first, no profound crisis within the apocalyptic movement occurred when the events of the Daniel and Enoch prophecies did not come about. The post-Daniel Qumran Habakkuk commentary indicates that the passages of Jeremiah (25:11f; 29:10–14) were not the only influence on his ideas about the *eschaton.* The text of Hab 2:3,

> for the vision still has its time, presses on to fulfillment, and will not disappoint; if it delays, wait for it, it will surely come, it will not be late,

played an even more important part in the thinking of the Qumran commentator and later apocalypticists. With reference to this passage, the expected final events could rather easily be reassessed. Still, it cannot be denied that the constantly pressing problems of the delayed *parousia* imposed difficult pastoral and psychological burdens upon the apocalypticists.[49]

#39 Their proclamations of salvation and ruin were not merely attempts to guard against invaders and sinners and to create a solid basis for the weak and loyal ones. The apocalypticists also tried to lay firm foundations of a spiritual and practical-religious nature. Next to, and linked with the view of history in the final age, a characteristic cue word for apocalyptic is "esoteric" (interior teaching, interior practice), which expresses the teaching as well as the life style developed by, and exclusively practiced within, a certain group. Such theories and practices do not represent simple conventions and possibilities but constitute guidelines of an authoritative and thereby internally binding character.

Insofar as apocalyptic is also esoteric, it could be called an interior experience in the regions of the unfathomable. What this actually means can be deduced from a saying in the Mishnah which deals with rampant speculations and practices regarding proto-history and meta-history, and the powers of heaven and the underworld:

> If anyone speculates about four things, it would have been better had he never come into the world; namely: what is above? what is below? what was before? and what will be hereafter? (mHag 2, 1).

This defensive formula in its polemical distortion lashes out not only against gnosticism but also against apocalyptic. In two main directions the apocalypticists sought the experience or path into the immeasurable: forward, toward the *eschaton,* and upward, into heavenly transcendence. We may even speak of a fourfold tendency, namely upward, below, backward, and forward because the *eschaton* cannot be described without reference to the beginnings (before), and a demonic sphere (below) which, according to the apocalyptic view, corresponded to the heavenly one.

#40 The apocalyptic pressing on toward the *eschaton* was accompanied by the attempt to elucidate it with reference to the primeval time of Israel or the world. Before the Deluge Enoch (1 En 1:3–9) saw a vision of the final theophany from Mount Sinai. Israel's beginnings were to be realized at the end of time in a most wonderful, terrible, decisive, and universal way:

> And the God of the world will come to earth on the Mount of Sinai. He will be seen on his couch. He will also be seen in the power of his strength from the heaven of heavens (v. 4).

This final Sinai theophany was to shake mankind and the world and bring about its collapse and consummation by fire. After this cosmic event, a judgment was to take place. When God at that time appears with his ten thousands to sit in judgment, the hour of the righteous' final bliss will have arrived.

J. Vanderkam reminds us of the genre of theophany descriptions in the Tanakh (Dt 33:2; Jgs 5:4f; Is 63:19ff; Mi 1:2–5; Hab 3) which are mirrored in the above Enoch verses.[50] The Enoch tradition almost always relies on narrations of primitive biblical history before Moses to describe the *eschaton*. The fall of the angels, also portrayed in Genesis 6, was very popular and, according to the Enoch tradition, actually brought about the original sin of mankind (cf. 1 En 6:1; 15:1–12). The *eschaton* includes the particular punishment of the wicked angels (cf. 1 En 18:13–19:1). The expectation of an eschatological Adam in 1 En 90:37f indicates the implied tie between primeval times and the *eschaton*.

Just as vision and stride were directed *forward* toward meta-history, an *upward* turning, toward the divine sphere, was also inherent in apocalyptic. The norms for living of early Jewish apocalypticists and related groups were contained not simply in the Torah and Prophets; heavenly tablets or scriptures seem to have been just as important. It says in the Book of Jubilees:

> And on the day when the sons of Jacob slew Shechem (cf. Gen 34) a writing was recorded in their favor in heaven that they had executed righteousness and uprightness and vengeance upon the sinner and it was written for a blessing (Jub 30:23).

Not only in the Book of Jubilees, written toward the end of the second century BCE, did passages occur mentioning that good and evil deeds of man are entered into heavenly books, but also in older portions of the First Book of Enoch, from which the Book of Jubilees derived. Other passages go even further to say that heavenly tablets or books are

> the foundations for the proper course of history, wherefore it was now considered necessary to conform one's own life to these heavenly tablets (cf. 1 En 81:1f; 93:1f; 103:2f; Jub 3:31; 4:5.32; T. Levi 5:4; T. Asher 7:5; etc.).[51]

The apocalypticists were not satisfied with looking toward heaven and the heavenly laws for the conduct of their life; they virtually tried to ascend to these spheres. We read of visions, auditions, ascensions, and journeys in the heavens.

In that respect, the apocalypticists are heirs to early Jewish Temple theology or mysticism or, rather, Temple esoterics. The latter, practiced by the priests, concentrated on the throne of God which, according to Isaiah 6, descended on the early Temple and deeply affected the prophet. Another important passage was Ezekiel 1 in which that priest-prophet had a vision of God's chariot (*merkabah*). Esoteric practice must be imagined as if the Temple priests could glimpse behind the Temple—as in a mysterious transparency—the throne (chariot) of God; accordingly, their Temple service was an earthly-heavenly function.[52] Various such ideas and traditions were seized upon by the apocalypticists and placed within a new context. They had a twofold interest in the notion of the chariot, namely as representation of judgment scenes at the end of time, and as authentication of their reception of a revelation. Typical is the eschatological judgment scene in Dan 7:9f, written in priestly-esoteric style:

> As I watched, thrones were set up and the Ancient One took his throne. His clothing was snow bright, and the hair on his head as white as wool; his throne was flames of fire, with wheels of burning fire. A surging stream of fire flowed out from where we sat; thousands upon thousands were ministering to him, and myriads upon myriads attended to him. The court was convened, and the books were opened.

1 En 46:1–6 and 2 Baruch 51:11 are comparable texts.

Relying on *merkabah* motifs in the priestly tradition, the apocalypticists could legitimize themselves as recipients of revelation and hence authorities concerning revelation. Representing the Temple, which penetrated into the heavenly spheres, as the place of revelation *par excellence* and considering themselves men elevated and blessed by grace, they gave their proclamations the highest imaginable justification. 1 En 14:8–25 illustrates this point:

> And a vision appeared to me as follows: Behold clouds called me in the vision, and mist called me, and the path of the stars and flashes of lightning hastened me and drove me, and in the vision winds caused me to fly and hastened me and lifted me up into heaven. And I proceeded until I came near to a wall which was built of hailstones, and a tongue of fire surrounded it, and it began to make me afraid. And I went into the tongue of fire and came near to a large house which was built of hailstones, and the wall of that house (was) like a mosaic (made) of hailstones, and its floor (was) snow. Its roof (was) like the path of the stars and flashes of lightning, and among them (were) fiery Cherubim, and their heaven (was like) water. And (there was) a fire burning around its wall, and its door was ablaze with fire. And I went into that house and (it was) hot as fire and cold as snow, and there was neither pleasure nor life in it. Fear covered me and trembling took hold of me. And as I was shaking and trembling, I fell on my face. And I saw in the vision, and behold, another house, which was larger than the former, and all its

doors (were) open before me, and (it was) built of a tongue of fire. And in everything it so excelled in glory and splendor and size that I am unable to describe to you its glory and its size. And its floor (was) fire, and above (were) lightning and the path of the stars, and its roof also (was) a burning fire. And I looked and I saw in it a high throne, and its appearance (was) like ice and its surrounds like the shining sun and the sound of Cherubim. And from underneath the high throne there flowed out rivers of burning fire so that it was impossible to look at it. And He who is great in glory sat on it, and his raiment was brighter than the sun, and whiter than any snow. And no angel could enter, and at the appearance of the face of him who is honored and praised no (creature of) flesh could look. A sea of fire burnt around him, and a great fire stood before him, and none of those around him came near to him. Ten thousand times ten thousand (stood) before him, but he needed no holy counsel. And the Holy Ones who were near to him did not leave by night or day, and did not depart from him. And until then I had a covering on my face, as I trembled. And the Lord called me with his own mouth and said to me: "Come hither, Enoch, to my holy word." And he lifted me up and brought me near to the door. And I looked, with my face down (Knibb, II, 97–100).

This text indicates that the apocalypticist did not presume that he could attain to the divine mysteries by his own efforts. Rather, he is catapulted into these spheres and borne up by the conviction of his being preferred to heavenly spirits and, even more, to all mortals. He receives revelations directly from God, and that is why men must obey him absolutely (cf. 1 En 60; 71; Apoc. Abr. 18; T. Levi 5; Ap 4–10; etc.).

We need not deal here with the apocalypticists' insights into the activities of the demonic powers. Such visions of "below" are sometimes to be found in visions relating to the *merkabah* sphere, and speculative descriptions occur in the Qumran literature (cf. IQS III, 13—IV, 26; IQM I).[53]

#41. The two related characteristics of apocalyptic, esoterics and an eschatological view of history, are not unambiguous signs, even in their occurrence together, whereby one can define apocalyptic literature in every case. This incertitude remains above all in the realm of Old Testament literature. The origin of apocalyptic in the Old Testament is to some extent unclear. The problems begin with the Book of Ezekiel which is definitely esoteric (Ez 1; 8; 9; 10) and contains passages of vehement and vivid eschatology (esp. 38; 39; cf. 21:13–22). The Gog-Magog section was not written by Ezekiel (Ez 38; 39) but is a later incorporation. It must be presumed that the redactors and glossators were thinking in apocalyptic terms, but it remains a supposition because the Gog-Magog descriptions do not carry great weight within the Book of Ezekiel.

#42 Hartmut Gese holds that the night visions experienced by the priest Zechariah ben Iddo in February 519 BCE (cf. Zech 1:7; 1:8—6:8) are the oldest apocalypse known. Deutero-Zechariah (Zech 9; 10; 11) and Trito-Zechariah (Zech 12; 13; 14) are said to be apocalyptic continuations of the First Zechariah, on the occasion of Alexander's expedition (cf. Zech 9:1–8) and the Ptolemaic era of the third century BCE (cf. Zech 12:10ff). Gese bases his view on the thrust of these night visions; unlike the earlier prophetic visions, they do not contain a proclamation but are initiations into a true reality that transcends history. He sums up his thesis as follows:

> We find here, not a collection of seven visions, but a system of seven dimensions of one night. I think that is a complete apocalypse, a system of a sevenfold revelation of the coming of a new age, the *basileia tou theou.* The qualitatively different time of the new aeon is determined by the transcendental intervention of God. The alleged absence of history in apocalyptic is contingent upon the totality of salvation which can be achieved by the action of God alone and must be understood as an intervention from above. In contrast to the totally New and Other of divine salvation, the contingent world experienced by man is nothing but a superficial reality. The seer can express true existence only in esoteric, mysterious symbols; however, his sapiential and disciplined discoveries of ideal truth as a sublimated experience of existence correspond to them.[54]

It is quite true that apocalyptic deals with the crisis in prophetic leadership and the search for a new divine authorization to bring the message to the people of God. It is equally correct that apocalyptic did not suddenly come with the Book of Daniel (164 BCE) but could at that time already look back on an earlier history and time of preparation. Yet, it is difficult to follow Gese without reservations because the historical basis for the night visions is too vague. The apocalypticists were neither systematic theologians nor mere speculators on the future. They produced very rigorous kerygmatic statements *for their own time,* a period they considered surfeited with sin, deprivations, and perversions. In order to lend their discourses more emphasis, they depicted the past of the nations and Israel as well as the *eschaton,* so that they addressed their admonitions to their contemporaries. We shall summarize five such apocalyptic homilies: 1 En

93:1–10; 91:12–17 (apocalypse of weeks); 1 En 85—90 (animal apocalypses); CD I, 1 - VIII, 21; XIX, 1 - XX, 34; and Jub 20—23. The following evils are there castigated: banding together of all the transgressors against the loyal Israel (that is, the group to which the apocalyptic writers belong); extremely frequent and ever increasing apostasy in Israel; harlotry, idolatry, intermarriage with pagans; brutality; desecration of the Temple and sacrilege by the priests. Past and future are represented in such a way that their reference to the present cannot be overlooked.

#43 Apocalyptic undoubtedly reached its pinnacle in the Book of Daniel (cf. #66f). But it is just as certain that an early apocalyptic period, beginning sometime after the Babylonian exile, preceded that culmination. The books of Ezekiel and Zechariah as well as passages in Malachi and the Apocalypse of Isaiah (24–27) are clear evidence for this fact. Through tradition-historical studies, the First Apocalypse of Enoch, which in its oldest parts (1–36; 93:3–10; 91:12–17) is pre-Daniel, can be traced to the third century BCE.

The Book of Jonah can be considered one of the first extant anti-apocalyptic writings. Perhaps it is a critique by irony of vulgar, threatening apocalyptic that counts on definite dates of catastrophes. "Forty days more and Nineveh shall be overthrown," is Jonah's threat (3:4). As becomes clear in the dialogue between God and Jonah in Chapter 4, the author turns against such fulminating preachers who in their threats and expectations of coming catastrophes do not give sufficient place to God's forbearance and human readiness to repent. This anti-apocalyptic criticism by the author of the Book of Jonah possesses a lasting validity.

#44 Apocalyptic proved an excellent means for proclaiming the message of early Christianity. The Christ event was conceived as an historical, eschatological, and transcendental act of salvation. In Christ the absolute future of God and man become transparent. Apocalyptic may, then, be called "the mother of all Christian theology"[55] or, more cautiously, its "midwife."[56] Yet, apocalyptic remained indispensable not only to Christianity but to Judaism as well. The basic reason is Jewish and Christian hope for unlimited fulfillment—beyond the distress, limitations, and inadequacies of history—as well as Jewish and Christian experience of the infinite God, an experience that can only be rendered in broken bizarre language. Apocalyptic cannot be squeezed into a Christian dogmatic system nor into a traditional Jewish order of conduct. Yet for Christians as well as Jews the task is to place apocalyptic into the focus of belief, while simultaneously guarding against extreme developments.

b. Messianic Hopes

#45 The theme of messiah served as an arena for polemicists. Jewish and Christian theologians and historians of religion held different views and used this topic to give a firm foundation to their own faith position and idea of the messiah. The same platitudes are always evident in these scholarly disputes. The often repeated phrase, "Christians believe in a messiah who has already come, but the Jews are still awaiting him," has in its emotional content and sweeping approach added to the obfuscation of the real relationship between Jews and Christians. The following clichés are being advanced, for example: Jesus Christ is no more nor less than *the* messiah. In the Hebrew Scriptures and at the time of Jesus, only *one* messianic idea was in circulation and tailored for Jesus. The Jews are obtuse in not recognizing the messiah in Jesus. Their ideas, then and now, are merely "carnal," and that prevents them from believing in Jesus Christ.

A long overdue disentanglement and simplification can be brought about only if the various Jewish messianic expectations at the time of Jesus and their different points of reference are considered, their roots in the Old Testament are investigated, and we learn to differentiate between genuine messianic hope and a flight into messianism. Long ago it was already shown not only that messianic hope is a true Jewish and Christian concern of faith but that it can also serve as alibi for all kinds of hostilities and substitutes disguised as religion.

#46 No clear understanding has been reached in the course of the history of research on the delimitation of the messiah concept. For that reason, the point in time at which we may speak of full messianic expectations has to remain vague, as does our knowledge of the groups representing and confessing this expectation. In the history of religion generally, such terms as messianism, messianic movements, messiah, etc., are quite broadly conceived. Messianism is said to be eschatological reverie with millenarian motifs and utopian yearnings. In the center of messianic movements asserting to be militant-activist stands the figure of a charismatic warrior messiah.[57] Scholars in the history of religion of biblical, early post-biblical, early Jewish, early Christian, and rabbinic times equally subscribe to such rather vague definitions.[58]

Joseph Klausner, a Jewish scholar on Jesus and messiahship, took great pains at defining the messiah. He was not content with the often presented characterization that the messiah was king of Israel at the end of time. Klausner's Jewish orientation is apparent in the differentiation he proposes between messianic hope and belief in the messiah. The former is the prophetic hope for a new era when political freedom, moral perfection, and earthly bliss will prevail for Israel in her own land, and for humanity as a whole. Belief in the messiah, however, refers to prophetic hope for a new age when a redeemer, by his power and spirit, will bring about political and spiritual salvation for Israel and, thereby, earthly bliss and moral perfection for all men.[59] None of the authors is so naive to assume that the difficult problem of the messiah could be solved by a long or short definition. A more profound understanding requires conceptual and religio-historical details to be taken into account. It must be realized above all that we cannot proceed from a messiah concept based exclusively on the Tanakh and New Testament. Judaism and Christianity have remained messianic movements, even in post-New Testament times.

#47 It would take us too far afield to trace the messiah concept, its contents and variations, from the time of the Tanakh; only the results are important in this context. Though the Tanakh contains all concepts and ideas constitutive to messianic notions, we speak with reservations and some hesitation of messianism in the Tanakh. We must take care not to confuse with messianic texts those merely referring to an interior historical restoration of the house of David. In pre-Daniel time, moreover, no universal notion of the *absolute* end of history and the "revolving of the times" (3 Sibylline Oracles 289) was at all current. Not before Jewish and intertestamental times did eschatological ideas circulate in such variety and depth as to make possible messianic images in the strictest sense of the word. The final event was called, among other definitions, *basileia tou theou,* the ultimate Kingdom of God. In 1 Cor 15:28 St. Paul refers to that meta-historical condition in which God, beyond all temporal confinements, will be "all in all." Still, a qualitatively different and ultimate tomorrow is already foreseen in the Tanakh (e.g., Is 1), and we may well speak of messianic expectations, though in a somewhat broader sense.

#48 Jewish history of religion does not recognize a messiah pure and simple whose powers and functions are defined unambiguously and immutably. Strongly divergent, constantly changing ideas were in circulation about the figure and actions of a messiah. At times a priestly messiah, at others a Davidic or prophetic one was expected. Messianic hope was sometimes placed in deceased and returning heroes of Jewish antiquity, or in contemporary rulers and charismatics, in heroes of a revolution, in fanatics or sapiential teachers. The palette of messianic ideas becomes even more colorful when we consider that quite often not just *one* but *several* (usually two) messianic figures were expected or appeared on the scene.

Keeping in mind that messianic expectations and figures cannot be fitted into official, doctrinal patterns and channels, we may accept the following general statements. Messiahs were representative figures who were to appear immediately before an absolute end of time, which was awaited with excitement and enthusiasm. They bore the features of sovereignty and power of great salvific personalities in the Hebrew Scriptures or at least they were symbols of an earlier deliverance. They appeared in situations when the people of God was in deepest distress which, in turn, was interpreted as the eve or beginning of the eschatological course of events. They were men who, owing to their God-given calling, stood in the midst of God's people, subject to its religious, social, economic, and political oppression, and admonished, corrected, and saved the people. As these men were no mere nationalists but concerned with universal as well as Jewish-national problems, it is not apposite at all to designate them "national messiah." Belief in the resurrection of the dead and in the God of Israel who will soon arrive for a final judgment and an all-new creation formed the most significant religious background for the development of messianic expectations.

#49 In theological and in the history of religion studies the son of man is the most effective parallel to the royal, Davidic messiah at the end of days. He appears in several early Jewish writings, and the New Testament applies the concept to Jesus. With the help of that figure it can be shown that the groups opposing the Jerusalem establishment, or at least hostile to or dissociated from it, did not expect a royal Davidic personality but a figure symbolic of their own group ideals.

The Septuagint translation of Num 24:17b has an interpretation of the Hebrew text which goes beyond the original meaning of this verse. The Hebrew has: "A star shall advance from Jacob, and a staff shall rise from Israel." The Greek version replaces the word "staff" with "man" (*anthropos*). "A star shall advance from Jacob, and a man shall rise (*anastesetai*) from Israel." Something similar happened to the saying of Baalam in Num 24:7. The Masoretic text is rather obscure. It seems that Samson Raphael Hirsch interpreted it particularly well:

> The waters flow from his (God's) buckets and his seed shall be in many waters. His king will be greater than Agag and his kingdom will be exalted. (RSV)

Hirsch paraphrases the sentence as follows:

> The waters flow from his buckets and his seed is every human shoot which is sown at these streams of the divine source of vivification; the

> full mystery which characterizes as good the tents and habitations of Jacob/Israel and forms all life there developing into such a "blessing and blessed" human plant lies in the moral, in the all-pervading sanctification and sanctity of sexual family life, which sees the power of human seed as most holy and belonging to God, and every human scion sown and planted according to God's instruction at the source of his teaching and law, for his glorification and the realization of his will on earth. . . . [60]

This interpretation in the light of Israelitic understanding of the holiness of sexuality and procreation probably conforms to the original meaning of the text. The reference to the great and exalted "king" indicates that the text was redacted in the Davidic-Solomonic period or a little later in monarchic times. The king and his empire are not explicitly described as the ideal David but simply as an historical, excellent king of many nations. The Septuagint version of Num 24:7 says: "A man will rise from his seed and he will rule over many nations. His rule will be greater than Gog." Just as in the Septuagint version of Num 24:17 a "man" is mentioned who will "rise," so the Amalekite king Agag of the Masoretic text becomes "Gog." According to Ezekiel 38 and 39, Gog is an extremely powerful eschatological enemy of Israel. The Septuagint translator wishes to say that the "man" whom he apparently expects to come in an exalted manner of existence after the destruction of Gog will be a redeemer figure sent by God in opposition to the eschatological enemy of Israel. The Septuagint avoids the word "king" for this luminous final figure, though the term might well have suggested itself in accord with the original. There are indications that the Septuagint version of Num 24:7 is based on a multifaceted understanding of the *eschaton*. The expected "man" was formulated in accordance with an eschatological passage in the Book of Ezekiel, whereby the original eschatological train of thought was even strengthened and broadened. In the Septuagint, it is only a short step from the expected "man" to the "son of man," *hyios anthropou*. In the Masoretic text the priest-prophet Ezekiel is called *ben adam,* son of man, ninety-three times, which the Septuagint renders as *hyios anthropou*. The term is always linked to solemn acclamation, exaltation, being called toward the divine sphere (cf. Ez 2:1.8; 3:1; 4:1; etc.). Since the translators of Num 24:7, 17 place the word "man" in relationship with the Book of Ezekiel and since it bears a note of authority, we could cautiously state that the expectation of an exalted man at the end of days antedates the expectation of a messiah of Davidic hues. Evidently that "man" belongs to the same category as the

Davidic messiah; he is a messianically conceived figure which is not clearly defined—provided the word "messianic" is given analogous value. What is remarkable and enigmatic is the fact that a messiah-expectation based on the pentateuchal tradition did not occur first in the Palestinian matrix of Judaism but in the Egyptian diaspora, where the Septuagint came into being. In the *Encyclopaedia Judaica,* Professor David Flusser concludes from the Septuagint translation of Num 24:7, 17:

> Possibly, the designation of the Messiah as "man" is a proof that the special concept of son of man already existed in the early third century BCE.[61]

The Septuagint translation suggests that the "son of man" should not be classified as a mere apocalyptic figure of expectation. Yet, many strands lead from the Septuagint to the Daniel and Enoch Apocalypses in which the "son of man" as well as the *adam*/man idea of primeval and final time plays an important part.[62]

Neither the authors of the Septuagint, nor the apocalypticists, nor the disciples of Christ belonged to the Jerusalem establishment, and it was they who preferred the term "son of man."[63] The early Jewish times' emphasis and tone concerning the final salvific figure depended on the structure, situation and main concerns of the various groups. He was a person in relation to and representing the different groups and movements. When the Pharisees, for example, awaited a Davidic messiah, they thereby gave expression to the still active influence of a

> loyalty to royalty dating back to the times of the kings . . . though now transformed by Davidic-messianic expectations, conformed to their own ideal of law and righteousness or the reign of God.[64]

#50 Messianic expectations set free enormous powers for hope and change within the people of God before Christ, within the Church, and within post-biblical Judaism. Yet, tragedy, impatience, dissension, and the development of ideologies also resulted. Right up to modern times, it proved difficult for Jews not to plunge into utopian, messianic adventures endangering the community, and not to seize the sword to force the coming of salvation. Again and again, messianic radicals disregarded innate Jewish traditions according to which messianic redemption sprouts slowly like a shoot and gradually grows to full flower and bears fruit. Christianity tended to ideologize messianic hope. The Messiah-already-come served as pretext for triumphalist, imperialistic ideas in the Church. Waiting in faith for the Coming of the Lord became stunted. Judaism and Christianity would be well advised to exchange experiences of messianism, its dangers and opportunities.

c. Sapiential and Law-Inspired Life Styles

#51 With surprising frequency certain terms occur in late books of the Hebrew Scriptures stating that the Torah is a revelation which must be studied, investigated, interpreted, read aloud, and taught by the scholarly and discerning (Ezra 7:11; Neh 8:7–9; 1 Chr 25:8; 2 Chr 27:32; 30:32; Dan 8:16; 9:22; 10:14; etc.). The religious reformers Ezra and Nehemiah (about 450 BCE) were the chief initiators of interpretation and actualization of traditional revelation.

The Chronicler's history subsequent to Ezra/Nehemiah reflects discord between conservative Jews who kept their well-measured distance from the sacred Scripture traditions (literalists) and those who wished to actualize those old traditions in an authoritative way. The latter are called princes (*sarim:* Ezra 8:24f; 9:1; 10:14; Neh 3:14; 7:2), elders (*zekenim:* Ezra 3:12; 10:8; 2 Chr 5:2, 4; 10:6, 8, 13), scribes (*sofrim:* Ezra 7:6, 11; Neh 8:4, 9, 13) and sons of captivity (*bne hagolah:* Ezra 10:7–16). They are the first more or less obvious representatives of that office of religious authority which later marked the rabbinic scholars (cf. #52, 91). The literalists resisted the new interpreters and adapters of traditional revelation who did not object, for example, to marriage with non-Jewish women (cf. Ezra 10:18; Neh 13:28) or treading the wine presses, bringing in grain, and carrying burdens on the sabbath (cf. Neh 13:15–18). Traces of such liberal-conservative groups that resisted a binding reinterpretation of the Torah appear again in later history. Those denying binding authority of the oral Torah, objecting to new principles of belief (for example, resurrection of the dead), and to autonomy of lay piety outside the Temple area before 70 CE, consisted mainly of the high priests and, since the middle of the second century BCE, of the *Sadducees* who were related to them in spirituality and by status. Josephus Flavius, who sympathized with the Pharisees, defined the Sadducees as a religious sect, "recognizing no other commandments but the laws" (*Ant* 18:16).[65]

#52 In contrast to the Sadducees, the group (fellowship, sect, religious party) of the *Pharisees* acknowledged oral revelation alongside the written one (*Ant* 13:297). They interpreted this twofold revelation not merely as literature but in conformity with the religious life style of their time. The synagogue was their typical institution and there as well as in

the "school" they cultivated a religious life independent of the Temple
(*Ant* 18:15). As Hugo Mantel recently pointed out, the Pharisees were
quite aware that they followed in the footsteps of Ezra/Nehemiah and
their adherents, namely the sons of the *golah,* the princes, elders, scribes,
men of the great assembly, and early pious men (cf. Ezra 10:7f; Neh 5:1–
13; 8:8; 10; 13:15–18; *Ant* 13:297; 18:15; *Avot* 1:1–12; and the Megillat
Ta'anit, Scroll of Fasting).[66]

#53 In order to understand the Pharisees, it will be helpful to con-
sider their doctrines, life style, and religio-political goals. The short sum-
maries given in Josephus (*Ant* 13:288–298; *Bellum* 2:162–166) and in the
Acts of the Apostles (23:6–8) do not give us a sufficiently clear picture of
the Pharisees. Their belief in a resurrection of the dead, in angels, and in
human freedom only partially limited by divine sovereignty and fate, as
well as their acceptance of written and oral revelation, must be seen within
the framework of their religious attitudes and life style. We previously referred (#27–31) to their basic skepticism with regard to radical expectations of the kingdom of God and radical defenders of Jewish-Hellenistic
progressivist piety. They were not always able to keep to the "middle
road," which is understandable in view of contemporary jealousy (cf. *Ant*
17:269f; 18:271; *Bellum* 1:648ff; 2:411–419). Their style and mode of life
were determined by the wish to live, according to their time and in confor-
mity with revelation, as a religiously effective group with strong inner cohesion (*havurah*). This was to be practiced in a life of prayer and cleanness,
independent of and yet related to the Temple, as well as by an intensive effort to present God's revelation as a practical norm of all situations of life.
Theirs could be called an attempt to prepare a divine realm on earth because the full eschatological rule of God was biding its time. This involved
a life according to the law of the Bible or derived from it, a sapientially in-
structed way conforming as far as possible to the will of God. We are allowed some glimpses of the Pharisees' manifold and provisional religious
views in certain scattered traditions and fragments of rabbinic literature
(the origins of which are sometimes doubtful)—for instance, in the "Mishnah of the early Pious" or "First Mishnah" (TJ *Ter* 8:10; TB *Ned* 91a), in
rules on membership in the Pharisaic fellowship (*havurah*) (Mishnah *Dem*
2:3; 3:4; Tosefta *Dem* 2:3; TJ *Ber* 9:14b), and in certain laws relating to
cleanness, festivals, and prayer (Mishnah *Ed* 8:4; *Hag* 2:2; *Meg* 1:5–11).

#54 Pharisaic spirituality also appears in early Jewish writings,
mainly in references to and modified developments of older apocalyptic
traditions. The parenetic part of the Ethiopic Enoch or Letter of Enoch
(1 Enoch 91–105, 108), for instance, is the work of an author of the second

to first century BCE who is familiar with Pharisaism; he takes up the traditions of the Enoch Apocalypse and discreetly applies them to Pharisaic views.[67] The Scroll of Fasting and the Second Book of the Maccabees also are close to Pharisaism, proving at the same time that Pharisaic influence was not confined to the Syriac-Palestinian sphere but took hold in the diaspora.[68]

It was by cooperating with the Great Council that the Pharisees chiefly tried to realize their religio-political goals, but their influence was limited because theirs was a minority party. As scholars of the law, they were successful and popular with the masses of the Galilean people. In the distressing war years of 66–70/73 CE, they gained esteem among the inhabitants of Jerusalem and Judea, first as opponents of the rebellion and later as representatives of as orderly a defense as possible against the Roman aggressors.

#55 Pharisaism was not only the tap-root of normative rabbinic Judaism; it also strongly influenced Christianity. Jesus responded to Pharisaic concerns and arguments (#124), and Paul was partly under Pharisaic influence (cf. Acts 23:6; 26:5; Phil 3:5). So-called Early Catholicism, insofar as it found expression in New Testament literature, attempted to bring the Christ event and Pharisaic-rabbinic spirituality and life styles into harmony. Precepts and exhortations in the Deutero-Pauline and Catholic Epistles have many strong parallels in rabbinic writings (cf., for example, 2 Pet 3; TB *San* 97b). Christians realized quite early that they also needed laws, precautionary measures, and rules together with their sustaining and healing spirituality (cf. #172–173). Christians were heirs to the Pharisees in this respect. It is one of the historical tragedies of theology, of the Gospel proclamation, and of humanity in general that the polemics of Jesus against the Pharisees were misinterpreted by absolutizing them and giving them the wrong emphasis. In the second century CE, Gentile Christians no longer understood the genre of Jewish "polemics," and Christian anti-Pharisaism became one with anti-Judaism. The great Pharisaic achievement in self-criticism was thereby changed into unalloyed reproaches against the Pharisees. The latter coined harsh, unrelenting words of self-criticism (e.g., TJ *Sot* 5:20c; Mishnah *Sot* 3:4) which were by no means milder than the anti-Pharisaic polemic in Matthew 23. Instead of appreciating that attitude, anti-Pharisaic, anti-Jewish positions called forth an arsenal of inflammatory speeches against the Pharisees, with whom no one was really familiar. In order to put a stop to the ideological circus against the Pharisees and their descendants in our time, knowledge of Pharisaism must become a required subject in Christian theological education.

5. The People of Qumran

#56 Among the first Qumran scholars, polemics ensued over the question whether Qumranites were Zealots, Sadducees, Pharisees, Essenes, Karaites, Jewish Christians, or whatever. Since the 1960's, interest in such classification has steadily diminished. Out of literary-critical analyses of Qumran literature and comparisons with related writings of the second to first century BCE as well as discoveries of new texts in various Qumran caves and environs and their publication, there developed the view that none of the early Jewish groups consisted exclusively of distinct elites. They all had members who lived up to specific group ideals but in a mitigated, blurred or distorted way.[69]

Even today the Qumranites are often called Essene or Essenic, but it is well known that such characterizations do not take us very far. Josephus Flavius' accounts on the Essenes (*Bellum* 2:119–161; *Ant* 18:18–22) and those of Philo of Alexandria (*De Vita Contemplativa* 18:68; *Quod Omnis Probus Sit Liber* 75–91), which are the mainstays for comparison, do not constitute exact historio-critical statements. We must rather think of disparate groups within Essenism that do not share all the same ideas. This becomes clear from the following example:

> ... for them (the community of Damascus) will God's covenant be an assurance that they shall live for a thousand generations.... And if they live in encampments, in accordance with the rule of the Land, and if they marry and beget children, they shall walk according to the Torah as an ordered community (in the sense) of the Torah (CD VII: 5b–8).

This text presupposes a group with strong interior cohesion which lives in tents. Contrary to the Josephus account that speaks of celibate Essenes (*Ant* 18:21; *Bellum* 2:160f), the members of the Damascus community were married. While in the "Community Rule" (1QS) the term *yahad* (union) is of considerable importance, it does not occur in CD; instead there is the word "camp." This is very significant because there is nothing objectively corresponding to *yahad* in the Hebrew Scriptures. The quoted CD text also allows us to assume that the Damascus community was not completely separated from the other Jews, while 1QS demands strict segregation from non-Qumran Jews.[70]

The War Scroll (1QM) makes the problem of the Qumran group's identity even more complicated. While the people of the "Community Rule" (1QS) seem to be almost quietist-pacifist, those of the War Scroll militantly take their part in the eschatological war. Several scholars assume that 1QM is not Qumran-Essenic but of Zealot origin. Others again say that 1QM reflects an early stage of the Qumran community, and still others date it later and take it as proof for serious changes in Qumran ideology.[71]

#57 From the beginning it has been particularly difficult to ascertain the temporal context of the Qumran community(ies). With the exception of one unclear example (Demetrius, king of Yawan, 4QpNah I:2), all persons and groups in Qumran literature are coded (teachers of justice, wicked priests, prophets of lies, men of violence, seekers of smooth things, scoffers, lion of wrath, house of Absalom, etc.). The hostility recounted in 1QpHab, 1QpNah, and 1QH, between the teacher of justice, the priest of sacrilege, and the men of violence, had to be placed in the context of a reasonable situation historically. Those assuming early dates decided on the years of about 200–160 BCE, the next group names the period of the Hasmonean Jonathan (152–143 BCE) or Hyrcanus I (134–104 BCE), and those deciding on a late date opted for the time of Alexander Janneus (103–76 BCE), Hyrcanus II (65–40 BCE), Herod I (37–4 BCE), or the time immediately before and during the first Jewish war against Rome (66–70 CE). Discussions on this topic continue as lively as ever,[72] even though it now seems certain that this dissident group lived between 200 BCE and 70 CE.

#58 Quite a number of identifying statements exist in Qumran literature. One section from the "Community Rule" will serve as example for the strong integration of the Qumran community within early Judaism, despite its distinctiveness:

> When these are in Israel, the council of the Community shall be established in truth. It will be an everlasting plantation, a house of holiness for Israel, and an assembly of supreme holiness for Aaron. They shall be witnesses to the truth at judgment and shall be the elect of (divine) favor, effecting atonement for the Land and ensuring the requital of the wicked. They will be, indeed, a "tested bulwark" and "precious cornerstone," whose foundations shall never be shaken or moved from their place (1QS VIII:4b–8).

This text contains seven short self-definitions of the Qumran community. They considered themselves a council of the community (*yahad*) founded in truth, an everlasting plantation, a temple consisting of a sanctuary and holy of holies, a tested bulwark, a precious cornerstone, witnesses of truth for the judgment, and elect of divine delight. We select the "everlasting plantation," without forgetting that it is just one among other, mainly cultic, definitions. The expression (eternal) plantation as a definition occurs several times in Qumran literature. It stands mostly close to terms such as those above, or similar ones (cf. esp. 1QS XI:8f; 1QH VI:15; VIII:6–10; CD I:7f). Such definitions and their context point toward communities characterized by priestly, apocalyptic, esoteric ·thinking, with hopes for an impending *eschaton.*[73]

Isaiah 60:21 is the background for the picture of planting (Isaiah 61:3 is similar):

> Your people shall all be just, they shall always possess the land, they, the bud of my planting, my handiwork (1QIs variant of plantation of YHWH) to show my glory (NAB).

Not to content oneself with the history of motifs, one must remember that Isaiah chapters 56–66 originated at least in part among people known for their piety of poverty (*anawim,* the downtrodden and the poor, are specially chosen). Among them, eschatological viewpoints stand in the foreground or at least in pregnant tension to life.[74] As Qumran was strongly influenced by ideas and sayings of these poor and pious people (e.g., 1QH V:22), Trito-Isaiah may be assumed to be their spiritual predecessor. The groups behind Trito-Isaiah were to a certain extent aloof from the contemporary Jewish establishment and, for that reason, socially disadvantaged.

The picture of the community as a plantation occurs also in some pseudepigrapha approximately contemporaneous with the Qumran writings. It is found in the oldest part of the Ethiopic Book of Enoch (93; 91:12–17, The Apocalypse of Weeks), probably written shortly before Daniel. We also find it in the Book of Jubilees which is from pre- or early Qumran times and is quoted in CD XVI:3f (cf. Jub 1:16; 16:26; 21:34; 36:7). In the Book of Jubilees as in the Apocalypse of Weeks we are dealing with a specifically priestly apocalypse because of the central interest in problems of the cultic calendar (cf. 1 En 93; Jub 30:18–23). Both of them mention the heavenly tablets on which are inscribed the festivals to be celebrated and the rules and conduct for man (cf. 1 En 91; Jub 30:18–23; etc.).

Qumran literature, the Daniel and Enoch Apocalypses, most of the Testaments of the Twelve Patriarchs, and the Book of Jubilees are closely related. They are based on a priestly apocalyptic and concerned with problems of the cultic calendar.[75]

#59 Before evaluating Qumran, we must analyze the religio-historical situation of that period. Great emphasis must be placed upon the defensive, religiously motivated *Kulturkampf* which Jews true to tradition (i.e., apocalyptic priests, laity, and many of the common people) were waging at the time of Antiochus IV Epiphanes against the Seleucid and Jewish "reformers." The usurping Hasmonean priest-princes and kings (Jonathan, Simon, Hyrcanus I, Aristobulus I, Alexander Janneus, Hyrcanus II, Aristobulus II) were still another historically important group. They moved with ever increasing speed in the wake of the earlier "reformers," that is, the radical Hellenizers (Jason, Menelaus, Alcimus).

From this study in history of religions and the analysis of Qumran literature, we can say that Qumran people were radical, anti-Hellenistic, priestly-apocalyptic groups that retreated to the desert, to this second place of eschatological salvation—next to Jerusalem—to be able to live in complete obedience to the Torah and await the final time of salvation. From its first beginnings, Qumran was a dissident movement calling for Torah revival. Torah fulfillment became for them the decisive factor in the history of revelation. Questions on the right interpretation of Torah and history thus became the explosive that sundered early Jewry into hostile groups.

Yet, the Qumran people were not exclusively preoccupied with the final events; in another way they were also hardy deniers of renewal. Here, too, the extremes of traditionalism and the expectation of an early Coming touched closely! Qumran separatists rejected the elite of Bible interpreters and actualizers who from Ezra-Nehemiah increasingly arrogated to themselves revelatory authority (cf. #51–55). With theological anachronism, they considered themselves the first generation of those returning from the Babylonian exile who were true to revelation and, with theological utopianism, they saw themselves as the last generation before the important final events. They skipped over and disregarded, as it were, the reforms begun by Ezra-Nehemiah and subsequent developments among the people of God.

Still, the Qumran groups did not refer their life entirely to the past and future; they also cultivated a strongly introverted spirituality in their daily life. They wanted to live "in glorious purity" (1QS IV:5). Requirements of ritual and moral purity stand at the core of community rules. After a probationary year, the novice was admitted to the bath of purification (cf. 1QS VI:13–23; *Bellum* 2:138). He was admonished that he was not a righteous man until he had resolved the stubbornness of his heart and walked blamelessly in the ways of God (cf. 1QS III:4.9f). The novice had to learn that sensual pleasures are wicked and continence and self-control virtuous (cf. 1QS IV:2–4; *Bellum* 2:119). The Holy Spirit was said to be active in the ritual bath to enlighten man and show him the revelation of God (1QS IV:20–22).

Qumran's eschatological orientation might suggest that the group was not concerned with social and religious structure, but such was not the case. Order by rank was very strictly observed:

> No man shall move down from his place or move up from his assigned position (1QS II:23). . . . This is the rule for an assembly of the Many. Each man shall sit in his place. The priests shall sit in the first place, the elders second and all the rest of the people according to their rank (1QS VI:8).

Every person is aware of and observes "the place of his lot," thereby decreeing a sign of assurance that the

> community is founded at once upon truth and virtuous humility, upon loving kindness and mutual fairness (1QS II:24).

#60 Qumran's importance can hardly be overrated in the history of religion and literature as well as in the history of the spirituality of God's people. It has become possible to explain many obscure Bible passages and Bible-theological contacts with the help of the Qumran discoveries. The latter play a minor role, however, in a Christian theology of Judaism. Though certain Qumran motifs may have continued to affect Christianity and Judaism, their history did not follow the Qumran initiatives. The sect disappeared about 70 CE, and their rigorous ideals of purity as well as intransigent claims to exclusivity were not taken up by any of the rival movements. It was similar for Qumran eschatological concepts and hierarchical order of rank. It would be erroneous to compare the Qumran Teacher of righteousness to the rabbinic sages who became so important to Judaism. A Christian theology of Judaism should not deal primarily with ancient modes of Jewish existence but concern itself with the ideas that have shaped Judaism to our day.

IV. Pseudepigraphical Literature

#61 The authors of the so-called pseudepigrapha of the Old Testament were convinced that they were in immediate contact with revelation. Most of them also believed that they were authoritative interpreters and trailblazers for their Jewish contemporaries. In the end, however, their writings were not accepted as canonical, neither in official Judaism nor in the Church. Their influence on the mainstream of faith communities gradually lessened. Unofficially, however, their effects on the New Testament, early Christian theology and rabbinic Judaism was quite considerable—if only as a source of secret or openly available material. Serious gaps within the source material make it quite impossible to disentangle theological and historic disputes. There remains the inescapable task, however, to bring the literature immediately before the advent of Christianity and normative Judaism into focus as clearly as possible. Were this task to be neglected, certain roots of Christian theology and rabbinic Judaism would be lost forever.

1. Sources for Research into History

#62 Translated literally pseudepigrapha would be false, mendacious, spurious documents, writings published under assumed names, that is, decadent literature. The authors, accordingly, would be fraudulent imitators, a malicious "band of Jewish forgers,"[76] or literary men of honor who for some reason—fear of denunciation, feelings of inferiority—were hiding behind a pseudonym, a literary mask, or a more or less harmless *nom de plume*.[77]

The term "pseudepigrapha," unfortunately adopted universally, should not be employed unambiguously or ideologically. It is admissible only as the designation for a genre of literature, and even in that case we must examine each piece of writing for its assumptions, context, and background. By no means is pseudepigrapha the most important or most useful term for extra-canonical early Jewish literature; "apocalyptic" or "Jewish-Hellenistic debates" would be much more pertinent. In the last resort, there is no terminological all-around solution to the problem. Even the intertestamental apocalypses, which are most strongly marked by formal indications of pseudepigraphy, could at times dispense with the term. A clear example is the fragment of a Daniel cycle (Pseudo-Daniel, 4 QpsDan) which quite openly speaks of the future, neither hiding time nor personalities. It has been suggested to call this piece *apokalypse im klartext*.[78]

#63 Contemporary scholarship has produced new editions of texts, translations and extensive secondary literature. Most important is the text series *Pseudepigrapha Veteris Testamenti Graece,* edited by M. Black, S. O. Brock, A. M. Denis, M. DeJonge, J. C. Picard, and others. A. M. Denis wrote an excellent introductory volume;[79] he is also trying to supply additional material for interpretations.[80] Marc Philonenko's *Joseph et Aséneth* provides a sound text edition and commentary of an individual book.[81]

Nothing much is to be gained from further pseudepigraphical research unless it were linked to Qumran literature. The latter (cf. #56–60) is a methodological aid that should not be foregone, particularly for editions and commentaries of pseudepigraphical texts that were found in Qumran,[82] however fragmentary. In the future we will also have to pay increased attention to Targum research. Since the publication of the Targum of Job from Qumran cave 11,[83] one has to keep in mind the interdependence of all the groups, Jewish literature, and literary genres of the time.

In order to clarify pseudepigrapha, we must examine, next to Jewish literature, non-Jewish or partly Jewish writings. The text editions by Alfons Kurfess, *Sybillinische Weissagungen* (Munich, 1951) and Menachem Stern, *Greek and Latin Authors on Jews and Judaism* (Jerusalem, 1974) are but two examples that alert us to the importance of that literature.

#64 It is beyond the scope of this volume to evaluate, however incompletely, the secondary literature. Roughly speaking we can distinguish three categories: (a) literature for the primary purpose of characterizing pseudepigrapha as a literary genre of late antiquity; in this group, the problems of early Jewish, early Christian, and Persian-Greek-Roman pseudepigrapha intersect;[84] (b) literature attempting primarily to clarify New Testament terms and statements, using pseudepigrapha as models or for similarities;[85] (c) literature to clarify early Jewish national and religious history; in this category New Testament references are subordinate.[86]

#65 Scholars have been increasingly faced with the puzzling question as to which statements could be of Jewish origin and which are Christian interpolations. We have become more cautious and diffident in assuming a large number of such additions.[87] In France at the end of the 1950's, the all too generous ascription of Christian interpolations by R. H. Charles, E. Kautzsch and others were refuted for the first time; almost nothing was interpolated by Christians. What had overhastily been called Christian was declared to be original early Jewish material. That approach, however, soon lost ground because it was inspired by an overestimation of the Qumran teacher of righteousness.[88] On the basis of new editions of texts and also from study of the Aramaic Targumin, we are still inclined to object to the frequent assumption of Christian interpolations. Much material is actually Jewish which previously had been declared non-Jewish, and that fact is of considerable importance to the history of biblical religion and a Christian theology of Judaism. We must beware of assigning too early a point in time for Christian disengagement from Judaism.

2. The Importance of Pseudepigraphical Statements

#66 In sizing up the intertestamental pseudepigrapha, the Book of Daniel, as a matter of course, must serve as the starting point because it unites Holy Scripture and pseudepigrapha.

H. H. Rowley held that the pseudonymity of the Book of Daniel was a genuine literary expression convenient to the time, while the pseudonymous successors, with the exception of the New Testament apocalypse of John, produced only epigonic works:

> When the author came to write his visions . . . also carrying a message of hope for the same circles, he wrote them under the guise of Daniel, not in order to deceive his readers, but in order to reveal his identity with the author of the Daniel stories. Pseudonymity was thus born of a living process, whose purpose was the precise opposite of deceit. It only became artificial when it was woodenly copied by imitators (here follow positive arguments for the Daniel pseudonymity). . . . All of this the imitators, always unable to distinguish between the accidents and the elements of what they copied, took over, and apocalyptic became esoteric.[89]

Rowley's arguments are apologetic. He feels obliged to present the canonical books to their best advantage, but this does not apply to the noncanonical ones. Such an approach is inadmissible in scholarship. A literary "stratagem," moreover, does not necessarily indicate decadence or an attempt at deception; we otherwise would have to condemn many a modern author of fiction. There remains no alternative but to examine each pseudonymous-pseudepigraphical work of early Judaism separately for the attitudes there expressed. The result must not be summarized as epigonic literature, affectation, deception, decadence, etc.; only ideological bias would produce such attributes.

#67 There are a number of reasons for the pseudonymity of the Book of Daniel. An intent to deceive is most certainly not one of them. Even historical misunderstandings, as Otto Ploeger implied, do not apply. The author of Daniel is said to have found the legendary Daniel figure in his favorite prophetic Book of Ezekiel (14:12–20; 28:3) and to have erroneously assumed that such a figure lived at the time of the Babylonian exile.[90]

We have good reason to think that the author was familiar with the tradition according to which Daniel was a heroic figure of the period before the Flood. The Book of Jubilees, written late in the second century BCE, calls Daniel the uncle and father-in-law of Enoch, the righteous one of pre-Israelite times (4:20). For the same reason we can take for granted that the name of the hero of the stories (Dan 1–6) and visions (Dan 7–12) was a subterfuge and that the historical mutilations were meant to serve the author's message at a time of difficulties and confusion. What he wanted to say was approximately this: Our time—the period under Antiochus IV (175–164 BCE) and of the Hellenizing Jewish priest/princes—is an era comparable to the Babylonian exile (587–538 BCE) in distress, punishment, and significance. Antiochus IV is a second Nebuchadnezzar, another destroyer of Israel. The persecutions by this pagan king and his Jewish followers and accomplices against traditional Jewry hit an even more sensitive nerve of God's people than did the destruction of the Temple and the deportations of our forefathers to Babylonia. The Daniel of my tales represents me and my fellows. We unswervingly keep to the covenantal obligations toward the God of Israel. We are prepared to risk our lives. We also consider ourselves radically responsible for the people of God. As far as we can see, we are the only ones still aware of Israel's mission, the only ones still heeding it, in traditional loyalty and by prayer. In this hour of decision we feel challenged and called upon to exhort, to reprimand, to ask for repentance, and to show the path toward the future. For this we rely on the most ancient traditions. The present is a time of unbelievable, supreme distress and sin, but it also points toward the imminent reign of God, when the oppressors and transgressors will be destroyed and the people of God will arise in glory, power, and happiness.[91]

In the first place, then, the pseudonymity of the Book of Daniel serves the message of the apocalyptic author. Deliberately and adroitly, he rearranges matters in order to stress the message all the more strongly. In a secondary aspect, there also seems to have been some literary mimicry. The alleged hero afforded some measure of protection, permitting the author to remain in the background. Both aspects were understood and approved by the recipients of the message.[92]

#68 Other contemporary or slightly later writings related in genre and content to the Book of Daniel have as chief hero the righteous Enoch of pre-Deluge times (cf. Gen 5:24) and other pre-Mosaic personalities. We are thinking of the First Book of Enoch, the Testament of the Twelve Patriarchs, and the Book of Jubilees. Enoch decries the sinfulness of the time as he prophesies the coming of God for judgment and for the salvation of the righteous; he is described as a sage, the beloved of God, a visionary of heavenly and eschatological mysteries. The basic texts are contained in the Apocalypse of Weeks (1 En 93:1–10; 91:12–17), and the Animal Apocalypse (1 En 85—90), as well as in the Book of Angels (1 En 1–36). Slightly later texts indicate more clearly certain traits and activities of this early hero, particularly his wisdom (Jub 4:16–20), his prophetic exhortations for the time of the second century BCE (T. Benjamin 9:1; T. Daniel 5:56; T. Judah 18:1; T. Levi 14:1–3; 16:1; T. Naphtali 4:1; T. Simeon 5:4), and his visions of heavenly and eschatological mysteries (1 En 39; 41; 46; 71). The Enoch traditions exerted some influence until the time after Christ (cf. Sir 44:16; Wis 4:10f; Heb 11:5; Jude 14f). Together with the Book of Daniel and the Qumran literature, 1 Enoch, Jubilees and the Testament of the Twelve Patriarchs are records of an influential Assidean literature,[93] characterized by apocalypses interspersed with exhortations and threats.[94]

#69 Why do the books of the Assidean Enoch traditions make use of pseudepigraphy? Akin to the Book of Daniel, first of all they share its interests and point, under the guise of mimicry, toward the approaching reign of God. They also are strongly hostile toward the Jerusalem establishment. The Jerusalem priests are said to have become a band of sinners (T. Levi 14—16); there must be restoration (Jub 30:18–20; T. Levi 18). The reflection on age-old Israelite (levitical and Enoch) traditions with all their particularities (worship and fear of angels, revelation by means of the cosmos, heavenly tablets) is therefore necessary (Jub 1:10–17). The struggle against symptoms of cultural degeneracy (lewdness, intermarriage with foreigners) must be continued with renewed strength (Jub 20:4; 22:20; 24:28–30; T. Daniel 5:4f). The heroes of antiquity with their esoteric-priestly traits serve as convenient reference points in radical, admonitory homilies meant to rally the few loyal supporters prepared to accept the rigorism of the Law, suffering of persecutions, and a new order of cultic life. The genre of pseudepigrapha was well suited to articulate such concerns, yet it was not the only means as the unknown historian Pseudo-Philo proves, since he showed similar interests without using pseudepigraphy (cf., e.g., *Liber Antiquitatum Biblicarum* 9:5–7: in-breeding is preferable to marriage with foreigners).

#70 In *Joseph et Aséneth,* a novel of the early second century CE, pseudepigraphy is mainly a literary device, not considered an end in itself but serving to make statements of the greatest importance to Egyptian Jews. The problem in question was the permissibility and possibility of Jews living with Greeks, in particular the problem of mixed marriages. The sojourn in Egypt of the patriarch Joseph must have suggested itself quite readily in that situation. Gen 41:45 relates how the Egyptian Pharaoh gave Asnath (Aséneth), daughter of the pagan priest Potiphar (Pentephres) of Heliopolis, in marriage to the patriarch Joseph. Gen 41:50–52 and 46:20 shows that the two Israelite ancestors Ephraim and Manasseh sprang from this union. A romantic embellishment of the Bible story enabled the pseudepigraphic author to say that living together, even marriage between Greek and Jew, was to be supported if it were to lead to renunciation of polytheism.[95] In the novel, Aséneth, who has the looks of a beautiful Jewish woman (JosAs 1:7–9), becomes the wife of Joseph and a symbol of the ideal people of God, or of a humankind inclining toward the acceptance of the God of Israel, after she has abjured the Egyptian gods and demons (10:11–13) and repented of her past deeds (12:5f).

The image of the young bride later on changes to that of happy first lovers (JosAs 15:2–7). The bridal couple symbolizes humanity, Jews and Gentiles beloved by God. Pseudepigraphy is here employed against Jewish agitators for the prohibition of intermingling with pagans (*amixia*).[96]

The author of the Testament of Abraham, also probably an Egyptian Jew of the first or second century CE, used pseudepigraphy for similar reasons. The Abraham-figure who struggles against death serves to oppose the Jews who overemphasized God's punishment and judgment without giving sufficient weight to divine mercy for sinners (T. Abraham 10; cf. Jos As 27:3–35; 29:1–4).[97] Philo of Alexandria was of a similar mind but did not use the artistic ploy of pseudepigraphy. He held close co-existence between Jews and non-Jews possible and desirable, as long as Roman power-Hellenism did not cause Jewish pogroms or demanded obligatory emperor cults (cf. *SpecLeg* I: 319–325; *LegGai* 118 Mos II:26–30).[98]

The struggle between uncompromising Jewish anti-Hellenists, suspicious of laxity and everything non-Jewish and the protagonists of a leveling and understanding attitude toward the non-Jews, eventually became very embittered. Both sides produced literary works, with or without pseudepigraphy. In these disputes we discover the beginnings of the New Testament message.

3. Chief Concerns of Pseudepigraphical Literature at the Time of Jesus

#71 There is no evidence of development, say from the genuine to the imitative, in intertestamental pseudepigraphy. Each document should be considered individually in its approach and purpose. The pseudepigrapha of the Egyptian diaspora argued somewhat differently from the Palestinian ones, even though there were similar tendencies. There are also certain main topics recurring in all these writings. They express a tenacious Jewish struggle for spiritual-religious (even physical) survival at a time of severe attacks and refined means of seduction by the Seleucid, Ptolemaic, and Roman power-Hellenists and their Jewish sympathizers and underlings. The older pseudepigrapha evince strong reactions against such assaults from within and without by threats against the sinners (older

Enoch traditions). In other passages there are complaints over the heavy
lot of the few loyal ones (cf. 1 En 103:9–15, and various passages in 4 Ezra
and 2 Baruch), as well as frequent references to the just judgment of God
(Jub 23:22f; T. Daniel 5:7f). There also were many attempts at remotivat-
ing the oppressed and gathering in the insecure, for instance in the colorful
pictures of the people of God (1QH III:6–8; JosAs 15:2–7; Apoc. Elijah
3:16–25). Such images were meant to win men of similar leanings over to
intimate cooperation. None of the images comparing the people of God to
a bride, wife, woman giving birth, etc., are applied to mere national unity.
Before the New Testament period already, unhappy experiences with the
Jerusalem priesthood had made national-religious thinking unacceptable
to many Jews. "People of God" always applied to those remaining true to
God, even under stress and oppression; it applied to a community of minds
rather than of descent. Opinions on the number of these loyal ones vary
greatly. The rigorists thought in very small numbers, while others were
dreaming of global expansion. The pseudepigraphical authors called upon
old traditions, mystical experiences and prophecies for the purpose of
gathering traditionalist Jews and motivating them to persevere, that is, to
oppose the ruling secular groups or to achieve a *modus vivendi* with the
surrounding cultures, religions, and powers. The New Testament and early
Christianity were recipients, therefore, of rich impulses toward a people-
of-God theology.

#72 A great number of problems resulted for that small group, dog-
gedly determined to persevere as the people of God under precarious conditions. Some of the problems—e.g., marriage to non-Jews, toleration of
non-Jewish customs and religious ideas, separation or assimilation—were
mentioned already. The question of God's transcendence and immanence
and his deeds in view of the people's loss of power was constantly recur-
ring in pseudepigraphical, religio-apologetic, targumic-talmudic and historical literature.

Here we will discuss only the aspect of religious service. Early Jewish
Essenic groups repudiated animal sacrifice in the Temple—in part because
of the Seleucid desecrations of the Temple—and were hostile to the Jerusalem Temple, its cult and cult functionaries. They contrasted Jerusalem cult
ideology and practice with the cult in heaven (cf. T. Levi 3:4–6) and with
the worship of the heart and the lips (1QS IX:3–5; *Ant* VIII:111–119).
Such theological-ideological notions must be seen in the context of the religious anguish of the time. Josephus' interpretation (*Ant* VIII:111–119) of
Solomon's prayer at the dedication of the Temple (1 Kgs 8:27–9:9; 2 Chr

7) indicates the importance of these questions, even outside of pseudepigraphy and Qumran.[99] Josephus' account is mainly within the biblical tradi-
ion, which contains everything but the divine praise by a human voice
111f) and justification against alleged Jewish misanthropy (117). Josephus, however, sets quite individual accents, clearly dictated by his impres-
ion of contemporary problems. He searches for a way out of the dead end
f Jewish isolationism within the pagan Roman environment (117) and the
pparently hopeless question of the cult after the destruction of the Tem-
le. Josephus does not wish to allegorize or spiritualize the Temple cult, as
s done by Philo. Even animal sacrifices he finds pleasing to God (118f),
et he relativizes them as "works" in spoken prayer, i.e., a service of the
vord, in a divine service without material gifts (111). Josephus' manner of
xpression harks back to Stoic models which, in their dependence on
ireek philosophy of religion, were promising in their application to the
iaspora situation.

Ways into Christianity

#73 Certain more general considerations are in order before we can
etermine how and to what extent intertestamental and pseudepigraphical
terature influenced the New Testament and early Christian theology. The
rst question concerns contents. All the religious ideas and ideals of the
ew Testament were circulating in some form among the contemporary
ws who did not believe in Christ. For each New Testament verse there
e a number of parallels or similarities that are outside this corpus. What
new and singular in the New Testament is the historical person of Jesus,
s activities and what happens to him, as well as the theological interpreta-
ns and initiatives called forth by his death and resurrection. This new
aterial, however, caused major shifts in value and accentuation. From
e Jewish point of view, the situation might be explained as follows: The
ew Testament and early Christianity radicalized and concentrated al-
ady extant Jewish material; that meant everything was taken too serious-
, was too heavily stressed. Many of these precisions of content had not
t been given sufficient consideration; they grew out of a play with ideas,
it also out of the wrestling with acute difficulties, for instance, the idea of
od's transcendence and immanence.[100] A Christian does not agree with
ch an assessment of "too much" or "too serious"; he feels that the Christ
ent called for a revaluation.[101] It will not be possible within the context
a Christian-Jewish dialogue to persuade him to draw back from his posi-

tion or to declare of no importance any of the essentials of whatever was new in Christ. That would mean a backing away from the Christ event.

#74 Though not of foremost importance, it is of theological relevance to consider from what particular movement certain Jewish ideas entered the presentation of the Christ event. Above all, no far-reaching conclusions can be drawn from a distinction between Hellenistic and Palestinian Judaism in regard to primitive and early Christian literature.[102] In recent times it was pointed out correctly that no purely Hellenistic Judaism existed at the time of Jesus nor was there a Palestinian Judaism untouched by Hellenism. The many Graeco-Palestinians institutionalized "blended Hellenism" (cf. #29) in the Palestinian cities, and the Jerusalem-centered ideas of Egyptian Jews[103] provide clear proof of this statement. Various Essenic groups and those sympathizing with them in the Jewish homeland and Western diaspora indicate the same trend.

The above observations must be kept in mind in order to resist the temptation of separating the New Testament from its Jewish matrix too frequently and too early.

#75 Early Jewish pseudepigrapha were used by Jewish and Christian groups alike. As early Rabbinism developed (beginning about 140 CE), pseudepigrapha maintained their influence particularly on Christianity. Some additions to certain long passages prove that those writing served many Christians as homiletic models and as instruction for moral exhortation. At the end of the twentieth chapter of the Testament of Abraham (Recension A), we find the following admonition and doxology (*berakha*):

> Brethren, let us imitate the hospitality of the Patriarch Abraham. Let us acquire his virtuous way of life that we may be worthy of eternal life, praising the Father, the Son, and the Holy Spirit. His is the glory and the power for ever and ever. Amen.[104]

The oldest parts of the Kaddish prayer indicate that it was customary to end the hours of teaching and study with doxologies, praising the power and glory of God. There are various reasons to think that before 140 CE the pseudepigrapha were employed in exchanges during Christian and Jewish catechesis and study. It is quite possible that only one part of the doxology, namely the Trinitarian addition, is specifically Christian. In other instances we may well wonder whether there were also Jewish gloss additions, based on Christian statements.

#76 Jewish and Christian interpolations in the pseudepigrapha indicate numerous seams and contacts between Judaism and Christianity. From various formulations and the point in time of their insertion, one notices that an active exchange of ideas and images took place, not only between the pseudepigrapha and the New Testament but also between the pseudepigrapha and extra-canonical early Christian literature. It is due to early Church leaders and thinkers (especially the authors of the Didache, Justin Martyr, Clement of Alexandria, Lactantius, Origen, Eusebius, and others) that many early Jewish writings and fragments were preserved and placed at the service of Christian theology.[105] A literary exchange took place particularly between the Septuagint, the Targumim, pseudepigrapha, and the early Midrashic and Aggadic literary and oral traditions. Rabbinic discussions, however, hardly entered into this exchange.

#77 How should such connecting strands between the pseudepigrapha and the New Testament be made visible, and what should develop in practice?

(1.) Just as the exegetes interpret the New Testament from its core, i.e., the Christ event, they must study the pseudepigrapha from their respective core, too. Any other interpretation would be one-sided: too emphatic on the one hand, too fundamentalistic on the other.

(2.) The contacts among groups must be investigated. How does a certain statement stand within the Essene, Pharisee, or other context? A clear line, for example, stretches from Qumran to the Apocalypse of John; there is continuity among exponents of eschatological war dualism (1QM; 1QMelch; Rev 12). Similar links in thought can be established from circles of Essenes to the teachings of Jesus.

(3.) Any attempt at pseudo-finality must be avoided. Concretely speaking, we should be satisfied to interpret the Gospel of John or the Pauline corpus with the aid, for example, of Joseph and Aséneth, the Apocalypse of Elijah, or the Fourth Book of Ezra as standard background material, drawing upon the current critical editions.

(4.) With regard to interpolations, we should accept any material not specifically Christian as early Jewish. Without such a "generous" attitude, we will be permanently frustrated, having to free allegedly Christian subject matter to its Jewish matrix.

These guidelines may sound rigorous; of course they should be employed with care. Yet, it is essential to a Christian theology of Judaism that we do not wrench prematurely from its Jewish context what actually belongs there.

V. JOSEPHUS FLAVIUS AND PHILO OF ALEXANDRIA

#78 Josephus Flavius (37–about 100 CE) is our chief witness to many of the most significant events of world history from 332 BCE (invasion of Judea by Alexander the Great) to about 90 CE. Without his writings, research would be unthinkable, for example, on the Samaritan schism, inner-Jewish and Jewish-Hellenistic struggles during the Hasmonean period (Pharisees, Sadducees, Qumran community, apocalypticists Seleucids, Ptolemies, Romans), the time of Herod and the first Jewish revolt against Rome. Most of all, Josephus

> is and remains the most important "commentator" on the New Testament by his "Antiquities of the Jews," "Wars of the Jews," the apology "Against Apion," and his autobiography.[106]

To this highly gifted and resourceful contemporary of the New Testament hagiographers, the Epicureans were the true intellectual and religious antipodes to the Jews:

> How mistaken are the Epicureans, who exclude Providence from human life and refuse to believe that God governs its affairs or that the universe is directed by a blessed and immortal Being to the end that the whole of it may endure, but say that the world runs by its own movement without knowing a guide or another's care (*Ant* 10:278).

To confess the God who acts on history was in Josephus' view what distinguished Judaism from paganism. He valued very highly human cooperation with that God of Israel. He considered himself and that part of the Jewish people which was not rebellious as united to God in friendship (*Ant* 14:22). As a friend of God, he wished to be a spiritual-religious strategist for his people. As such, he went from one extreme to another, from rebellious fighter against Rome to court biographer to the Roman emperor

> The basic features of his personality were vanity and complacency. . . .
> His going over to the Romans and his intimate alliance with the Flavian imperial house was performed with more ingenuity and indifference than was seemly in a person mourning the downfall of his nation.[107]

Josephus was very self-centered, and success and fame counted for everything. He lacked even the slightest sympathy with the needs of the socially deprived, and certain signs of unscrupulosity cannot be denied. Yet even what makes him little and shallow makes him an indispensable witness for us.[108]

Though his personal life was in part influenced by Jewish Hellenism, he is mainly a witness not of Hellenistic, but of Palestinian Judaism. His historical and apologetic works usually present the conservative views of Pharisaic and early rabbinic Judaism, which makes him an even more important witness to the time of Jesus.

#79 Philo of Alexandria (died shortly after 40 CE) must also be mentioned in the context of a Christian theology of Judaism. His stature is often underrated because his writings were of no consequence for Judaism. For reasons of religious politics, he was at times even placed in a somewhat dubious light. His naively dialogic thinking was considered prone to the influence of Christianity and paganism.[109] But a Christian theology of Judaism is undertaken in a hopeful spirit, and negative experiences of the past should not become absolute and perpetuated. Philo's ideas and his influence on the history of theology should be reconsidered. He was the first Jewish philosopher of religion who intensively and comprehensively attempted to combine philosophy with a theology oriented toward revelation (cf. his teaching on God in *De Opificio Mundi* 171f). He honestly considered himself a citizen of the Jewish diaspora and Hellenistic civilization; we cannot prove any interior or external apostasy from Judaism. In his allegorizing interpretations of Scripture he remained within the confines of Jewish understanding of the Law (cf. *De Migratione Abrahae* 89).

Without being aware of the birth of Christianity, he became the most important ecumenical figure of diaspora Judaism in his time. His ideas proved a most fruitful soil for the growth of Christianity. Soon after his death, Christian communities sprang up spontaneously in Alexandria. Jews and Christians should take these and other ideas of Philo into their dialogue. They should also try, of course, to elucidate the effects of Philo's writings (cf. #70).

3.
Rabbinic Judaism

#80 As already explained (#53, 54), it was due mainly to the Pharisees that chaos did not break out among the Jews after the destruction of the Temple in 70 CE. The decisive influence in the time of dispersal and oppression was exercised by a small group of Pharisees who gathered around their leader, Yohanan ben Zakkai. Tradition has it that, while wars raged in Jerusalem, he foresaw the destruction of the Temple and took organizational and spiritual-religious measures to prepare for a time without a Temple (TB *Git* 56b). After the destruction, he re-emphasized his earlier opinion that Judaism's existence does not depend on the Temple:

> It happened that Rabban Johanan b. Zakkai was coming out of Jerusalem, followed by R. Joshua, and he beheld the Temple in ruins. Woe to us, cried R. Joshua, for this house that lies in ruins, the place where atonement was made for the sins of Israel. Rabban Johanan said to him, My son, be not grieved, for we have another means of atonement which is as effective, and that is the practice of loving kindness. (ARN 4).[110]

In its beginnings, rabbinic Judaism was Pharisaic: a Pharisaism already transformed, called from its former existence as a separate group to a position of responsibility for all the Jews, now bereft of their hierarchic leadership. In the narrow sense, rabbinic Judaism ended with the conclusion of the two Talmuds (cf. #81). Beyond that time, however, it remained an important religious and social factor within Judaism. Apart from some marginal groups, even present-day Judaism in its various branches is influenced more or less clearly by rabbinic teachings. A Christian theologian, then, cannot bypass it or, even worse, pit rabbinic Judaism against an allegedly more attractive Hasidic-mystical Judaism. Yet, it is a laborious task for an outsider to come to understand the situation.

One misunderstanding must be cleared up immediately. We cannot say that Judaism today, as far as it continues in the tradition of the rabbis, is Pharisaic Judaism. Beginning with 70 CE, Pharisaism by necessity had to change, because more encompassing responsibilities were placed upon it which were not there previously. During that period of decision Pharisees saved Pharisaic spirituality and religio-political experience for a new time. But their inheritance had to be fitted into new situations and for that reason it had to be adapted. As time went on, Pharisaic influence diminished (particularly after 120/140 CE) in accord with the participation of other Jewish groups—apocalypticists, esoterics, and priests—in guiding God's dispersed, insecure people, the Jews.[111]

Jewish-Christian dialogue in our time would suffer if such findings of religious history were disregarded. When we discuss the Pharisees, however, the study will lead to their complete vindication, even if Jewish tradition does not give exclusively favorable accounts of them (cf. #55). Again, were the dialogue to concentrate too much on the Pharisees, it would amount to no more than historio-critical research. The characteristics and significance of modern Judaism and post-Pharisaic and post-New Testament history would in that case not be taken seriously enough. In order to pave the way for solid Christian consideration of the various expressions and consequences of Pharisaic rabbinic Judaism, we must point first of all to the rich rabbinic literature and the Jewish religious life and practices deriving from rabbinic ideas.

I. Rabbinic Literature, Acceptable and Unacceptable Evaluations

1. Talmuds, Midrashim, Targumim, Prayers, and "Underground" Literature

#81 The most important parts of rabbinic literature are the two Talmuds, the Babylonian (completed about 500/550 CE) and the Jerusalem (Palestinian) (completed about 400 CE). The Babylonian Talmud became authoritative for later Jewish tradition, and for traditional Jews it is the Talmud pure and simple.[112] Together with the Old Testament, the New Testament, the Koran, the Vedas, etc., the Talmud is one of the great primary religious works. Of all the books mentioned, it is the most voluminous, so that we speak of the "sea of the Talmud" which nobody can traverse by plunging in and swimming. A good modern Talmudic scholar compares it to a mountain which can never be climbed to the top. He speaks of his own attempts to conquer it all the same and to make it intelligible to others, in the following sarcastic words:

> If now, with offensive brevity and ecumenical ignorance, we attempt to sketch some phases of this immense Talmud that entered into every cranny of medieval Hebrew life, let us confess that we are but scratching a mountain, and that our external approach condemns us to error.[113]

The Talmud consists of the Mishnah (repetition, teaching) and the Gemara (accomplishment, completion, discussions of the sages about the Mishnah). The Mishnah is the foundation of the Talmud, consisting of six orders, divided into sixty-three tractates. It mainly contains legal traditions (Halakhot) of the two centuries before and the two after Christ.[114] The Gemara is largely made up of narrative traditions (Aggadot). We must also mention the Tosefta, various Midrashic books, Targumim, prayers, and other works. The Tosefta (addition) is like a para-Mishnah, or secondary Mishnah, a collection of laws and traditions not included in the official Mishnah of Yehuda Ha Nassi (died 217 CE). It has no binding authority but contains some traditions older than the Mishnah.

#82 Next to the Mishnah-Talmud, the rabbinic-midrashic works are of great importance. Midrash means investigation, searching, exegesis. Early Jewish preaching, from the second century BCE at the latest, was presented in the form of Midrash. The people were made familiar with Bible verses by means of examples adapted to the contemporary situation. The midrashic sermon at the synagogue service consisted of *pshat* (explanation of the literal meaning of the biblical text) and *drash* (actualization of the meaning of the Bible). Midrash signified the intellectual effort to find an explanation and suitable actualization of the biblical reading as well as the final result of such efforts. The most important question asked by Midrash teachers was: "What should it teach me?" There are Tannaic and Amoraic Midrashim. The former are older, hailing from the time of the Tannaim (transmitters) who are identical with the teachers of the Mishnah. Tannaitic Midrashim include the Mekhilta, an interpretation of the Book of Exodus (beginning with Ex 12), Sifra, an interpretation of the Book of Leviticus, and Sifre, an interpretation of Numbers and Deuteronomy. The Amoraic Midrash collections derive from the time of the Amoraim, Talmudic scholars of the period from about 220 to 550 CE, though the redaction sometimes took place in post-Talmudic time. Most important among those works are Midrash Rabba, a continuous (verse by verse) interpretation of the Pentateuch; Midrash Tanchuma, especially on Genesis and Leviticus; Midrash of Rabbi Nathan on the Sayings of the Fathers (Abot); Midrash on Psalms; Midrash on the Five Scrolls (Song of Songs, Ruth, Qohelet, Esther, Lamentations); and Midrashim in a certain thematic order: Pesikta de Rav Kahana; Pesikta Rabbati, Seder Eliahu Rabba and Eliahu Zuta.[115]

#83 Research on the Aramaic Targumim developed immensely in modern times, stimulated by new discoveries and editions. The pre-Christian Targum Job,[116] found in Qumran, and even more so the Palestinian-rabbinic Targum, Codex Neophyti, discovered in a most sensational way in the Vatican Library by Alejandro Diez Macho,[117] have exercised considerable influence. Targum Onkelos, Targum Jonathan and other Targumim also are available in good editions.[118]

Yet, the real reason for such great interest in early Jewish and rabbinic Targum literature must be sought elsewhere. Targum means, literally, interpretation, translation; that implies translation of the Hebrew Bible into Aramaic for purposes of divine worship. Such translations are not concerned with literal renderings of the Hebrew text but with explanations, actualizations, and qualifications of difficult biblical passages (cf. TB *Meg* 2:1; 4:4.10; *Kid* 49a-b). Not only are the Targumim of considerable interest to religious history because some of their traditions possibly date back to pre-Christian times, but they also have great theological significance. They indicate, more or less, how the Bible was read and interpreted at the time of Jesus. That is interesting not only because of Jesus and the language and manner of argumentation in New Testament writings, but also, and most of all, as proof that ever since the beginning of the period after the Old Testament, it never was

the letter of the Torah which was considered royal law, but the prevailing interpretation and application, the historically actual form of the Torah.[119]

Final codification of the Targumim as we know them probably took place in late Talmudic or even post-Talmudic times. That fact implies very difficult problems for form-critical and history of tradition studies, and that work is still in its infancy. The main problems continue to be questions of the oral, pre-literary tradition of the Targumim (cf. Ezra 4:7; Neh 8:8). The usual methods of literary criticism are hardly adequate for rabbinic writings. We must allow for wide temporal differences in oral tradition. Long-known Targumim as well as newly discovered ones have thrown new light on the interpretative influence of the Tanakh on the New Testament. What previously was classified in the New Testament as Greek-Hellenistic has now been recognized as belonging to the Palestinian Targum tradition.[120]

#84 Talmudic writings include many prayers and hymns which developed among Mishnaic and Talmudic scholars and became part of the Jewish liturgy. The most central prayers—Kaddish, Tefilla (Sh'moneh Esreh) and Sh'ma Yisrael—have been transmitted in several separate fragments, but liturgical prayer books (*siddurim, machzorim*) came into being only in post-Talmudic times.[121] What applies to Talmudic writings in general is particularly true regarding the prayers. From the point of view of form-critical and history of tradition investigations we are in a predicament regarding the origin and antiquity of these texts. The question of original versions has proved dubious in any case. In 1896, Solomon Schechter discovered a vast number of Jewish liturgical, Midrashic, Targumic and esoteric manuscripts in the Genizah of the Ezra synagogue in Cairo. Only an insignificant portion of these more than 200,000 fragments has been published so far.[122]

#85 Next to these more or less official or semi-official Talmudic writings, there existed an "underground" literature. For pastoral reasons and as a matter of principle, rabbinic Judaism placed a taboo on radical apocalyptic, mystic-esoteric, and magical ideas. Yet, these could not be fully banned. We find traces of magic, sorcery, mysticism, and apocalyptic in the Babylonian Talmud itself, though in a very modified form. In spite of threats by rabbis, apocalypticists, mystics, esoterics, and magicians maintained themselves at the fringes of society during rabbinic times. At the beginning of the Middle Ages, they again appeared openly in times of dire need, causing much unhappiness and confusion.[123]

2. Christian Anti-Judaism and Jewish Anti-Christianism

#86 Christians have discredited the Talmud quite continuously throughout their history. At very low points there were political agitations, burning of Talmuds, sermons against the Talmud, calumny and persecution of Jews, all based on quotations of the Talmud.

The medieval preacher Berthold of Regensburg (about 1210-1272

CE), who was immensely popular, said in one of his sermons that all the Jews had become heretics and broken the covenant:

> Twelve of them have made a book which is called Talmud; it is all heresy and so much is in it that is heretical that it is a wonder they are still alive.[124]

Popular sermons against the Talmud were not the only tragic experience. Ecclesiastical authorities ordered that Talmuds be burned; several popes, between 1220 and 1420 CE in particular, were prominent in such undertakings. The reformers of the sixteenth century continued this antisemitic tradition. During the nineteenth century it was mainly German nationalistic and Christian-Socialist clerics and politicians who used the Talmud at the service of antisemitic demagogy. The famous Old Testament scholar Julius Wellhausen (1844–1918) judged Talmudic Judaism in these words:

> Even the most insignificant good deed is counted so that finally a garment of justice develops woven of threads, or an armor consisting of small rings.[125]

The assessment of these people was plagiarized later in publications by National Socialist ideologues and hate publications such as *Der Stuermer.*

Christian anti-Talmudists and antisemites justify their attitude by insisting that in the Talmud Jesus was being reviled and Christianity cursed. They also would discuss, without direct acquaintance with the text, what the Talmud has to say on God and man.

It is true that in the Talmud, and in rabbinic writings generally, the figure of Jesus is distorted and diminished (cf., for example, TB *San* 43a; *Git* 56b-57a; *BerR* 98:9 on Gn 49:11).[126] Sayings against Jesus are rare, however, filling no more than about twenty small pages, and are of little consequence for theology and the history of religion. Moreover, it must be noted that sayings hostile to Jesus date to the time after the fourth century CE and the changes under Constantine, when the Church in her position as imperial power acted with hostility toward Jews. The Mishnah, that basic component of the Talmud, does not contain a single passage clearly denouncing Jesus or Christianity. At a time when the Church Fathers loudly and aggressively preached and wrote against the Jews, such refraining from polemics is proof of considerable inner strength. During the first post-Christian centuries, the rabbinic sages had accepted almost without exception the tactics of silence; but beginning with the fourth century, they believed that they had to immunize the Jews against Christian pressure. This was done by means of legends about Jesus and Christianity, to mobilize counter-forces against an increasingly stronger Church. Rabbinic legends about Jesus, then, are not an expression of a Jewish anti-Christian attitude but belong to religious apologetic folklore. For that reason, they should not be employed in theological controversy.

3. An Attempt at Evaluation

#87 In the present context, some brief indications of literary criticism and religious history will suffice. The Talmud is not homogenous, and a survey of it is exceedingly difficult.

> Talmudic thought grasps problems in an isolated way and nowhere attempts to consolidate the results into a larger frame of thinking.[127]

#88. We can appreciate the diversity and unsystematic approach of the Talmud most profitably by seeing it—in a highly simplified manner—as a "place of deposit" for "minutes" to refresh the memory concerning rabbinic scholarly discussions over several centuries. Some form of orderly arrangement was eventually applied to this deposit and it was made available to the general reader in folio volumes. The thematic and systematic disorder of the Talmud is the chief reason for the "unsuitable, vague shape in which the faith contents of Judaism remained."[128] Liturgical sayings stand next to edifying ones, speculation on the Law alongside problems of everyday life, profound matters next to insignificant ones, and ancient traditions are interspersed with later information, etc.

#89 A Christian theologian cannot agree, of course, with the judgments on Jesus contained in the Talmud, but he must beware of isolating the few statements against Jesus from their immense Talmudic context (cf. #86). It would be most unfair and destructive to point only to these few dark spots. In order to protect the Talmud and the Church Fathers against an equally wholesale condemnation, a Christian theologian of Judaism should point out the historical and social conditions of that period. Thoughts and actions in late antiquity were not determined by historical criticism, religious ecumenism, or social openness. The various political, politico-religious, economic, and social communities were bent on mutual hostility and rivalry. They maligned one another with the high authorities in order to obtain some small indulgence for their own group. That situation is well documented in patristic literature as in the Talmud, and we should beware of interpreting the anti-Jewish statements of the Church Fathers and the anti-Christian ones in the Talmud in a fundamentalistic manner.

It makes a considerable difference whether certain Christian anti-Jewish statements were made before or after medieval, early modern or contemporary Jewish pogroms. Similarly, it makes a difference for Jewish anti-Christian sayings whether they date from before or after a time when Jews were able to obtain more information about Christianity. The oft-cited "normative power of what happened" (*Kraft des Geschehenen*) must be taken into account regarding such sayings and legends. A Christian speaking out against Jews after Auschwitz is much more irresponsible than some Church Father who, without realizing the harm his words could inflict, believed that degradation of the Jews belonged to Christian preaching.

#90 In the present context, the usefulness of the Talmud for Christian theology is important for a Christian assessment of this literature. Would certain New Testament passages become more intelligible if we were to find Talmudic parallels? Could some statements and institutions of the Apostolic Church be more comprehensible to us with the help of the Talmud? These two questions must be answered positively. Up to this time, Christians have not made sufficient use of the Talmud. For that reason, large parts of the New Testament have remained without shape and color. Many primitive (Apostolic) and early Church institutions (especially Church order and liturgy), therefore, are hidden in partial darkness.

#91 Finally, we must inquire into the evaluation of Judaism itself concerning the Talmud. In the eyes of traditional Jews, the Babylonian Talmud is an expression of God's oral revelation to Israel. As such, it is accorded a status similar to the written revelation laid down in the Tanakh (cf. TB *Ned* 37b; *Ber* 26b). Commandments not in the Bible but contained in the Talmud are considered as laws already given to Moses on Mount Sinai. According to this interpretation, intellectual and dialogic preoccupations of the rabbinic scholars are opportunities granted by God to revive revelations given in previous eras and to make them fruitful for Judaism (cf. John 14:26; 16:13). Liberal and Reform Jews do not go quite as far in their esteem for the Talmud, but even they perceive it as the religious foundation which must not be neglected by Jews in their life and philosophy.

#92 How, then, should Christians judge the Talmud? First of all, it is a significant religious work of God's people who are in some hidden way one with us (cf. Rom 11:28). Secondly, it is a mine of information for a more profound understanding of the Hebrew Scriptures and the New Testament. Finally, it is a resource for the Church in her constant quest for reform and reconsideration of her foundation, as well as a goad to a renewed understanding of her traditions.

II. Religious Life and Practices According to Rabbinic Ideals

#93 Without sufficient information on the meaning of Judaism, Christians have often maintained that from early Jewish and rabbinic times it had become a religion of legalism. Rabbinic piety was said to be a mere matter of reason and will which also dominated Jewish ethics; Judaism was often contemptuously categorized as "piety of works," "justification by works," etc. (cf. #15, 86). Jewish apologists reacted in a rather unfortunate manner to such accusations. Fascinated with the Enlightenment and modern philosophies, nineteenth-century Jews, for example, very one-sidedly emphasized that Judaism was a rational alternative to romantic, mystical, mythical Christian religion. Judaism does not know original sin, ideas of expiation, irrational mysticism, dogmas, or mysteries.[129] Unintentionally, such Jewish views served to strengthen Christian belief that Judaism was in the grip of a rigid law. Research by Martin Buber, Gershom Scholem, and others led the way to rediscovery and revaluation of the mystical, esoteric aspects of Judaism,[130] which obviously influenced modern Judaism to some extent (cf. #211).

Generally speaking, Jewish religious life consists of a mysterious interplay of an interior attitude and an activity which conforms to God's will as expressed in biblical and post-biblical teachings. In order to understand Jewish religious attitudes of life and practices we must consider the spiritual and legal components; we must also ask how these components find expression.

1. Spirituality

#94 We use the term "spirituality" mainly in Christian theology, but it can be adapted to Judaism without great effort. It means a subjective, religious relationship of human beings to God, applying to all situations of life, but particularly in distressing, extreme situations, to keep one from perishing or breaking down. Spirituality means plucking up courage, derived from strength and motivation offered by revelation. It is an interior actualization of revelation for concrete life situations, in reliance on the Spirit of God.[131]

a. Akedah

#95 We can best explain Jewish spirituality by the influence of Gen 22 in rabbinic times. This requires an examination of early Jewish ideas.

Genesis relates Abraham's readiness, at the command of God, to sacrifice his son Isaac on Mount Moriah. At the time of Jesus, and probably already in the Old Testament context, this divine command was counted as the most difficult trial to which Israel's progenitor could possibly have submitted (cf. *Liber Antiquitatum Biblicarum* 32:1–4). The interpretations of this profound Bible story were known in rabbinic times as *akedah Itzhak* ("binding of Isaac"), or simply *akedah* ("binding"). The word is taken from Gen 22:9, according to which Isaac was bound by Abraham on the sacrificial altar. In Jewish tradition, *akedah* is a complex of significant religious ideas expressed in mysticism as in religious practice.[132]

#96 Already in pre-Christian times, *akedah* belonged to the mysteries of the Passover festival. The Book of Jubilees, composed around 100 BCE, contains an amplification of Gen 22:9, according to which Abraham happily and gratefully celebrated for seven days after having passed the trial. Since that day, it is held, Israelites must observe that festival:

> And accordingly has it been ordained and written on the heavenly tablets regarding Israel and its seed that they should observe this festival seven days with the joys of festival (Jub 18:18).

At the time that the Book of Jubilees was written, this passage could be understood only in connection with the Passover feast of seven (possibly eight) days. It is also possible that the typical division of Passover into animal sacrifice at the Temple and a festive meal in the home was based on the original link between, and theological equality of, the *akedah* and the Exodus from Egypt. The fact that in later and post-biblical times Mount Moriah, the place of the Abraham-Isaac trial, was identified as the place of the Temple in Jerusalem points in the same direction (cf. 2 Chron 3:1; Jub 18:13; *Ant* 1:224; 7:333).[133]

According to a Jerusalem Targum tradition on Ex 12:42, preserved in the Codex Neophyti, the Jewish Passover feast in rabbinic times consisted of four mysteries: creation, *akedah,* exodus, and final redemption. The version contained in Codex Neophyti 1 was probably used as a brief liturgical formula in Palestine to call the festive mysteries to mind. The *akedah* passage says:

> The second night: when the Lord was revealed to Abram, a man at the age of a hundred years, and as Sarah his wife was a woman of ninety years. Thus was fulfilled what the Scripture says: "Will Abram, a man of a hundred years, beget, and will his wife Sarah, a woman of ninety years, bear?" (Gen 17:17). And Isaac was thirty-seven years when he was offered upon the altar. The heavens were let down and descended and Isaac saw their perfections. His eyes were dimmed because of their perfections. And he called it the Second Night.[134]

As the *akedah* was firmly linked to the theme of mysteries in the early Jewish and rabbinic Passover (cf. MekhY on Ex 12:41, Horovitz 51), it was understood as a primary event (*Urereignis*) of Jewish faith such as creation, the exodus, and the *eschaton*. Accordingly, past salvation history (creation, *akedah,* exodus) and the salvific future (*eschaton*) have a bearing on the celebration of the Passover. Christians have, then, rightly called the Passover festival the "sacrament of Israel."[135]

#97 The Jewish concept of merit is no mere "justification by works." It is closely linked to the conviction, which also finds expression in the Passover, that the divine influence of the past and future may become effective in the present time (cf. Mish *Pes* 10:5). Jewish tradition, therefore, called *akedah* primary merit, thanks to which weaknesses and sins of later generations would be expiated and taken away (e.g., *Liber Antiquitatum Biblicarum* 18:5; Mish *Ta'an* 2:4; *BerR* 56:1 on Gen 22:4, and 56:2 on Gen 22:5). The words "on the merit of Abraham" (*bizekut Abraham*) or "on the merit of the patriarchs" (*bizekut avot*) frequently occur together with demands to fulfill certain duties (*hobah,* etc.).[136] Behind this stands the conviction that fulfillment of Torah by the individual can be accounted a merit to be rewarded by God only in union with Abraham's trial of faith and his and the other patriarchs' fulfillment of Torah.

#98 The previously quoted Targum text (CN 1 on Ex 12:42) indicates still another aspect of *akedah,* that is, Isaac's complete self-sacrifice. The narrator calculates Isaac to be thirty-seven years old in order to emphasize this fact. He describes Isaac's attitude as *'tkrb*—he surrendered himself, he was of a sacrificial mind, he was prepared to be sacrificed. In his interpretation, the Targumist clearly indicates the unity of mind between Abraham's sacrifice and Isaac's sacrificial offering. Twice he em phasizes (in Gen 22:6 and 22:8) that "they walked together as one, in the same spirit."

Twice the Targumist has Isaac address his father Abraham with the intimately familiar *abba* (in Gen 22:7 and 22:10). The Tiberian Midrash tradition also stresses their harmony of mind:

> "And they went both of them together": one to bind and the other to be bound, one to slaughter and the other to be slaughtered (*BerR* 56:3 on Gn 22:6).

This very intimate father-son relationship between Abraham and Isaac on the occasion of a most unprecedented trial was possibly the background for the account of Jesus' baptism in the Jordan River (Mk 1:1–11). It could be that the New Testament authors considered the Abraham figure in this narrative in the direction of God the Father while Jesus was seen as the perfect Isaac. The voice from heaven, "This is my beloved son" (Matt 3:17), then, would express the very intimate familiarity and harmony of will between Jesus and the Father.[137]

#99 In rabbinic-Targumic understanding, the *akedah* was not a unique event that concerned only Abraham and Isaac. It applies as well to later generations who, as descendants of the two patriarchs, must try to accomplish the *akedah* in accordance with their example:

> And Abraham worshiped and prayed in the name of the Word of the Lord and said: I beseech by the mercy that is before you, O Lord. All things are manifest and known before you: that there was no division in my heart for the first time that you said to me to sacrifice my son Isaac, to make him dust and ashes before you, but that I immediately arose early in the morning and diligently put your words into practice with gladness and fulfilled your decree. And now, when his sons are in the hour of affliction, remember the *akedah* of their father Isaac and listen to the voice of their supplication and hear them and deliver them from all tribulation. . . . (CN 1 on Gen 22:14; similarly *BerR* 56:10 on Gen 22:14).

Isaac's attitude of devotion is to be imitated by his descendants, parcularly in moments of anguish, pointing to the primary event of Isaac's anguish. The theological key word in Aramaic is *dkr,* corresponding to the Hebrew *zkr,* "to remember."

According to the Tanakh and also prevailing in New Testament and

Talmudic-Targumic times, zkr/zkrwn/dkr/anamnesis/memoria/remembrance is a petitioning, summoning signal toward God and the members of his people. God may remember his earlier covenant—particularly with Abraham, Isaac, and Jacob, but also with Moses, Aaron, David. Human beings should remember God's kindnesses in the past, for which they owe him gratitude (cf., e.g., Pss 105:8–48; 132:17; Luke 1:54–75). This divine-human reference and recollection is a revival of the first covenant within the community of those who gratefully remember, for God's remembrance is gracious and active. These ideas and beliefs stand in Christian tradition at the beginning of all worship and sacramental thought and activity.[138] Such ideas also indicate that Jewish tradition, in many of its aspects, is not a-sacramental or anti-sacramental. The history of *akedah* shows, however that in Judaism the concept of fulfillment is not so much grounded in communal prayer as in achievements of life, in the sight of danger under harsh everyday circumstances (cf., e.g., Jdt 8:24–27).

b. Kiddush Ha-Shem and Hillul Ha-Shem

#100 Beginning with the second to first century BCE, *akedah* became significant as a means to strengthen the individual's readiness for martyrdom.[139] Looking back on the Maccabean martyrs of the second century BCE, it says in the Fourth Book of Maccabees, which was composed about the time of Jesus:

> Remember that for the sake of God ye have come into the world, and have enjoyed life, and that therefore ye owe it to God to endure all pain for his sake; for whom also our father Abraham made haste to sacrifice his son Isaac, the ancestor of our nation; and Isaac, seeing his father's hand lifting the knife against him, did not shrink (4 Macc 16:18–20).

In the two centuries before and after Christ, martyrdom was extremely frequent, and every Jew had to prepare to be led unexpectedly to his execution.

Yet, Isaac was not killed on Mount Moriah but was only on the brink of death. This explains why in rabbinic Judaism the *akedah* was not the central theme in preparing for the acceptance of martyrdom. Probably under Pharisaic influence, the term *kiddush ha-Shem* (sanctification of the divine Name) came into use.

#101 *Kiddush ha-Shem* signifies the greatest sacrifice for God, acceptance of a martyr's death or accomplishment of an act transcending all Jewish and non-Jewish expectations. *Hillul ha-Shem* is the opposite, the is, desecration of the Name. Blasphemy, capital crime, idolatry, sexual violations, shedding of blood and apostasy were all considered *hillul ha-Shem.*

"You must not profane my holy name, so that I may be proclaimed holy among the sons of Israel. I am Yahweh who sanctify you" (Lev 22:32) is the Bible verse most frequently quoted on the significance of the sanctification and desecreation of the Name. This and other quotations (e.g., Lev 10:1–3) enable us to understand that sanctification and desecration not only set the highest and lowest limits (martyrdom, apostasy) of moral conduct; they regulate not only matters between God and the human conscience but, as the rabbis understood it, *kiddush* and *hillul* can also take place in the encounter between Jews and non-Jews.

On the insistence of non-Jews that certain Jewish laws were hostile to strangers, R. Gamliel (about 100 CE) decreed their abolition:

> At that hour, R. Gamliel decreed that it was forbidden to rob a non-Jew because it could (possibly) desecrate the Divine Name (TJ *BK* 4:3).

To prevent non-Jews from similarly blaspheming God and persecuting the Jews, it was taught:

> Where a suit arises between an Israelite and a heathen, if you can justify the former according to the laws of Israel, justify him and say: "This is *our* law"; so also if you can justify him by the laws of the heathens justify him and say (to the other party): "This is *your* law"; but if this cannot be done, we use subterfuges to circumvent him. This is the view of R. Ishmael, but R. Akiba said that we should not attempt to circumvent him on account of the sanctification of the Name (TB *BK* 113a).

In order to keep peace among Jews and between Jews and non-Jews (*mipne darke shalom,* Mish *Git* 5:7–8; TB *Git* 59b), a unified attitude was demanded for inner-Jewish and general social conduct (*toko kebaro,* TB *Ber* 28b), as well as acknowledgment of the authority of the laws of the (pagan) state (*dina de makuta dina,* TB *BK* 113a). This touches on the foundation of rabbinic interpretation of the Law.

2. The Law

#102 In discussing Jewish law from a Christian theological point of view, care must be taken to consider the vibration of undertones and acces-

sory terms. Whenever the word "nomocracy," government by law, is lev-
eled at Judaism, or when the alleged Jewish-Christian dichotomy
law/grace and law/freedom is applied in favor of Christianity, we must
suspect that "the Law" is used merely as a polemic formula. It is part of
ecumenical fairness that outsiders not harp on actual or alleged misuse of
Jewish piety and practice of the Law. Such an approach could only go contrary to one's own Christian interests; the Law of the Hebrew Scriptures is,
after all, a part of Christian revelation. Christian opinion of the Law must
be based on the fact that, wherever the Law is properly understood and
practiced, law/grace and law/freedom are not opposites but belong together. One can verify this easily from the Old Testament (for example, Ps
119).

#103 There is good reason to understand Matt 5:17 as follows: "Do
not imagine that I have come to sever the Law or the prophets from their
context, but, on the contrary, I have come to place them within their context." According to the teaching of the Matthean Christ, his disciples are
forbidden to be antinomians. Christians do not do away with, or express
contempt for, the Law, but they place it into a favored context by linking it
to Christ who fulfilled all God's laws. Paul held a similar conviction when
he said: "Do we therefore through faith destroy the Law? By no means.
Rather we establish the Law" (Rom 3:31). Since the disciples of Christ,
then, are to accept and fulfill what the Law means at its deepest level, we
must take a look at the meaning and rank it has in the Hebrew Scriptures.

According to the Old Testament, the people of God is a community-
in-pilgrimage following divine instruction (Torah), that is, acting according to the will of God in history. The Five Books of Moses are rightly
called Torah or instruction. It is the divine Will which stands behind the
biblical instruction and individual commandments and prohibitions. The
instructions proper are not absolute and independent. Accordingly, Deut
8:1f should read: "All the commandments I enjoin on you today you must
keep and observe so that you may live and increase in numbers and enter
into the land that the Lord promised on oath to your fathers and make it
your own. Remember all of the way that YHWH your God has led you in
the wilderness, to humble you, to test you and know your innermost
heart—whether you would keep his commandments or not."

There is a broad biblical tradition which—never asking for an explanation for Israel's existence, Israel's laws, or one's own humanity—is solely directed toward the will of the God of revelation. It is he who instructs,
shows his way to Israel and illumines it; he also indicates the goal. Israel
must walk this way, whether or not it can understand. The Israelite is a

person who "must walk all the paths of God" (Deut 11:22; cf. Deut 5:32f; Pss 23:3; 139:23; etc.). Judaism, then, does not acknowledge government by the Law but government by God. The establishment of God's reign is the innermost meaning of the Jewish Law.[140]

#104 In late Old Testament times and even more so during the rabbinic era, the many instructions, decrees, commandments, exhortations, and precepts of the Hebrew Scriptures received actualizations, modifications and additions in many ways. It was a question of adapting to new times, to different problems and changed ways of life (cf. #81–82).[141] Many rabbinic sages considered their own decrees, derived and adapted from the Bible, as equivalent to biblical commandments:

> R. Levi b. Hama says . . . in the name of R. Simeon b. Lakish (about 250 CE): What is the meaning of the verse: "And I will give thee the tables of stone, and the law and the commandment, which I have written that thou mayest teach them" (Ex 24:12)? "Tables of stone": these are the ten commandments; "the law": this is the Pentateuch; "the commandment": this is the Mishnah; "which I have written": these are the Prophets and the Hagiographa; "that thou mayest teach them": this is the Gemara. It teaches (us) that all these things were given to Moses on Sinai (TB *Ber* 5a).

A single commandment, a *halakhah,* declared as binding by the Pharisaic-rabbinic scholars after long discussions and an experimental phase, was in their view

> a particular explanation of divine Will, brought to bear on a given case, and as such binding on all who recognize the Torah as highest authority and who committed themselves to live in the way prescribed by it.[142]

This view is based on the theological notion of a twofold Torah, Written (*shebiktav*) and Oral (*shebealpeh*). Written Torah (Tanakh, particularly the Pentateuch) and Oral Torah (Mishnah, Talmud) were both revealed to Moses on Sinai. The laws of the Mishnah and Talmud are said to be revivals of that which God revealed to Moses (*Avot* 1:1; Mish*Pea* 2:6; TB *Shab* 31a; *Er* 54b, *Naz* 56b; *Ned* 35b–37b; cf. #91).

#105 Within the framework of rabbinic law, explanations, misrepresentations, exaggerations, and errors occurred. Time and again, rigorous Halakhists had to be restrained by Aggadists—that is, scholars whose teaching contained religious tales (*aggadot*) and parables (*meshalim*)— from making intolerable demands (cf. TB *Mak* 23b; *Shab* 31a–32a). As a result of such arguments and at the urging of Hillel's followers, particularly the mild R. Joshua b. Hananya (120 CE), the following popular principle prevailed:

> We do not lay a hardship *(gzarah)* on the community unless the majority can endure it (TB *BB* 60b).

#106 "Making a hedge around the Torah" (Mish*Avot* 1:1), a principle stated already in pre-Christian times, was often misunderstood; the people of Qumran already criticized the Pharisees because of it. Sarcastically they said, "The hedge is built; far is the statute" (CD IV:12; see Micah 7:11). Disregarding polemical distortions, we know from the Mekhilta on Ex 12:6 what the rabbis actually intended by the "hedge around the Torah." They meant additional laws which were to keep people from transgressing the biblical commandments. The rabbis asked for precautionary measures as moral guidance to the Jews in small matters in order to guard against unforeseen temptations to disregard major commandments. This hedge principle easily lent itself to petty, nervous moralizing. Later outsiders discerned here a soft spot in Judaism that they could trample on by maintaining that Jews hold to a narrow, hair-splitting interpretation and application of the Scriptures.

#107 Although *halakhah* played an important part, Jewish history was not exclusively determined by it. What Jacob Katz said with regard to the Middle Ages holds more or less equally true for rabbinic times:

> Its *(halakhah's)* function was that of holding the balance between the two driving forces, namely the necessary adjustment to new conditions and the preservation of Jewish identity. That the halakhah followed in the wake of social change has been observed very often by historians. . . . But the other function, that of safeguarding Jewish identity by means of rationalization, is no less conspicuous a task. It was the achievement of the halakhah that it prevented the community and the individual from being engulfed by the social and religious life of the Christian environment. . . . [143]

#108 In view of the relativity and occasional misuse of the Law, great Jewish personalities not only embraced it lovingly and obediently, but they also held their critical distance. In varying degrees, such a dialectic relationship obtained for instance with Hillel I (died about 20 BCE; cf. his *Prosbul;* TB *Git* 36a–b), Jesus of Nazareth, Paul of Tarsus, R. Joshua b. Hananya (ab. 120 CE), R. Meir (140 CE), Isaac Luria (1534–

1572), Sabbatai Zvi (1626–1676), and the Hasidic teachers of the eighteenth century. On Jesus' relationship to the Law, the Jewish scholar David Flusser has this to say:

> For Jesus there was, of course, the peculiar problem of his relationship
> to the Law and its precepts; but this arises for every believing Jew who
> takes his Judaism seriously.[144]

We must beware, then, of prematurely hailing Jesus and Paul as transgressors of the Law, or to derive an interpretation of their identity from their activities allegedly abolishing the Law (cf. #103, 130, 193f).

3. Divine Worship

#109 Jewish worship is an expression of Jewish piety. The rabbis were at pains to emphasize that piety is not an isolated outcry to God, no mere irrational emotionality. Piety must conform to spiritual-intellectual striving, manifested in knowledge of the Scriptures, study of the Law, etc., and to a way of life. Awareness of this unity between piety, study, and practice led to uniformity of concepts applied to them. The verb *sms* for instance, an equivalent of the biblical verb *srt* (to serve), is applied in rabbinic writings to the liturgical service of the angels in heaven and to the priests in the Temple. *Sms* is also used in theoretical reflections on the Torah, as in the relationship between student and teacher, the former's services, willingness to learn, and serving at table.[145] In liturgical speculation and social contexts, Josephus Flavius used without differentiation the terms *diakonein/diakonia* (to serve, service) (cf. *Ant* 5:344; 7:365.378; *Bellum* 3:354; 4:626). He

> could hardly have done so without the influence of the homely *sms,*
> which is used for every service to God, as much as for serving meals and
> for services which the disciple has to render to his master.[146]

In awareness of this background, certain gestures and words of Christ should not overhastily be called un-cultic or anti-cultic, thereby perhaps designating them as un-Jewish or anti-Jewish. Such circumspection applies, for example, to the story in John 13:1–17 of the washing of feet. It is an exemplary service of Christ to his disciples and teaches that they should be prepared to serve one another. (It is of no consequence that the word *duluein* is used instead of *diakonein.*) In the eyes of the Johannine Christ and his Jewish disciples, the washing of feet was simultaneously service to

God and service to man. According to the understanding of the time, those two types of services should not be separated; they are two expressions of one and the same mental attitude.

#110 Piety is circumscribed in the Talmud as "awe of Heaven," that is, awe of God (TB *Ber* 33b). It is expressed chiefly in communal prayer. TB *Ta'anit* 2a calls prayer *abodah* (service) accomplished in the heart. That definition was often degraded to a mere cultic substitution formula because *abodah* is a cultic term. In the Talmud, however, *abodah* of the heart is a midrashic explanation of Deut 11:13f which speaks of obedient service to God with all one's heart and all one's love and of the divine reward for such service. Accordingly this Talmudic definition of prayer can be expanded to mean that prayer is service to God, in discernment, obedience, and love, in full interior engagement, so that God may make his promises come to pass. In the rabbinic meaning, the praying individual should be united to all of Israel and all of Israel's expectations with all his being. His prayer thereby becomes more than a striving for transcendence; it is service in the temporal life of God's people.

#111 Pharisaic-rabbinic piety at the time of Jesus impresses many people in our day as somewhat dubious, and they find their arguments for such an attitude in the New Testament. Jesus accuses the contemporary cult leaders of performing their prayer without heed to the acute needs of their fellow men (Luke 10:25–37). Pharisaic prayer is called self-complacent, based on false appearances, and emphasizing the praying person's merits (Luke 18:9–14; Matt 23). There are many who interpret such New Testament statements not simply as a warning against the perversion of Jewish or any other religious experience, but as historical illustrations of a declining Jewish prayer life. For example, Paul Billerbeck writes:

> The thanksgiving prayer on the lips of the Pharisee in Lk 18:11f is not freely or even tendentiously invented but true to facts.[147]

The *Begriffslexikon zum Neuen Testament* says that Jewish prayer of the time was dominated "by the idea of merit which prevailed in their piety."[148]

As far as we can tell from records, piety inspired by Pharisees was by no means decadent; such documents, on the contrary, seem to prove an exceedingly elevated attitude toward prayer and its practice. Because of dialogue between the people and the scholars, the time of Jesus was a period of consolidation of piety.[149] Jesus' words against the false piety of the cult leaders and Pharisees mean that he was a very discerning critic of the contemporary life of prayer. His critical stance, however, applies not only to Jewish piety but to any praying community and every praying person, also to the Church and each one of her faithful. Even among the most pious individuals—whether Pharisees, Christian monks or others—there are tendencies toward sham appearances and running away from social responsibilities.

#112 Certain "classic" contrasts between Jewish synagogue service and Christian liturgy prove, upon closer inspection, to be nothing but the results of well-established Jewish and Christian apologetic positions. That is the case, for example, when Jewish and Protestant service (service of the Word) is placed over against Catholic service (celebration of the Mystery). Ever since rabbinic times, it has not been a modern Christian service of the Word but the traditional institution of prayer in choir by communities of monks and priests that has come closest in form to the Jewish synagogue service. In either situation it is not so much the personal intention of each praying person that counts, but obedient execution as such, an expression of the awareness that the praying community officially represents "all Israel" or "all of the Church." In both, the service builds upon alternation of hymns, psalms, responses, supplications, praises, reading of texts, and relatively sparse ceremonies—all of it elaborate and difficult to understand because of accretions which have accumulated in the course of history. In both, it is not primarily the case of an individual struggling with God but of official, deputized praise of God.

Here we must briefly discuss the theme of Mystery in Christian liturgical service. Some Jewish colleagues seem to consider it in acute contrast to Jewish synagogue service because they assume that the Christian Eucharist in particular is nothing but an adaptation of the mystery cults and sacrificial celebrations of late pagan antiquity. They contrast such a liturgy to the anti-mystic and anti-mythic character of the Jewish synagogue service. But such assumptions are not correct. Christian liturgy wants to make the redemptive God present; it is not a question of magic practices, but of a personal encounter with this God. To this day, synagogue liturgy contains similar elements of Mystery. It also comprises much of the old Temple mystic and apocalyptic esotericism (cf. #39–41). It is imbued, moreover, with a theology of remembrance, of re-presentation, for example, in the Passover festival (cf. #96–99). Such elements are most evident in the *kedushah* (*trisaghion, sanctus*) of the synagogue service.[150]

#113 Between the liturgical services of Judaism and Christianity there exist only two weighty differences: Jesus Christ and the cult leaders. The *doxa* of Jesus Christ, mysteriously present in the Eucharist, is rejected by Jews. The related Christian idea that (in Christ) the cult is perfect is rejected also. In those portions of the *kaddish* prayer which are probably pre-Christian, God is praised in accordance with Neh 9:5: "He who is high above all the blessings and hymns, praises and consolations, which are uttered in the world." Of course, Christians should point out that Christian liturgy, as it is celebrated by the faithful, is also imperfect. A further convergence can be detected in the fact that the New Testament and liturgical doxologies (Rom 11:33–36 and the final doxology of the Roman Canon) and all "classic" liturgical prayers are not directed to Jesus but to the "Father."

Jews reject all statements on the mediating action of cult functionaries. The Christian stand, for instance, that in the liturgy the bishop symbolizes Christ and/or the unity of the Church is unacceptable to Jews. Even at the time of Jesus and the rabbis, the office of synagogue-president was an inferior one not linked to ordination. In Pharisaic-rabbinic Judaism, the high Jewish office of patriarch, the Babylonian "head of diaspora," scholarly bodies, and teachers were not linked *ex officio* to the arrangement of liturgical services, but to the interpretation of Scripture, the court of religious law, charitable and pastoral leadership of communities, etc. The synagogue service was and is a meeting of lay people.[151]

#114 The three interrelated topics—spirituality, law, and liturgical service—contain much material that could be significant for a new theological beginning and in discussions with Jewish colleagues. Further discussions on such themes would yield many more approaches. It is incomprehensible that, to my knowledge, no direct or indirect contact has been made between Jewish halakhists and Christian moralists, ethicists, and casuists. I do not know whose fault this is; each side accuses the other. Far too much prejudice and distrust, it seems, adhere to the concept of the Law. Basic Jewish notions on biblical and post-biblical laws would be highly significant for Christian moral theology and Christian ethics generally. It would also be helpful if Christian masters of the spiritual life were to discover Jewish spiritual experiences. Even more puzzling is the fact that Christian liturgists are very fainthearted in their approach to the flourishing Jewish scholarship in liturgical life.

4.
Jesus Christ

#115 Up to this point, Jesus Christ has been mentioned only spo-
radically. An integrating presentation of his person, dignity, and importance can now be given, based on a description and theological evaluation
of his early Jewish and rabbinic environment. We sketched a picture of the
Jews of his time, their creativity and humanity, and, having done this, we
may now talk of the Jew Jesus of Nazareth in his uniqueness. To do so prematurely—without giving the appropriate background—would ill befit a
Christian theology of Judaism. We will first consider Christian and Jewish
scholarship in the field, then the human, historical Jewish Jesus (based on
insights gained in previous chapters), and finally Jewish and Christian differences of belief with regard to Jesus Christ.

Each generation must confront anew the various approaches to Jesus
Christ, his place in history, and his significance for human history. It
would be a lack of scholarship and good will were we to undertake research about Jesus and Christology without regard to contemporary methods of approach. A Christian theology of Judaism must try to fathom the
interpretation of Jesus Christ on Jewish terms and by Jewish ways of
thinking. Appreciation of the Jewish literature at the time of Jesus clearly
demonstrates that the Jewish contribution is not limited to the human Jesus up to the moment of his death. Jewish theology of the period was
dominated by ideas that the New Testament hagiographers and early
Church writers employed in their presentation of the risen Christ.

I. Modern Jewish and Christian Interpreters
of the Risen Christ

#116 It has always been known that Jesus was born, lived and died a Jew; only extremely anti-Jewish movements, for example, the German National Socialists, attempted, for obvious reasons, to deny this fact. Since the time when Julius Wellhausen's (1844–1918) remark, "Jesus was not a Christian; he was a Jew,"[152] was elevated to a hermeneutical principle in New Testament scholarship, the Jewishness of Jesus has become an ever more important question, even though some emotional and ideological undercurrents could not always be stilled. The Jewish scholar Joseph Klausner (1874–1958) referred to Wellhausen when he wrote:

> Jesus of Nazareth . . . was a product of Palestine alone, a product of Judaism unaffected by any foreign admixture. There were many Gentiles in Galilee, but Jesus was in no way influenced by them. In his days Galilee was the stronghold of the most enthusiastic Jewish patriotism. Jesus spoke Aramaic and there is no hint that he knew Greek—none of his sayings show any clear mark of Greek literary influence. Without any exception he is wholly explainable by the scriptural and Pharisaic Judaism of his time.[153]

Though many Christian exegetes could not be fully reconciled to Klausner's words that Jesus' teaching could "without any exception" be explained in a Jewish sense, they nevertheless continued in that direction, specifically after the Second World War. Even the message of Jesus belongs "within the framework of Jewish religion."[154] Jesus did not found a new religion but wanted to "assert the meaning of the Jewish religion."[155]

#117 Lately, the Christian exegete Siegfried Schulz had the following very radical words to say about Jesus' Jewishness:

> Not only Jesus himself but conservative apocalyptic Jewish-Christianity remained within Israel and forms a part not of Christianity, but of the history of late Judaism. As apocalyptic prophet and wisdom teacher of the last age, Jesus did preach the promises, but most of all the Law. Even his prophetic polemics against the Pharisees form part of the great anti-Pharisaic critique by the apocalyptists within Israel. . . . Even though, from the viewpoint of historical criticism, Jesus' eschatological possession of the spirit and his apocalyptic expectation of the early coming of the *basileia* made the Torah and proclamation of the approaching Creator God more acute, from the viewpoint of theological criticism,

the eschatological possession of the spirit, apocalyptic eschatological expectation, and proclamation of the Coming of the Creator God become
functions of Law and ethics. Frequently held opposite views notwith-
standing, Jesus and his message are only apparently universal, radical,
and unique, while on the other hand any immediate actualization becomes impossible.[156]

Appealing to the oldest pre-Easter Q-material, with these remarks
Schulz erects barriers between the pre-Easter period of Jesus and the post-
Easter time of Christ, between Jesus and Paul, between the Pauline teaching on justification of the sinner by faith and early Catholic/Jewish-Chris-
tian piety of works, between Judaism and the Church. Yet it is not
appropriate in biblical research to pit individual layers of the material
against the transmitted text as a whole and the redacted additions and
modifications within individual writings. All of the New Testament and
later literature, moreover, bears witness to "lasting fidelity to the normative beginnings," to Jesus Christ, his words, actions, attitudes, and experience, and demand the same (cf. Luke 1:2; John 1:1; 1 John 2:24a; 2 John 9;
etc.).[157]

#118 Jewish research on Jesus since the beginning of this century
clearly insists on his Jewishness. On the one hand, that is based on findings
of historical criticism; on the other, most Jewish authors, implicitly or explicitly, pose the question existentially. They have come to realize that un-
Jewish or anti-Jewish interpretations of Jesus serve as an alibi for Christian
anti-Judaism. Whenever Jewish authors emphasize and elaborate on Jesus'
Jewishness, they have at the back of their mind their own fate and that of
their people. Many Jews feel personally affected whenever Christians voice
their opinion on Jesus and the Judaism of his time. We cannot help it if
judgment of Judaism is considered a judgment on the Jewish existence.[158]

Reproaches and objections by influential, critically inclined Jewish
scholars since 1900 could be summarized as follows: Christians have torn
Jesus from the soil of Israel. They have de-Judaized, uprooted, alienated,
Hellenized, and Europeanized him. The consequences of these manipula-
tions and whitewashings are hopeless confusion about the person of Jesus,
the nature and tasks of Christianity, and the meaning of Judaism in religious history. [159]

#119 Because of frequently intersecting results of Jewish and Chris-
tian research concerning Jesus, we cannot make a clean division between
the two. It would be naive to think that only Jewish, or Christian, or religiously uncommitted Jesus scholars can be objective. It is true, however,

that Jewish scholarship has not been sufficiently taken into account by Christian and non-Christian colleagues. Jewish authors often have a much better knowledge of non-New Testament sources, while their non-Jewish counterparts sometimes have to their credit the appropriate use of methodological tools. Jewish authors must at times be suspected of carrying their leanings toward the state of Israel into their research on Jesus, while traditional Christian exegetes must often be reproached for interpreting New Testament texts overhastily as anti-Jewish because of their lack of familiarity with sources outside of the New Testament and insufficient empathy for Jewish ways of life and the interaction of Jewish groups.

However that may be, it would be wrong to isolate the person of Jesus Christ from the Tanakh and Judaism of his time. Anyone wishing to understand him thoroughly must undertake extensive studies of the mystery of Israel's election and the link between Jesus and Judaism. In order to gain an insight, moreover, into the historical Jesus, considerable attention must be paid to the ideas, events, and personalities of the time:

> The Jewish material is important, therefore, not just because it allows us to place Jesus in his own time, but because it allows us to interpret his sayings aright.[160]

Certain vague statements and differences in accentuation within the New Testament will continue to cause divergent Jesus interpretations. The postulate, however, remains that the various theological projections of the Bible must be classified critically according to the measure of the Bible. We must try to overcome certain barriers, as was attempted, for example, by Martin Buber (1878–1965) in *Two Types of Faith*.[161] He speaks there of two ways of faith, *emunah* and *pistis*, which fundamentally differ from one another. *Emunah* was realized mainly in the early time of the people Israel, he says. It means trust, confidence in God, an attitude always held by the community of Israel. *Pistis*, on the other hand, was clearly expressed by the early Church; it emphatically means individual belief in a certain faith content. This analysis by Buber was to fall on fruitful Christian soil. There hardly was a Bible scholar or preacher in the 1950's or 1960's who would not call for a Christian world view in the meaning of *emunah*. The first critic of this opinion of Buber was the Jewish philosopher of religion, Samuel Hugo Bergmann (1883–1975). He read Buber's manuscript and already in 1949 called it unconvincing and apologetic. Not only Jews but Christians, too, are borne up by *emunah*, feel sheltered in God, Bergmann

maintained. The historical Jesus in his *emunah* attitude should not be pit-
ted against Christianity because,

> not the living but the dead and risen Jesus is the "founder" of Christian-
> ity. . . . This resurrection is a real or alleged fact in the world. In what
> other way, then, can we confront a fact than by either accepting or de-
> nying it, "I believe that" or "I do not believe that"? And if it really hap-
> pened, it was such an important fact, such a new beginning of human
> history that Paul was correct in ascribing an overriding importance to
> faith in that fact. And is it not possible that *pistis* is so pervaded by trust
> of *emunah* that the conceptual separation, which is probably justified, is
> cancelled out in a higher synthesis?[162]

David Flusser, who drew attention to this important Bergmann letter,
also suggests that *emunah* in rabbinic texts sometimes means faith, plain
and simple,

> just like the Greek *pistis* which in that language also has the secondary
> meaning of trust. . . . But the New Testament term *pistis* is a correct
> translation of the Hebrew *emunah*.[163]

Beyond that, Flusser makes the following important critical remark on
Bergmann's first sentence above:

> Perhaps this applies partly to Paul because of his Damascus experience,
> and perhaps the "pre-Easter" Jesus is not accorded sufficient attention
> in the modern churches. But does it have to be that way, and has it al-
> ways been that way? Jesus' words and message have always been influ-
> ential, perhaps not sufficiently so. And perhaps it would be more than
> worthwhile to attempt somehow to link the message of the "historical"
> Jesus with a theology of the cross, so that not the cross would be the be-
> ginning but the beatitudes.[163a]

Buber's presentation of *pistis* and *emunah* erected still another barrier
between Jesus and Christianity, between Judaism and Christianity. It was
beneficial, however, that this happened because many Christians were
alerted to the unacceptability of a faith based merely on formulas and content. Bergmann indicated that not the historical Jesus as a person caused
Christian faith to come about, but the Risen One. Finally, Flusser touched
upon an important point within the Jewish-Christian dialogue on Jesus: we

must try to place the message even of the human Jesus (Flusser mentions the Sermon on the Mount as an example) within a Christian-ecclesial context. We must search at least for true links between the message of the pre-Easter Jesus and the post-Easter Christian communities. When one fails to do that and rests content with constructing new barriers, he neglects the Jew Jesus, the Christ proclaimed, early Judaism, the early Church, and today's Christian-Jewish dialogue bases. If we will take the pains to build well-established bridges, however, we will find that Jesus is, to express it somewhat carelessly, much more Jewish and much more Christian than many people think.

II. Jesus and His Jewish Home

1. Public Activities

#120 Among other things, everyone is a product of his environment, but environment alone will not fully explain him. Next to it, his uniqueness and singularity shine through. Such an understanding of the human personality has always been familiar to Jews. It is based on the biblical teaching that man was created in the image and likeness of God (Gen 1:26f). That teaching was very significant, particularly at the time of Jesus.[164] About 200 CE, the Mishnah indicated its great importance for Judaism, in connection with an admonition to court witnesses not to give false testimony against a defendant:

> Therefore but a single man was created in the world, to teach that if any man has caused a single soul to perish from Israel, Scripture imputes it to him as though he had caused a whole world to perish; and if any man saves alive a single soul (from Israel), Scripture imputes it to him as though he had saved alive a whole world. Again (but a single man was created) for the sake of peace among mankind, that none should say to his fellow, "My father was greater than thy father"; also that the heretics should not say, "There are many ruling powers in heaven." Again (but a single man was created) to proclaim the greatness of the Holy One, blessed is he: for man stamps many coins with the same seal and they are all like one another; but the King of kings, the Holy One, blessed is he, has stamped every man with the seal of the first man, yet not one of them is like his fellow (Mish *San* 4:5).

When we apply this to Jesus, it means that we much too often and frivolously talk, write, and preach about his self-awareness. What does it convey to an outsider if we say that his attitude was prophetic, apocalyptic, non-sectarian, Jewish, or universal? None of these categories could make him transparent. Like any human being, he remains as behind a veil or mystery, in his uniqueness, his feeling of himself. Since his hearers experienced him as a fascinating, extremely profound personality, there must be in him an even greater expanse of hiddenness. Some of the misunderstandings during his public life (cf. Mark 3:20–35) and in regard to his Passion (Mark 14:10f) are, in the last resort, due to the veiled, inexplicable mystery of his personality.

#121 Jesus was not a member of any Jewish religious party or esoteric group, nor did he stand apart as on a pedestal. He did not live in a desolate environment, far from civilization. He obviously chose to remain outside of parties, groups, and classes, but, within the Jewish community afflicted by crises and wars and moved by great expectations, he evidently wished to talk to all groups and individuals, from an unfettered, independent position. That position, however, was not equally removed from all the parties and trends; certain movements, ideas, and hopes were closer to his heart than others.

#122 It seems that Jesus avoided only the highest religious and political rulers who directly imperiled his message. The following, for example, were to meet him only as defendant: Herod Antipas (cf. Luke 13:31–33), the Sadducean high priests, the Roman procurator Pontius Pilate, Herod, and probably the chief priests, particularly the High Priest (cf., e.g., Luke 22:3–6; 23:6–12). Those harsh words which, according to Luke 12:32, Jesus applied to Herod, "tell this fox," reveal him as a counter-type to the informers (*mesorot*) and slanderers (*malsinim*) of the period who were hated by the people and parties alike. There existed clever tacticians who, by exploiting the turbulent yet politically impotent situation of Judea, Samaria, and Galilee with the Roman imperial court, hatched intrigues with the Roman court, the Roman governors, or any other person in authority against their own fellow men. They caused much suffering and discord among the Jews. In Talmudic times already, curses and prayers against such intriguers were invoked (Tos *San* 13:4f; TB *RH* 17a).[165] Jesus probably avoided those in high authority because he did not find there the desired climate of freedom, dialogue, and expectation of God's reign; they represented the very opposite.

#123 Jesus' best, closest, and most varied relationships were with the simple, everyday Jewish folk. They were by no means quiet, jolly, unprejudiced, patient people. Contemporary scholarship has rightly rejected the formerly often evoked "silent ones in the country," those allegedly neutral, childishly devout, and prudent ones who were said to be particularly close to Jesus. They were much rather crowds of people harboring a wide variety of ideas, sympathies, confusions, enmities, and depravities. Some of them were under the influence of apocalyptic wishful thinking; others would clench their fists against the harsh Roman occupation forces and the collaborating Jewish leaders. These were ripe for anarchic, messianic zealotism. Others, again, sympathized with the realistic religious policy of the Pharisees. There also were many disappointed, religiously and socially impoverished ones, more or less broken and despised individuals and tradesfolk, such as fishermen, tanners, shepherds, tradesmen, publicans, harlots, etc.

David Flusser may be correct when he says that Luke's description in the traditional and redacted passages, of the crowd's attitude toward the Crucified Jesus is historically clearer than that of the other evangelists. Referring to Luke 23:27, 35, 47–49, he writes:

> The sympathy of the Jewish crowd with the one to be crucified is expressed three times in Luke's report, which never mentions any mockery by the Jews present: the multitude of the people accompanies him and the women lament him, the people attend the Crucifixion, and when the whole crowd sees that Jesus is dead they beat their breasts as a sign of grief and go home mourning. The sympathy of the people is understandable. The crowd was with Jesus the whole time he was in Jerusalem and the high priests did not dare to arrest him in public because "they feared the people" (Luke 20:19; Mark 12:12).[166]

Only the Romans and leading Jewish dignitaries are described by Luke as enemies and scoffers of Jesus. His love for the simple people was due to several reasons. Obviously, all hardened fixations of mind and heart, rigidities of social and religious structures were distasteful to him. He found in the common people, assembling for various reasons and in ever changing groups, an open, uncommitted receptacle for his message of the coming Kingdom of God. He recognized those who were insecure, despised and marked as sinners, as human beings who were inwardly shaken and jolted, receptive for that very reason to the Kingdom of God (cf. Luke 19:1–10). His solidarity with the lowest and most despised laid him open to the reproach of being a drunkard, glutton, friend of publicans and sinners (Luke 7:34f). Nowhere is it mentioned that Jesus attempted to extricate himself from this scandalous image, while with similar words he himself accused his opponents, evidently Pharisees, of conduct displeasing to God. According to Luke 20:47, he calls them people who "swallow" the widows' property while saying long prayers He was so much concerned with the poor, the oppressed, the sinners, that he never made light of his relationship to them or betrayed it, even though misunderstanding and hostilities dangerously threatened him because of this attitude.

#124 Though Jesus' attention was first and foremost directed toward the open, unorganized, unstructured masses of the people and individuals, his relations with the fellowships of religious parties, esoteric groups, and anarchistic movements were not negative on principle. Friends of Jesus were to be found among all of these groups. He used their manner of speaking, particularly in his relationship with the Pharisees. Like them, he conducted "controversies on the Name of Heaven" (*mahalokat l'shem shamayim, Avot* 5:17). In order to understand Jesus and the New Testament, it is most important not to interpret his disputes with the Pharisees as basically anti-Pharisaic. Such inter-Jewish controversies had been customary since the times of the Tanakh, and their asperity is easy to understand in view of the importance of the coming of God's reign, a topic very vital to the Jews. Jesus had friends among the Pharisees; according to the Lukan tradition, he sometimes dined with Pharisees (Luke 11:37; 14:1–6); it also was Pharisees who warned him of Herod Antipas' persecution (Luke 19:31–33).

It would be wrong, on the other hand, to make Pharisaic opposition appear quite innocuous. We previously mentioned Pharisaic self-criticism and their occasionally unfavorable reputation; we also indicated their refusal to place the approach of God's Kingdom at the heart of their religious thinking (#52–55, 106). These were inflammable matters in their encounter with Jesus. Not only the final, redacted parts of the New Testament but even earlier ones indicate opposition as well as affinity between Jesus and the Pharisees.

#125 In the year 6 CE, the Zealot movement came into being, in rebellion against Roman authority and their Jewish accomplices. From his early youth, Jesus was familiar with this religio-messianic group of terrorists.[166a] His activities in Galilee took place amid a dangerously crackling pre-war atmosphere. At least one of his closest disciples, Simon the Zealot (Luke 6:15; Acts 1:13), belonged to that group. Other disciples were, if only temporarily, touched by militant Zealotism (cf. Mark 10:35–45; 14:47; Matt 26:14–16; Luke 9:51–56; etc.). Zealot terminology also was familiar to Jesus (cf. Matt 10:34–36); he employed it realistically tempered, however, or in connection with opposite notions. There is an example of such realistic use in Luke 14:26f, where the following words occur which must in part be interpreted in the Zealotic sense: "If any man comes to me without hating his father, mother, wife, children, brothers, sisters, yes and his own life too, he cannot be my disciple. Anyone who does not carry his cross and come after me cannot be my disciple."

Immediately following (Luke 14:28–32), there are two examples stressing the need for exact calculations and reasonable deliberations—in the construction of a tower and when waging war. Such realistic attitudes were in complete contrast to Zealotic fanaticism and radicalism. Even more in opposition to the Zealots was Jesus' turning toward the unclean and the collaborators with the Romans, namely the publicans, and so was his "golden rule" (Matt 7:12) and his commandment to love one's enemies (Matt 5:44).

#126 The apocalypticists at the time of Jesus were not institutionalized groups, the only exception being the Qumran community with its strictly ritualistic and hierarchically ordered way of life. Other apocalypticists would come together for worship and meetings, but they did not have any group structure. Their influence, nevertheless, was immense, and Galilee and Judea were in the grip of their ideas. All of the groups, especially the Essenes, the Zealots, and in part the Pharisees, were motivated apocalyptically, and Jesus' message of the Kingdom of God was in fact apocalyptic. Later on, the evangelists employed the apocalyptic view of history to make the Christ event intelligible. Nevertheless, Jesus cannot be called simply an apocalyptic preacher, nor could the Gospels be interpreted as apocalyptic literature. Neither Jesus nor the evangelists entered, for instance, the intra-apocalyptic dispute on whether the Kingdom of God should be fought for, prayed for, or passively awaited. Jesus rejected all ideas of the "sword," according to which the final events must be prepared for by war (cf. 1 En 91:12; Matt 26:52; Luke 22:38), nor was he interested in apocalyptic chronology (cf. Mark 13:32). An apocalypticist would not have dared to say, as Jesus did: "If I cast out devils by the spirit of God, then the Kingdom of God has come upon you" (Matt 12:28). He absolutely linked the Kingdom of God to his activities and his person; on this point he was unique. Yet, he was in agreement with the apocalypticists in being deeply imbued with the penetrating, assertive power of God in the world.[167]

#127 We could continue this comparative analysis with Jesus' attitude to the Essenes, the Hellenists, etc. Our results would hardly be changed thereby. Jesus knew all the parties, ranks and groups. His terminology and positions must be interpreted in conjunction with all of them. He entered into all their problems, yet he refused blind conformism and did not permit himself to be taken into tow by any one group. He did not wish to dilute by partisanship his honesty and the seriousness of his mission. He took sides exclusively in his commitment to the despised, the weak, the poor, the outlawed, and the sinners.

#128 In the last resort, Jesus was not concerned with an elaborate dialogue with any groups or personalities; his message of the Final Age was not, narrowly speaking, his only topic. Next to his eschatological message and his caring for human beings, he also had theocentric concerns. He preached about God as Lord and Father. The "Our Father" in its central passages probably originated with him (Luke 11:2b–4). Jesus did not wish to surrender the Lord and Father-God to arbitrary human interpretation:

> Jesus did not expose God to human beings by permitting apocalyptic calculations for the determination of his Coming, nor did he give them apocalyptic images that would make available to their imagination the splendors of the future.[168]

In his relationship to the God and Father, Jesus gathered together Old Testament Jewish traditions of piety in an original way and endowed them with new beauty. Yet, it would be a radical mistake to represent Jesus, on principle and in any way at all, as being in opposition to the God of the Torah.[169] However, he did experience this God in a uniquely close and intimate way.

#129 Even Jesus' admonitions to the malcontent and the leaders of the people express his close association with the fate of the Jews in his time. Had the Jewish public taken more seriously Jesus' preaching against apocalyptic dreams of the future, against Zealot and Pharisee fanaticism toward sin and ritual impurity, against human intolerance and group hostilities, against the amassing of riches, and against religious chauvinism, the fateful Jewish revolt against Rome (66–73 CE), the destruction of the Temple, and the decimation and deportations of the people might not have occurred. Jesus did not wish to act merely as an arbiter in questions of day-to-day dispute but was mainly concerned with the future of his people.[170] In a similar vein, R. Yohanan ben Zakkai, R. Zadok (TB *Git* 56a–b) and others (cf. Acts 11:3–14) warned of developments within Judaism which would lead to a national and religious catastrophe.

#130 Something must be said here against scholars who deduce an awareness of sovereignty in the man Jesus from the alleged evidence of violations of the Sabbath commandment (the plucking of ears of grain and the healing of the man with a withered hand, Matt 12:14, etc.). Jesus, the so-called sovereign transgressor of the Law, does not exist! Simply because some bigoted Law interpreters made the accusation, we cannot say that Jesus acted against the Law. He certainly did not practice a narrow-minded interpretation of it, but he also opposed all excesses. He wanted the Law to be understood in its most profound meaning and in its original context. Paul, for instance, attests to Jesus' obedience to the Law: "But when the fullness of time came, God sent his Son, born of a woman, born under the Law, that he might redeem those who were under the Law, that we might receive the adoption as sons" (Gal 4:4f). A much closer examination of the circumstances in Galilee would be required before an opinion could be advanced on Jesus' transgression of the prevailing interpretation of the Law. Which Christian exegete really knows enough about this complicated matter? It is quite indispensable that we have increased contacts with Jewish specialists in the Law.

If we take seriously Jesus' solidarity with his people, their faith and ways of life, as well as his care for their future, then it is not unreasonable to assume that he kept the Jewish Law in its genuine meaning, in order to guide his people. Fulfillment of the Law was not tantamount to contempt for those who neglected or violated it. Jesus wanted the Law to be observed without sacrificing any human being. That meant opposition to any form of struggle between the "sons of the light" and the "sons of darkness" (cf. Qumran, Zealotism). Again, if his example of obedience to the Law had been followed, the internecine massacres and wars between Jews and Romans might never have taken place.

2. The Passion of Jesus

#131 About the year 30 CE, when the Jewish Passover festival was about to be celebrated, Jesus was condemned to death on the cross, on instructions from Pontius Pilate, the highest representative of the Roman invader. The sentence was carried out immediately, on the place of the skull opposite the Jerusalem wall. Gradually a consensus is forming among those scholars who incline to a critical view of history with regard to the persons repsonsible for the death of Jesus and their motivation.[171] The Roman procurator was the man chiefly responsible for the crucifixion of Jesus. His motives were power-political, not religious. It was not a question of guilt or innocence, true accusations or false. The personality of Pilate and his part in politics can be grasped only when it is understood that the Passion narratives do not present us with an unvarnished historical Pilate, but as he was presented in sermons. The evangelists described a more moderate Pilate because they did not want to endanger unnecessarily the young Christian communities within the Roman Empire. They did not wish to make even more acute the antagonism between Romans and Christians by speaking of a cruel Pilate. The historical truth about this man, who was notorious for his cruelty, his greed, and his animosity to Jews, was well known among the Romans in any case (*LegGai* 37–39; *Bellum* 2:169–174; *Ant* 18:55–59; Luke 13:1).

#132 Among the Jews, it was the high priest Caiaphas, the chief priests with him, and probably some representatives of the Sanhedrin, whose majority consisted of Sadducees with some Pharisees in the minority, who were responsible for the death of Jesus. This was the upper crust of the Jerusalem authorities. They were dominated by high priests and the liberal-conservative Sadducee party. According to *Ant* 20:251, since the year 6 CE,

> the Jewish state was administered aristocratically, while supervision of the people was in the hands of the high priests.

That made the Sanhedrin the most important government authority. The high priest as leader of that institution became the political-spiritual head of the Jews under the Roman rod. Jesus' words and actions criticizing the Temple (Mk 11:15–19) and all his influence among the people must have appeared to the high priest as a danger to the Temple-national order which he so arduously tried to maintain. It is impossible, however, to determine the extent of ill-will among the high priest and his followers. There seems to be no doubt that they acted against Jesus not for religious reasons but chiefly from religio-political considerations.

#133 One passage of the Gospel of John defines with some theological benevolence the actions against Jesus by the high priest and his attendants. John 11:45–52 relates the meeting of the high council and their annoyance at the signs effected by Jesus, his constantly growing influence, and the council's fears that he might be a danger to people and country. The Jesus movement, so they thought, could serve the Roman as an alibi to destroy the people and their Temple. The text continues: "But one of them, Caiaphas, being high priest that year, said to them, 'You know nothing at all; nor do you reflect that it is expedient for us that one man die for the people, instead of the whole nation perishing.' This, however, he said not of himself; but being high priest that year, he prophesied that Jesus was to die for the nation; and not only for the nation, but that he might gather into one the children of God who are scattered abroad."

In the extra-New Testament Jewish tradition, this Johannine interpretation would not have been admissible. Jewish tradition judges very harshly a person who surrenders another to the enemy in order to possibly save others. The Jerusalem Talmud contains the reminiscence of a pre-Christian Jewish Law code, probably a mishnaic text of the "early pious" (Assideans, cf. #26), of the second century BCE:

> Given the case: A number of Israelites are on a long journey. They encounter some pagans who say to them: "Give us one of you; we want to kill him. If you do not do so, we will kill all of you." In such a case, they must not surrender a single Israelite, even if for that reason they will all be killed (TJ *Ter* 8:10).

The Talmud continues, with some regret, that some of the strictness of the instruction had to be mitigated during the third century CE. At that time, the following consideration had come to prevail: If the (pagan) authorities asked for the surrender of a Jew, to be punished for a crime of which he had been found guilty, it would be permissible to give him up; the rabbis were aware that they laid themselves open to the accusation of being "collaborators."

The Talmud passage indicates in passing the pagan terrorist climate in which the Jews were forced to live at that time. Extortionist kidnapings were more or less the order of the day, and the Jewish community attempted to defend itself vigorously. Nobody was to be handed over, even if others would be killed for that reason. The tactics of Caiaphas and his followers, as also the "paid" clamoring rabble before Pilate (cf. Matt 27:15–26), in no way are justified by Jewish law. These considerations are most significant for catechetical instruction; they could serve to close loopholes in the presentation of the Passion and to prevent incitement to anti-Judaism.

#134 From an ominous secondary point of view, the question of guilt in the death of Christ has, unfortunately, become a very important one. Vagueness over the mystery of Jesus' suffering became an excuse for stirring up trouble. It was trumpeted about piously that the Jews, all of them, brought Jesus to the cross. Jews were accused of deicide, and ecclesial hostility found its ready-made vocabulary in the account of Jesus' Passion. It could easily have been quite different. In the person of Jesus, human rights were shackled; pagan power-imperialism, toying with human life, raged against Jesus; semi-religious authorities, fearing for their power, trampled on the unfortunate man Jesus. Any victim in our day of political systems and power blocs, anyone in fear of terror, murky assassins or slanderers, should be able to understand that Jesus suffered and died a victim of inscrutable slander and political machinations. Jews, Christians, anyone in fact, could easily enter into a situation similar to that which broke Jesus. His Passion, then, should unite rather than separate Jews and Christians.[172]

III. THE CHRIST OF FAITH

1. The Man Jesus Can Be Regarded as Belonging to Judaism and Christianity

#135 How can we bridge the gaps between the earthly Jesus and the Christ proclaimed as risen Lord, between Jesus the Jew and the Savior of the world whom Christians believe in and confess, between the claim that Jesus belongs to early Jewish history and spirituality and the just as vehemently argued disignation of Christ as the founder of Christianity? Since the founding of the Church can hardly be ascribed to the man Jesus, this problem is a very acute one for scholars. Theologically speaking, the Church is the work of the Spirit of the risen Christ. Many answers have been given to this question which neither Bible scholars nor dogmatic theologians can evade. We will speak here of only two, thoroughly Jewish, arguments, to supplement whatever can be said on the problem in dogmatic and systematic theology.

#136 Old Testament and Jewish tradition does not recognize respect of persons. Just as God cannot be forced into any system, no person may be claimed fully for one particular organization. Pharaoh's daughter (clearly not a Jew) who took part in saving Moses is called a Jewess by the rabbis because of her action (TB *Meg* 13a). Abraham, who originally was not a Jew, is named the archetype of Judaism and the non-Jewish nations, according to Jewish tradition.[173] The founder of the Achaemenian Empire, the Persian emperor Cyrus (559–520 BCE), gave the deported Judeans the opportunity to return to their land. Deutero-Isaiah therefore calls him "shepherd of God" (Is 44:28), "anointed" (Is 45:1), "champion of justice" (Is 41:2). With regard to great personalities, ascription of membership among God's people was not judged by criteria of historical criticism or genealogy but according to their contributions to the benefit of God's people. Applying these standards to Jesus, even before his suffering and death he becomes the primary cause, the *arche,* of Christianity. As a human being living in history, he is the model of every Christian. Any separation of Jesus from Christianity, then, is nonsense from the viewpoint of revelation history.

#137 We will arrive at similar results when considering biblical Jewish notions on the imitation of God. The first disciples of Jesus were fully convinced that in the suffering, dying, and risen Christ, the God of Israel revealed himself in an unprecedented and ultimately decisive manner for all mankind. In Christ, so they believed, the final revelation of God for judgment and salvation had come. It was this Christ they wished to imitate in their personal and community life and proclaim to human beings.

The idea was not new. The Hebrew Scriptures speak of the Israelite as a person imitating God and clinging to his ways in the world (cf., for example, Ex 34:6; Lev 19:2f; Deut 4:31; Jer 9:22f; Pss 78:38; 86:15; 103:8; 139:21f). At the time of Jesus, every Jewish group gave its own imprint and hue to the imitation of God (cf. 1QS 1:9b–11a; 10:17b–19; Tob 12:7b–9; TAbr 12:1–12; TBenj 3:3–5; 4:2f). Jesus himself called for imitation of God (cf. Matt 5:45, 48). In Pauline writings, imitation of God and imitation of Christ are placed on the same level. As practiced by the disciples, imitation of God or of Christ is held up as a model (cf. Eph 5:1f; etc.).[174] While the imitation of Christ takes its inspiration from the risen Lord, it always remained an imitation of the man Jesus. Since these are ethical dimensions, the notion of imitation forms a bridge between the earthly Jesus and the risen Christ. It would be absurd and against all human rights to forbid a person from living according to the spirit of Jesus.

Once more, when it concerns the person of Jesus and his influence, we find that Jewish and Christian ideas cannot be neatly kept apart. The manner of Jesus' Jewishness is not such that it should somehow be dogmatized, added to the dogma of Incarnation.[175] There is no justification for this in the New Testament. It is quite sufficient for Christians to become aware that they can better understand and appreciate Jesus and Christianity when they inquire into his Jewishness. Such an approach could also lessen prejudice and arrogance toward Jews, Jesus' brothers and ours.

> A return to teaching historical, basic facts of faith is much more urgent than elaborate sermons. It is a danger inherent in non-biblical theology that it may lead to an abstract Christ who has nothing in common with the historical Christ.[176]

2. A Weakening of Monotheism?

#138 It is not so much the historical pre-Easter earthly Jewish Jesus who is disputed between Jews and Christians, but the post-Easter risen proclaimed Christ of faith. The stories of the pre-Easter Jesus are not nearly as offensive to Jews as Christian faith in Jesus Christ.[177] Yet, a division between the earthly Jesus and the Christ proclaimed as risen is possible only in abstract methodology, not in his person. For that reason, from the Christian standpoint, placing Jesus in the history of the Jewish and Christian religious and national history is possible only in a relative way, not absolutely.

#139 Before going into details about the relationship between the Christ of faith and Jewish tradition, we must ask whether a Christological understanding of God is, absolutely and on principle, incompatible with Jewish notions of God. Should that be the case, Christian statements on the divinity of Christ could not even come under consideration by Jews but must be repudiated by them as blasphemies. The Nicene-Constantinopolitan creed, for instance—"We believe in one Lord, Jesus Christ, only begotten Son of God. Born of the Father before all ages. God from God, Light from Light, true God of true God. Begotten not made, one in being with the Father by whom all things were made"—would be, even apart from the historical figure of Jesus Christ, a pagan, anti-Jewish statement and the central attack against Jewish faith-consciousness.

#140 There can be no doubt that in rabbinic times and later, until our day, confession of the one and only God of Israel and his continuing bond as partner of the Jewish people has been and still is at the heart of Judaism. Anyone denying the oneness of God and his unique turning toward the people of God was called a *kofer ba'ikkar*, a denier of the main thing.[178]

#141 It is not quite clear at what time Christian faith in the Trinity came under acute Jewish suspicion as offending against the oneness of God. There are certain sayings in rabbinic literature which in the first place were probably not directed against the Trinitarian dogma, but Jews and Christians alike discerned in them at least a secondary anti-Trinitarian or anti-Christological meaning. Beginning with the second century CE, rabbinic scholars took a strong stand against Jewish defenders of metaphysical dualism (gnostics, heterodox esoterics, extremely pessimistic apocalyptics). They were concerned with preventing division on God and his providence. One such passage against dualistic Jewish heterodoxy, dating from the late second century, states:

"I am the Lord thy God": why is this said? For this reason. At the sea he appeared to them as a mighty hero doing battles, as it is said: "The Lord is a man of war" (Ex 15:3). At Sinai he appeared to them as an old man full of mercy. It is said: "And they saw the God of Israel" (Ex 24:10). And of the time after they had been redeemed what does it say? "And the like of the very heaven for clearness" (Ex 24:10). Again it

says: "I beheld till thrones were placed" (Dan 7:9). . . . Scripture, therefore, would not let the nations of the world have an excuse for saying
that there are two Powers, but declares: "I am the Lord thy God!" I am
he who was in Egypt and I am he who was at sea. I am he who was at
Sinai. I am he who was in the past and I am he who will be in the future
(*MekY* on Ex 20:2; cf. TB *Ber* 33b; *Hag* 15a; *BerR* 1:7 on Gen 1:1).

BerR 26:5 on Gen 6:2 indicates that the rabbis of the second to third
century prohibited the use of "son of God/sons of God/sons of gods"
whenever such terms were employed to question the oneness of God. A
midrash says that R. Simon ben Yohai (about 150 CE) used to curse anyone who interpreted *ben elohim* literally, that is "sons of God." The term
was said to mean "sons of judges." The midrash then continues:

> R. Simeon b. Yohai said: "If division (*p'rasah,* lit. rupture) does not pro-
> ceed from the leaders, it is not a real division (*BerR* 26:5 on Gn 6:2).

The "leaders" here applies to God and all the heavenly powers. R.
Simeon ben Yohai saw a primary heresy in the projection of disunity and
divisiveness onto God and his sovereignty. Whenever there was no danger
of theological straying, the rabbis would not hesitate to confer the dignity
of "son of God" or "sons of God" upon the people of God as a whole or
upon some charismatic personality (cf. Mish *Abot* 3:14; *Ta'an* 3:8; *Sifre
Devarim* 308 on Dt 32:5; TB *Ta'an* 24b-25a; 3 En 1:8; *Liber Antiquitatum
Biblicarum* III:1). The rabbinic meaning of "son of God" gives many clues
to the philological origin and content applied in Palestinian understanding
to Christ's designation as son of God, and also to the variations under
which the first Jewish Christians received and proclaimed this message.

Rabbinic literature also contains certain polemics against those who
speak of "several powers" (in heaven) (e.g., Mish *San* 4:5). These texts
must have been directed against opponents, that is, Jewish apostates in the
rabbinic sense who maintained that God was not the only one in heaven,
that he must share his sovereignty of the world and the people of God with
one or several divine or semi-divine competitors. The tactics of the rabbis
entailed not naming religious deviators and their teaching and concerns.
They called opponents by one cue word which could, more or less, be applied to various heterodoxies; they tried not to confront already insecure
Jews with additional problems and dangers. This method was guided by
the rabbinic opinion that, despite certain variations, all heretics (*minim*)

belonged basically to one and the same, uniformly motivated clique. If, next to gnostics and others, Christians (because of their theological profession of Christ) were called advocates of two or more powers in heaven— di-theists or tri-theists—then there was one limitation: Only Jewish Christians, not Gentile Christians, were the immediate subjects of rabbinic polemic. The Talmudic proof, from the third or fourth century CE, runs as follows:

> R. Nahman in the name of Rabbah b. Abbuha answered: There are no "minim" among the Gentiles. But we see that there are. Say: The majority of Gentiles are not "minim." For he accepts the opinion expressed by R. Hiyya b. Abba in the name of R. Johanan: The Gentiles outside the land (of Israel) are not idolaters; they only continue the customs of their ancestors (TB *Hul* 13b).

#142 During the Middle Ages and later, when Jewish scholars (decisors, philosophers of religion) were more directly confronted with the dogma of the Trinity, many of them accused Christians of weakening the idea of the one and only God of Israel. This interpretation, they said, came about by a mingling of Jewish and non-Jewish faith elements. They classified Christianity as *shittuf,* a term in religious law.[179]

Hermann Cohen translated *shittuf* as "association, partnership" (*Vergesellschaftung*).[180] That implies in the Jewish meaning a deformation or weakening of pure monotheism by the mystery of the Trinity and the linking of God with the man Jesus Christ. It must be remembered, though, that *shittuf* does not imply idolatry or polytheism. Since non-Jews had not been given the revelation on Sinai where such association was proscribed, the Jewish decisors believed that they were not to be punished for joining certain human additions and vague obscurities with the Name of God. It was understandable that such hazy monotheism prevailed with them, they decided, but the people of God, true to the revelation on Sinai, confesses the absolute oneness and uniqueness of God.[181]

#143 Even in modern times, we encounter among Jews the notion that Christianity was a diminished and hazy monotheism, while Judaism in its theological presupposition was a-Christological and anti-Christological. It was particularly the liberal Jews of the nineteenth and twentieth centuries who argued in this direction.[182] Isolated examples of an even harsher term are known where Christianity is called a renewed version of Baalism, against which the Prophets, the Assideans and Maccabees defended themselves already (cf. #23–26). Accordingly, because of its Trinitarian dogma and its Christology, Christianity is accused of syncretism, even of theocrasy (mingling of deities).[183]

#144 To proceed with the idea of God, we must point out that neither in the Tanakh nor in the New Testament, in Talmudic or Jewish esoteric literature do we find such "strict transcendence-monotheism," as is often maintained today.[184] The God of Israel has always been a covenantal God who not only ruled but entered the life situations of his people, permitting himself to be affected by them. During the exodus through the desert toward the promised land, he preceded the people. He went with them into exile and misery. The term "panentheism" was proposed for this bond of God with his people and all his creatures. God has a "real pathos." The biblical prophets were considered worthy to approach in sympathy the "intimacy of God." That enabled them, in "lively emotion," to make the word of God fruitful for the people. This view of God, linked to the destiny of his people, has been an "original Hebrew attitude" since biblical times, in distinct contrast to all deistic, dualistic, and pantheistic world views.[185]

#145 Talmudic literature contains the most beautiful testimonies to God who lives with his people. The importance in rabbinic Judaism of faith in this God is indicated by the fact that it is associated with the revelation of the Name of God to Moses.

> "I am that I am" (Ex 3:14). The Holy One, blessed be he, said to Moses: Go and say to Israel: I was with you in this (Egyptian) servitude and I shall be with you in the servitude of the (other) kingdoms (TB *Ber* 9b).

#146 When rabbinic scholars speak of the special, involved existence and actions of God among his people, they assume a dual meaning: God in his immeasurable, ineffable, unattainable, non-manipulative greatness, and God in his lowliness and union with his people. *Shekhinah* theology in particular contains a glimmer of this. *Shekhinah* means God's indwelling, his special way of being and acting. Originally, the word was used in Temple theology; in early Jewish and rabbinic times it was extended to all spheres of the divine presence on earth:[186]

> "And it came to pass on the day Moses finished. . . . " (Num 7:1). This can also be read (because of the consonants) as *way hayah*, that is, "woe." They said: "Now the Holy One, blessed be he, will leave us and

go down and dwell on earth." However, the Holy One, blessed be he, re-assured them and said to them: "By your life: My chief abode is on high. . . . " R. Simon in the name of R. Joshua b. Levi explained that when the Holy One, blessed be he, told them that his chief abode was on high he smiled upon them (because that was but a temporary arrange-ment). . . . Now that they (the Israelites) have made him a tabernacle . . . he is all the more certain to stand by them. . . . I . . . will accommo-date my shechinah to the confined space in their midst below (Tanhuma *Naso* 12 on Nm 7:1).

Considering certain biblical references in the above text (here omit-ted), we find that *shekhinah* can stand, e.g., for dwelling (*miskan*), glory (*kabod*), and magnificence (*hod*). Theologically speaking, it is even more significant that God himself moves, removes, rests his *shekhinah* (*hif,* of *sur, zuz, sarah*). The Infinite One also causes his own humiliation. The cul-mination of the above quotations, however, is that the main aspect, the nu-cleus, the root of the *shekhinah* is not in heaven with the angels, but on earth with human beings. Peter Schaefer is correct when he says that in the many rabbinic texts speaking of God, man and the angels, it is mostly a question of God's turning toward man, that is, his favoring man over all other beings.[187]

#147 In mystical, esoteric Jewish tradition, particularly in the Kab-balah, withdrawal of God (*tsimtsum*) played a most important part. The kabbalists speak of divine powers (manifestations, forces, characteristics, spheres, *sefirot*) which are gradually poured into creation from the infinity of God (*En-Sof*). The world was created by a gradual drawing back of God. The world will be brought to completion (*tikkun*) when the divine powers in the cosmos will, with the assistance of the people of God, be re-united in their original home, the *En-Sof.*[188]

Jewish esotericism also wrestles with the infinite God and the God who acts on earth; there is awareness of the two aspects of God, without ever relinquishing his oneness. We could even speak of three, four or five aspects of God, since his involvement in the world is said to take place in several thrusts. The kabbalists repeatedly had to defend themselves against their opponents who unfairly accused them of Christian-Trinitarian or even polytheistic trends.[189]

#148 Among certain esoteric groups, the Jewish notion that God graciously retreats upon himself was further developed to mean that God has a mysterious astral body. Moses Maimonides (1138–1204), from his

point of view as philosopher of religion, polemicized against the advocates of God's "corporeality" (*hagsama*):

> People have thought that in the Hebrew language "image" denotes the
> shape and configuration of a thing. This supposition led them to the
> pure doctrine of the corporeality of God, on account of his saying: "Let
> us make man in our image, after our likeness" (Gen 1:26). For they
> thought that God has a man's form—I mean his shape and configura-
> tion. The pure doctrine of the corporeality of God was a necessary con-
> sequence to be accepted by them. They accordingly believed in it and
> deemed that if they abandoned this belief, they would give the lie to the
> biblical text; that they would even make the deity to be nothing at all
> unless they thought that God was a body provided with a face and a
> hand, like them in shape and configuration. However, he is in their view
> bigger and more resplendent than they themselves, and the matter of
> which he is composed is not flesh and blood. As they see it, this is as far
> as one can go in establishing the separateness of God from other things.
> Now with respect to that which ought to be said in order to refute the
> doctrine of the corporeality of God and to establish his real unity—
> which can have no true reality unless one disproves his corporeality—
> you shall know the demonstration of all this from this treatise (*The
> Guide of the Perplexed 1:1*).

As an exponent of a rationalistic Judaism, Maimonides was not sensitive to the esoteric, mystic idea of divine "corporeality," expressed not in
materially confined thinking but in faith in the God of Israel as a partner
who sometimes acts as if he was human. Nor did Maimonides see that
such ideas, just as the Christian Trinitarian dogma, were not directed
against the oneness, spirituality, and uniqueness of God.

#149 This short excursus into historically relevant Jewish ideas
about God affords certain insights. Martin Buber correctly speaks of Jewish monotheism, "so often misunderstood and cruelly rationalized" in history.[190] Jews far removed from the kabbalists understand that God is not
an isolationist, imperialist, static Being but one who lives in himself, holds
mysterious exchange with himself, manifests himself to man in free affabil-
ity and is even affected by events among men. As Christians we would,
therefore, assume that Jews should not immediately consider a Trinitarian
view of God as theologically incompatible with or in opposition to, a Jewish understanding of God. Similar to Christians, Jews profess belief in a
God who is not rationally comprehensible. They avoid, just as Christians

do, too facile an explanation of the inconceivable and paradoxical in God. Followers of Jewish mysticism emphatically deny the Christian Trinity because it is necessarily linked to the revelation of Christ. Yet together with Christians, they admit of a rich life within the Deity, various manners of God's efficacy outside of himself, and unfathomable dialectical and dialogic movements between the infinity of God and his efficacy in the world. As a Christian observer of the Jewish theological scene, one cannot but conclude that a Christological perception of God—apart from its historical realization—is not un-Jewish. Of course, we must not infer a theological unity or near-unity between Jewish and Christian ideas of God. What separates us is Jesus Christ who, according to Christian belief, is a Person within the life of the Deity.

It is comforting for a Christian to know that in Jewish eyes his idea of God is not necessarily a weakened monotheism. There remains, however, the eminent Christian concern to make credible to Jews that the oneness and uniqueness of God is just as central to Christianity as it is to Judaism.

3. The Incarnation of God: A Reversal of Jewish Faith?

#150 The above considerations of certain fundamental traits in Jewish-Christian monotheism lead to additional theological and Christological questions: What are the God of Israel's limits of condescension? Can he become man at all? Does the Incarnation of God contradict his essence and the tradition of revelation? Such questions have often been raised among Christians. Some marginal aspects of Jewish tradition may be helpful in this respect, but we must be aware that any answer cannot but be a search among potentialities and realities which are not open to human sensibility, or at best are accessible to man only at their very peak.

#151 Philo of Alexandria (about 30 BCE–40 CE) was not familiar with the Christian dogma of the Incarnation. He was confronted, however, with the idolatrous tendencies of the megalomaniac emperor Gaius Caligula (37–41 CE). Philo wrote in an apologetic vein because the emperor cult which tended to become an apotheosis was highly dangerous to the Jews in Alexandria and Palestine. Emphatically, he called out:

> . . . but of the greatest of all that exists, when the created and corruptible nature of man was made to appear uncreated and incorruptible by a deification which our nation judged to be the most grievous impiety, since sooner could God change into a man than a man into God (*LegGai* 118).

Had Philo known of the early Church's proclamation of God's Incarnation, he would probably have changed that sentence. Justin Martyr, in his *Dialogue with Trypho* (about 160 CE), reacts to the tradition that Jews are convinced that the Incarnation of God is unacceptable to them. Justin has his Jewish opponent say:

> You have gravely blasphemed with your assertion that this crucified man was with Moses and Aaron and spoke with them in the pillar of the cloud. That he became man and after his crucifixion ascended into heaven. That he will return to this earth and that he should be worshiped (PG VI;557).

Similarly it says in rabbinic literature of approximately the same time

> When a man says to you, "I am God," then he is lying. "Son of man," he will repent in the end. "I ascend into heaven," he will not adhere to it (TJ *Ta'an* 2:1).

This polemic was probably directed against the gnostic dogma of the descending and ascending primal man and savior. In the context of Num 23:19, it could also be interpreted as an open challenge to the Christian profession of the incarnate God and the glorified Christ. Since the beginnings of the ever-expanding influence of the Christian message and until our time, Jews have usually insisted that divine incarnation is impossible. Most of the time, such statements are polemics against Christianity.[191]

#152 In isolated cases after the time of Christ, Judaism has insisted that apotheosis (divinization of a human being) is absolute blasphemy (*gid duf*) but that the motif of incarnation might to some extent be intelligible to Jews. The following words by Michael Wyschogrod—professor for philosophy, expert on Karl Barth, and an orthodox Jew—may serve as an example:

> If Judaism cannot accept the Incarnation, it is because Jews do not hear that story, because the word of God as it is heard in Judaism does not tell them this, and because Jewish faith does not witness to it. When the Church accepts the Incarnation, it does not do so because it somehow discovered that such an event should take place, but because it hears that it was the free and gracious decision of God, a decision that could not have been foretold by man. Strangely enough, viewed in this light, the antagonism between Judaism and Christianity could be, though not

dissolved, at least brought into a context within which it is a matter of differences in faith, with regard to the free and sovereign action of the God of Israel.[192]

These words show profound understanding for Christian reasoning. We must listen closely because Wyschogrod does not simply make counter-dogmatic statements but places Christian words on the Incarnation of God within the context of Bible history and witness to the God of Israel in his sovereign freedom and free descent.

#153 According to Wyschogrod, who does not write as an apologist but, in this instance, as an historian of the Bible, the Incarnation was not foreseeable in the Hebrew Scriptures nor possible as a prophecy. It must be regarded as a wholly unexpected, unforeseen gift. After the unexpected had happened and been the subject of abundant attestation—after the fact, that is—it is now possible to discuss whether or not the Incarnation is in opposition to the spirit of the Tanakh.

An unambiguous contrast, we think, does not exist. If God walks in the cool of the day in paradise (Gen 3:8), is seen on the mountain by the elders in Israel (Ex 24:9–11), "with his strong hand and outstretched arm" brings Israel out of Egyptian slavery (Deut 5:15), and has the "appearance of man" (Ez 1:26), could he not, if he so decided, become man? In the quoted passages, the Bible speaks mythologically and organically, of course, but what else can one do with mysteries, such as God's talking to men, manifesting himself to them, leading them, etc.?

#154 The chief advocates of Jewish apologetics, who during the first post-Christian centuries fought against the possibility and reality of incarnation, perceived it either as metaphysical dualism or as pre-Chalcedon verbal monophysitism. We previously mentioned (#146) that the rabbis stamped it as metaphysical dualism; as an example of pre-Chalcedon verbal monophysitism, we need refer only to the *Dialogue with Trypho* (#151). The basic view was that Christ's message served to blur and dilute the differences between God and man. Certain Christian churches cling to this day to verbal monophysitism.[193] The Coptic, Ethiopian, West-Syriac, and Armenian churches, for example, have always lived in close proximity to Jewish groups and—despite massive polemics against Jews—bear the marks of Jewish anti-Hellenistic features.

#155 Christology should not neglect one particular Jewish concern: that the role of Christ might jeopardize the sovereignty of God. The Pharisee and apocalypticist Paul took great pains in all his statements on Christ to make manifest the sovereignty of the Father as the beginning and end of all Christology. 1 Cor 15:20–28 is a good example which Oscar Cullman quite rightly considers a "very important passage for Christology."

> It is thus very significant that the final fulfillment of all redemptive activity is described precisely as a final "subjection of the Son" to the Father. . . . Here lies the key to all New Testament Christology. It is only meaningful to speak of the Son in view of God's revelatory action, not in view of his being. But precisely for this reason, Father and Son are really one in this activity.[194]

It is possible to prove that in 1 Cor 15:20–28 Paul fully expresses Pharisaic-rabbinic and apocalyptic concerns. As far as the Pharisees espoused a fervent messianic expectation, he was anxious to shield the sovereignty of God from competition by a rule of the messiah. The Psalms of Solomon, of Pharisaic origin toward the end of the first century BCE, contain as their most salient messianic idea the words that the messianic rule is absolutely subordinate and conformed to the sovereignty of God (PsSol 17–18). Here, in a most unprecedented way, we have statements about the unique rule of God (PsSol 17:21–23, 35–44; 18:6–9).[195]

In the *Shemoneh Esreh* (Prayer of Eighteen Benedictions), acknowledgment of God's sole sovereignty is the core theme. It dates in its final redaction to the second century CE, but in great part goes back to pre-Christian blessings (cf. Sir 51:12a–p; TB *Ber* 28b–29a). The ninth blessing says: "Rule over us as King, you alone." The fourteenth blessing voices messianic hope, yet it cannot be in doubt that "the rule of David, the anointed of your justice," is but an interim phase, preparing for and pointing toward the reign of God who is "all in all."[196]

#156 Franz Rosenzweig (1886–1929) was chiefly referring to 1 Cor 15:28 and John 14:6 when he wrote:

> Christianity recognizes the God of Judaism, not as God but as Father of Jesus Christ. They cling to the "Lord" because they know that only he is the way to the Father. He remains as Lord with his Church, all the days till the end of the world. Then, however, he ceases to be Lord because he, too, becomes subject to the Father and, at that, God will be all in all. What Christ and his Church mean to the world, that we agree upon: nobody comes to the Father but through him. Nobody *comes* to the Father, yet it is different with one who no longer needs to come to the Father because he already *is* with him. And such is the case with the people Israel (not the individual Jew). The people Israel, chosen by its

Father, looks fixedly—beyond history and the world—at that ultimate, far-away point when he himself, the one and only, will be its Father, the "all in all." At this point, when Christ ceases to be Lord, Israel ceases to be chosen; on that day, God loses the Name by which Israel alone calls to him, God. Until that day, however, the life of Israel consists in anticipating that eternal day in faith and in action, as a living sign to that day, a people of priests under the law, sanctifying the Name of God by its own holiness.[197]

Rosenzweig's grandiose and generous view of salvation history contains one harsh, anti-Christian supposition, which in a Jew is justifiable: Christians are said to recognize God not as the God of Judaism but as Father of Christ. As Christian theologians of Judaism, we must correct this view. Christians do recognize God as the God of Judaism and as Father of Jesus Christ. Christian theologians would be well advised, though, to consider Jewish exceptions to their theological and Christological statements. Taken altogether, Jewish ideas are not mere negations, opposition for opposition's sake, but warnings of potential perversions of faith in the God of Israel.

4. The Scandal of the Cross

#157 The New Testament speaks of many Jews who were annoyed by the Christ as he was preached to them. Paul writes: "For the Jews ask for signs, and the Greeks look for 'wisdom'; but we, for our part, preach a crucified Christ—to the Jews indeed a stumbling-block and to the Gentiles foolishness" (1 Cor 1:22f; cf. Gal 3:13).

This passage makes it evident that not the Incarnation but the consequences revealed in Christ—his Passion, Cross, and Resurrection—brought antagonism between Pauline preaching and Jewish rejection of Christ. Deut 21:23 says, "God's curse rests on him who hangs on a tree." From the New Testament point of view, the controversy comes to a head with this man "who was hanged." The Jewish opponents could not remain neutral and aloof to this message (cf. Matt 14:55–65; Acts 7:54–60; etc.). That first reaction of Jewish scholars and authorities is quite understandable. The Cross is and remains a scandal, to Jews as well as to Christians, and we do not wish to diminish this aspect.

Beyond all Jewish-Christian polemics, however, we must speak of the God of Israel who shares the afflictions and suffering of his people. Anyone who even vaguely apprehends the God of Israel as the God who suffers with his people will proclaim and experience the scandal of the Cross in a manner that will be fruitful and lead to further developments.

#158 In an early rabbinic passage it says:

> Whenever Israel is enslaved, the Shekinah, as it were, is enslaved with them, as it is said . . . : "In all their affliction he was afflicted" (Is 63:9; different from Masoretic text). So far I know only that he shares in the affliction of the community (that is, that God is also affected). How about the affliction of the individual? Scripture says: "He shall call upon me and I will answer him. I will be with him in trouble" (Ps 91:15). It also says: "And Joseph's master took him" (Gen 39:20, Potiphar put Joseph undeservedly into jail but YHWH was with Joseph in the jail). . . . And thus it says: "From before thy people, whom thou didst redeem to thee out of Egypt, the nation and its God" (2 Sam 7–23; different from Masoretic text). . . . R. Akiba says: Were it not expressly written in Scripture, it would be impossible to say it: Israel said to God: Thou hadst redeemed thyself, as though one could conceive such a thing (*asmeka padita*). Likewise you find that whithersoever Israel was exiled, the Shekinah, as it were, went into exile with them. When they went into exile to Egypt, the Shekinah went into exile with them . . . they were exiled to Edom, the Shekinah went into exile with them. . . . And when they return in the future, the Shekinah, as it were, will return with them (*MekY* on Ex 12:41).

The above is a typical example of Jewish theology of exile which should be investigated, together with all that was said under #145–149. The covenantal God who goes into exile with his people, who divests and exposes himself for the sake of his people, is the foundation. Very vivid expressions are used: God became a slave with his people; he, too, is in distress whenever his people or an individual is; he was exiled together with the people; he must redeem himself from slavery (cf. the dual meaning of God, mentioned in #146); in the final age, he will return from exile with his people. The rabbis evidently held that the Hebrew Scriptures reveal not only the sovereign redeemer but also the One who is affected by human fate, who suffers with man, is exiled with them and made a slave.[198]

#159 The God of Israel is not pure spirit, unaffected by the world, by man, or by fate. Even less is he an unfeeling potentate removed from the people, but together with man the God of Israel is ensnared by fate and suffering. The Mishnah says that God suffers agony when a man, his image, groans in the agony of execution; he says to himself, "My head hurts, my arm hurts" (Mish *San* 6:7; cf. Tg. Jonathan on Dt 21:23). This highly graphic description shows the influence of rabbinic thinking on the divine likeness in man (Gen 1:26). Man is said to be so much like God, and God so much like man, that man senses reality as God does, and God senses reality as man does. Whenever man is reviled, so is God. Whenever God is abused, so is man.[199] In his deepest distress, man could even be mistaken for God, as one twin for another.

The following parable was told in this context:

> To what is this matter comparable? To twin brothers (who lived) in one city; one was appointed king, and the other took to highway robbery. At the king's command they hanged him. But all who saw him exclaimed "The king is hanged!" whereupon the king issued a command and he was taken down (TB *San* 46b).

#160 This exposed God who may be mistaken for suffering man is alive in contemporary Jewish holocaust theology (cf. #186–188). Elie Wiesel tells the story of a young boy sentenced to death by the Nazis who was too light to hang; he slowly struggles to death on the rope. To a man asking "Where is God now?" one of the other witnesses answers, "Here he is—he is hanging here on this gallows. . . . "[200]

#161 These and other statements about the suffering God of Israel must not be taken too "carnally" incarnationally, but they call our attention to what is probably the most moving belief held in common by Jews and Christians: God is our partner, even in suffering, distress and death. Jurgen Moltmann, to some extent influenced by Abraham J. Heschel and André Néher (cf. discussion of their ideas, #144), says:

> The New Testament tells in essence the Passion story of Jesus Christ. But how can the Son of God suffer? How can he change? How can he love and feel pain? How can he die on the Cross abandoned by God? The Passion story did not correspond to the ideals of Stoicism. One either had to break through the axiom of apathy or to reinterpret the Passion story. . . . There are various God-situations in which man finds himself and various ways in which he experiences himself and leads his life. The God-situation of *apatheia* leads man into transcendent freedom from his body and environment. Faith in the apathetic God leads to the ethics of man's liberation from need and drive, and to dominion over body and nature. However the God-situation in which Israel discovers itself as God's people is different. It is the situation of the pathos of God and the sympathy of man. The God-situation in which Christians dis-

cover themselves as Christians is once again different. It is the situation
of the incarnate, crucified God and the loving man.[201]

Christ on the cross as an expression of God in the situation of suffering and death is not part of Jewish belief, but Judaism recognizes that, in
his love, God becomes involved in human need.

5. The Messianic Question

#162 It is not correct to say that the decisive or even the sole differ-
ence between Judaism and Christianity consists in the Christian affirma-
tion of Jesus as the messiah and its denial by Jews. There are certain
asymmetries and considerations on both sides that render unacceptable
such absolute statements on the messianic question. For a better evaluation we must consider and compare the relative importance and place accorded the question in Judaism and Christianity.

#163 We have already sketched (#48–49) the rich palette of messi-
anic notions within Judaism at the time of Jesus. A redeemer figure, not
yet arrived but expected, is endowed in the popular imagination with
dreamlike and phantastic features; each generation adds certain new traits.
The conclusion is evident that there is no fully established, universally portrayed Jewish messiah figure which should be contrasted to the human Jesus. David Flusser could very well say, then:

> I do not think many Jews would object if the messiah when he came
> again was the Jew Jesus. But wouldn't many Christians be uneasy if they
> found that the messianic ideas of the Old Testament prophets were ful-
> filled, even though the Old Testament is also Scripture for them?[202]

#164 Even more important is the fact that often in Judaism the mes-
siah has been relativized; at times, he was even considered a dispensable
figure. Jewish tradition has sometimes interpreted certain Bible passages—
notably, Is 24:21–23; 25:6–12; 36:18; 40:9–11; 52:7; 65:17; Ps 25:22—as if
God alone is the final redeemer of Israel and as if no messiah was to be expected. Far more prevalent, however, is the hope that in the final days of
history a messiah will appear to announce and represent the eschatological
and ultimate coming God and his reign. Yet even in that case, the messiah
does not fulfill all salvific expectations. At a time of upheaval, he is hardly
more than a figure referring to ultimate and universal redemption. Typical
for this view is a rabbinic interpretation of Ps 107:1–4 and Is 48:11.

"O give thanks unto the Lord, for he is good, for his mercy endureth forever. So let the redeemed of the Lord say whom he hath redeemed from the hand of the adversary" (Ps 107:1–2). Elsewhere this is what Scripture says: "For my own sake, for my own sake will I do it" (Is 48:11). . . . But why is "for my own sake" said twice? Because the Holy One, blessed be he, said: Even as when you were in Egypt, I redeemed you for the sake of my name, so in Edom (the Roman world power, the nations of the end time) I shall save you for the sake of my name. . . . And even as I redeemed you in this world, so I shall redeem you in the world-to-come. Therefore . . . "My glory will I not give to another" (Is 48:11). . . . Also, "Not for thy righteousness, or for the uprightness of thy heart, dost thou go in to possess the land" (Dt 9:3–5). . . . The Holy One, blessed be he, said further: Nor have I done this for the sake of Abraham, Isaac and Jacob; for whose sake then? For my great name's sake. . . . R. Berechiah said . . . Who are meant by "the redeemed" in "Let the redeemed of the Lord say"? The people of Israel. This, Isaiah made explicit in saying, "And the ransomed of the Lord shall return and come with singing unto Zion" (Is 35:10). He did not say "the ransomed of Elijah," nor "the ransomed of the King Messiah," but "the ransomed of the Lord" (Midr *Teh* 107:1–4).

In the last resort, neither in Judaism nor in Christianity is it a question of the messiah but of the Kingdom of God, of "God who is all in all" (1 Cor 15:28; cf. #155).

#165 Christians perceive in Christ far more than a Jewish messiah. According to Mark 8:30, we must assume that the man Jesus was quite reserved in regard to the appellation "messiah." The Christ of faith, however, receives this designation in many New Testament passages, even though in the beginning it is a supplementary title. It is of major importance that in Christ the God of Israel himself appeared to bring ultimate salvation to all men. Above the Christ of faith, the heavens are opened and the angels of God are ascending and descending (cf. John 1:51). In him "dwells bodily the fullness of God" (Col 2:9); he and the father "are one" (John 10:30); in him is the glory of God (cf. John 17:24). If in Christ God himself has appeared as a person and is effective in him, then—and only on that condition—can all the biblical and traditional honors be transferred on him: he is the Son of Man, the high priest, the messiah. In that context, however, many of these concepts lose some of their contingency. The name of Christ is originally the Greek translation of the Hebrew/Aramaic *mashiah/meshiha*. In many passages, however, particularly of Paul's writings, it has become a proper name without close reference to the concrete Jewish messianic ideas and expectations.

#166 Although there is priority of faith with regard to the Christ in whom the God of Israel has appeared, Christianity must insist on the true messiahship of Christ. This is of particular significance because Christ as messiah remains indissolubly linked to the earthly Israel. The Apostolic and early Church perceived Jesus Christ as Son of God and, just as emphatically, as Son of David, the messiah.

As Son of David, that is, as messiah, "Jesus is inserted into the continuum of Israel." It is part of Christian identity

> to be aware of the inseparable link between the Church and Israel. Were the Church not to recognize or not willing to recognize this link, it would bring about a loss of identity.[203]

#167 Christian-Jewish discussion about Jesus the messiah must be held with great circumspection. Wherever the unreflected statement is bandied about, "Here is the true messiah, there he is denied," we must ask whether the speaker really knows what the Jewish messiah looks like, what his rank and functions are. After serious study of the Jewish tradition, only one continuous characteristic of the Jewish messiah stands out: he is a man, not God. The Christ of faith can also be linked to and made known by a great many Jewish ideas concerning God who reveals himself, who is condescending, who is among his people. We will also find that Paul proclaimed that this Christ is rooted in God and in Israel: "Paul, the servant of Jesus Christ, called to be an apostle, set apart for the Gospel of God, which he had promised beforehand through his prophets in the holy Scriptures, concerning his Son who was born to him according to the flesh of the offspring of David; who was foreordained Son of God by an act of power in keeping with the holiness of his spirit" (Rom 1:1–4).

PART III
JEWS AND CHRISTIANS
SINCE THE TIME OF CHRIST

5.
Early Relations between Judaism and Christianity

#168 Since Golgatha, Christians—at first, mainly Jewish Christians, later almost exclusively Gentiles—and Jews who do not accept Christ's message have been living in the same environment. In New Testament times, the disciples of Christ were accustomed to visit the synagogues and proclaim their message (cf. Acts 13:5, 14–50; 14:1; 17). During the Middle Ages, many important Jewish centers came into being in Europe where society was dominated by Christians. (We will not discuss the simultaneous Jewish-Islamic symbiosis here.) When at the beginning of modern times traditional formations of society tended to disintegrate, the alternating tendencies of attraction and rejection between Jews and Christians continued or took on new hues and intensities. Such a state of relations exists even in our day whenever we discuss, for example, Hitler's attempted "final solution," the state of Israel, the dangers of war in the Middle East, and a newly awakened Christian interest in Jewish traditions.

In medieval times, Jews as well as Christians attempted systematizations of whatever divides, and is common to, Christianity and Judaism. They tried to apply insights gained in that process to social institutions. The Jewish ghetto was a typical expression of Christian and Jewish modes of thinking and the power politics they reflected. Jews were considered physical descendants of the biblical people of Israel, which placed them in a particular position. Not only did ties of common issue unite the Jews but even more so the biblical tradition, as they interpreted it. Christian interpretations were repudiated by Jews.

During the Middle Ages, Jews were allowed a relative right to existence. Any other group of people denying the truths of the Christian religion. for example the heretics, were not usually permitted to remain in a Christian country. The Jews, however, were more or less conditionally tolerated by the Church. Still, they were not permitted to hold manorial rights, in order to demonstrate that they were a repudiated community. Although Jews did not accept such an interpretation, of course, they had their own theological explanation for their provisional, conditional existence: It was due to their transgressions and, with the help of God, they hoped for a change in their situation.

It was the Christian majority that decided on the physical conditions of Jewish life. Although according to Christian theology they were to be tolerated, no rules for this toleration were issued by the Church. Generally speaking there prevailed the view that Jews should not be converted forcibly, yet those in political power were under no obligation to accept them in their land. Thus it happened that Jews were tolerated in one place and persecuted in another. In countries with divided political power, it was up to the local authorities to decide the question. For economic reasons, Jews were invited at times and, for the same reasons, confined or exiled again.

Jewish community existence was determined by religion because the contrast between Judaism and Christianity was in the foreground of life. Life within the Jewish communities, however, was not just a question of religious principles, but of tradition and a complete, independent culture. That culture accompanied the Jews from their homeland to the countries of the diaspora, linking them to the past and, at the same time, permitting them to take up elements from their environment. They spoke, for example, the language of the country in which they lived, as well as Hebrew and Aramaic, the languages in which the internal communal affairs were transacted. Only a person familiar with Hebrew could truly share in the tradition, which was not handed on primarily by means of books but within the living community, particularly on the occasion of Jewish festivals. Prayers, instruction, etc., were held in the synagogue without great need for the written word.

Soon after constituting itself in a new locality, a Jewish community would attempt to create an elite of scholars, from among their own ranks or by inviting some from abroad. Academies came into being wherever consolidated Jewish communities existed. Such communities were never unsophisticated but intellectually co-determined or controlled by traditions of previous periods.[204]

The main impression of the history of Jewish-Christian relations is negative and irritating. It could be likened to a brutal boxing match without a referee and hardly any rules, and where most blows were below the belt. Ever since the second century CE, slanders, persecutions, and murders occurred. A Christian theology of Judaism must present the causes and extent of animosity between Jews and Christians, their inability—in spite of everything—to leave each other alone, their reciprocal bias and rash judgments, and, finally, alternatives for a new Christian-Jewish future. We must come to grips with our life against one another, side by side, and for one another.

#169 Positions taken up against one another are particularly manifest in the separation of Christians and Jews, in Christian hostility against Jews (antisemitism and anti-Judaism), and in Jewish reactions to such animosity. Though the latter will be touched upon briefly (cf. #171, 177–180), this aspect should be the prerogative of a Jewish theology of Christianity. Separation from and hostility toward Jews, on the other hand, must be treated and explained by Christian theologians. The two phenomena are unfortunately linked inextricably. Yet, theoretically, Christian-Jewish separation must be distinguished from antisemitism in order to promote greater clarity and more precise evaluations.

We must avoid the term "schism" in the contemporary situation. Christianity has not broken with Judaism in the same sense as applies, for instance, to the schism between the churches of the East and West. The opposition between Judaism and Christianity is more profound, less symmetrically distributed, wavering, yet charged with much more hope for healing than could be said for any intra-Christian antagonism. In the following pages we will explain this enigmatic statement. The terms selected—"separation" and "divorce"—do not fully indicate the difficult, diffuse Jewish-Christian situation; they are used for want of any better and to avoid the even more problematic concept of "schism."

I
JEWISH ANTAGONISM

1. Jewish-Christian Separation

#170 Neither Jesus of Nazareth nor Paul of Tarsus pronounced a ban against the Jews, nor did they preach that the Jews were rejected or cursed by God; nor did Christians of the New Testament era. Between the first and second century CE, however, alienation and hostility between the disciples of Christ and the Jews who did not accept him increased to such an extent that it resulted in the exclusion of Jewish Christians from the synagogues and in a fundamental hardening of positions against non-Jewish Christians. The redactional parts of the New Testament, the rabbinic writings, and the works of the Church Fathers clearly indicate that a separation between Jews and Christians began soon after 70 CE, that there were fears on that score, and that counter-measures were attempted. In rabbinic and patristic literature we find reflections of an already completed, mutual rejection and isolation.[205]

a. Fear of Possible Exclusion

#171 The Gospel of John emphatically testifies to the Christians' fear of the Jews who did not believe in Christ, and to Christian disappointment and embitterment because of imminently expected exclusion from the synagogues. On relating Christ's healing of the man born blind, it says in John 9:22: "These things his parents said because they feared the Jews. For already the Jews had agreed that if anyone were to confess him to be the Christ, he should be put out of the synagogue" (cf. also John 7:13; 12:42; 19:38; 20:19). John 16:1f presents the expulsion from the synagogue as foretold by Christ himself. Christians were to expect that event without being led astray. Mark and Matthew consider the possibility of Christians being scourged in the synagogues (Mk 13:9; Matt 10:17). Luke tells that Jesus was put out of the synagogue in his home town of Nazareth when he first appeared there, and that he was nearly pushed over a cliff (Luke 4:28f).

Passages which according to form critical and tradition history studies date back to the time before 70 CE (Mark 13:9; Matt 10:17; Luke 4:28; cf. also Matt 23:37–39) clearly indicate that from the beginning of Jesus' appearance in public, some confrontations occurred with Jewish functionaries and some of the groups. Nobody before 70 CE, however, ever considered the exclusion of Jesus and his disciples from the people of Israel. Polemics on both sides merely expressed inner-Jewish disputes (#53, 124).

The Johannine passages, however, were redacted and written after 70 CE, and besides reflecting the transmitted tradition, they express early Christian fears. Many pastoral leaders and their flocks, weakened as they were by persecution and interior difficulties, were perplexed and dismayed as Pharisaism had emerged rapidly and unexpectedly from its sectarian existence to represent with a sure hand the concerns of all of Judaism (#52–

55, 80). It was easy to foresee that sometime in the near future the rabbis would refuse membership in the synagogue to the disciples of Christ.

b. Growing Pharisaic Influence on Jewish Christianity

#172 Things did not develop in the same way everywhere and did not lead to an inevitable separation. So-called early Catholicism which is reflected in Acts and the Deutero-Pauline and "Catholic" epistles was greatly influenced by Pharisaic interpretations and community structures. The word "Pharisaizing" is greatly to be preferred to the overly used "Judaizing."[206]

#173 Pharisaic influence is particularly evident in the New Testament Book of Acts. The author of the Gamaliel pericope emphasizes that even leading Pharisees did not necessarily consider faith in Christ displeasing to God and un-Jewish (Acts 5:34–39). We are also told that quite a number of Pharisees became Jewish Christians, thereby creating many problems: "But some of the Pharisees' sect, who had accepted the faith, got up and said, 'They must be circumcised and also told to observe the Law of Moses' " (Acts 15:5).

The Book of Acts also emphasizes Paul's Pharisaic past. Recalling that period of his life, Paul says that he was "zealous for the Law" (Acts 22:3). Similarly, Jewish Christians are called "zealous upholders of the Law" (Acts 21:20). The Deutero-Pauline passage of 2 Timothy suggests unity in prayer and likeness of mind and genealogy between early Catholic Jewish Christians and pre-Christian Jewry: "I give thanks to God, whom I serve as did my forefathers, with a clear conscience, that I remember you without ceasing in my prayers night and day."

The relationship between Pharisees and Jewish Christians was probably never without its problems, as is stated indirectly in Acts 12. It was the friend, nay pupil, of the Pharisees, Agrippa I, who initiated the execution of James, the son of Zebedee, and the incarceration of Peter. The latter fled from Jerusalem after his liberation.

#174 The execution in 63 CE of James, the brother of the Lord, under the reign of Agrippa II (28/50–94 CE) is particularly important in this context. Following that execution, there occurred what H. J. Schoeps calls the "Pharisaic revolution."[207] Josephus writes about this event:

> Upon learning of the death of Festus, Caesar sent Albinus to Judaea as procurator. The king . . . bestowed the succession to this office (of the high priest) upon the son of Ananus, who was likewise called Ananus. It is said that the elder Ananus was extremely fortunate. For he had five

sons, all of whom, after he had previously enjoyed the office for a very long period, became high priests of God. . . . The younger Ananus, who, as we have said, had been appointed to the high priesthood, was rash in his temper and unusually daring. He followed the school of the Sadducees, who are indeed more heartless than any of the other Jews, as I have already explained, when they sit in judgment. Possessed of such a character, Ananus thought that he had a favorable opportunity because Festus was dead and Albinus was still on the way. And so he convened the judges of the Sanhedrin and brought before them a man named James, the brother of Jesus, who was called the Christ, and certain others. He accused them of having transgressed the Law and delivered them up to be stoned. Those of the inhabitants of the city who were considered the most fair-minded and who were strict in observance of the Law were offended at this. They therefore secretly sent to King Agrippa urging him, for Ananus had not even been correct in this first step, to order him to desist from any further such actions. Certain of them even went to meet Albinus, who was on his way from Alexandria, and informed him that Ananus had no authority to convene the Sanhedrin without his consent (*Ant* 20:197–203).

This paragraph is partially disputed because of the inserted "Little Flavian Testiomony" (verse 200).[208] The point that interests us is mainly that non-Sadducees protested against the judicial murder of James, or at least against his over-hasty execution, instigated by a high priest. The nucleus of that group must have consisted of Pharisees whose program included "deliberateness in judging" (*Avot* 1:1). They also were probably the official protesters under Agrippa II and Albinus because, next to the Sadducees, theirs was the only officially recognized religious party. If this hypothesis is correct, it would be the last time that Pharisees took up the defense of Jewish Christians. Their protests may not have been for the sake of that group but possibly because of zeal for the Law and opposition of Sadduceeism. It should not be forgotten, however, that such Pharisaic errors benefited Christ's disciples.

Eusebius' account of the execution of the Lord's brother (*Hist Eccl* II:23) merits much less confidence than the older description by Josephus. According to Eusebius, it was not a rabid Sadducee high priest who instigated James' execution but the "scribes and Pharisees." We find in Eusebius certain after-effects of the New Testament style. Also, he was no longer interested in the Sadducees but only in Pharisaic-rabbinic Judaism devoted to scriptural scholarship. It was Eusebius' environment, which was hostile to the Jews, that caused him to describe the execution as highly tumultuous, discovering therein one of the causes for the destruction of the Temple in 70 CE. Josephus Flavius is a more trustworthy witness in this respect than the anti-Jewish Eusebius.

c. Competition within the People of God

#175 Not only did apostolic and early Christianity waver between fear of the measures taken by Jewish authorities and assimilation to a Pharisaic way of life. It was also characterized by missionary tendencies and intense theological and historical self-reflection. Paul was the most important, indefatigable preacher of Christianity and, at the same time, its greatest theologian.

In Rom 1:5 Paul says that he received from Christ "grace and apostolic mission to preach the obedience of faith to all the pagan nations." He considered himself an apostle to the nations, his missionary field knowing no boundaries. He says: "I owe a duty to Greeks and barbarians, to the educated and the uneducated. So for my part, I am ready to preach the Gospel to you also who are at Rome. For I am not ashamed of the Gospel, for it is the power of God unto salvation to everyone who believes, to Jews first and then to Greek" (Rom 1:14–16).

Taken together, the above verses indicate a new dimension destined to lead to the disintegration of the Jewish community as a religio-sociological formation. Paul's attempt to convert all the nations was not the seed, however, that caused the separation. The trend among Jews of Alexandria, Babylonia, and Palestine to gain converts among the nations is well known (cf. Matt 23:15). What gave offense was Paul's conviction that none of the religious-national features—Jerusalem, Jewish descent, the Jewish people, the word of revelation as such, the Temple cult, the Law, etc.—were inevitable pre-conditions for a particular bestowal of divine grace. He rejected all human insistence on inviolable holy institutions, all self-complacency, and calculations regarding unmerited bestowal of grace by God. He envisioned a divinely chosen community, obedient to faith, among the nations. He declared that all institutions linked to religious peoplehood are of merely relative significance (circumcision, dietary laws, marital rules, revelation as a bond of unity). He was concerned with a frame of mind imprinted by Christ, which was to be the unifying link and pledge of future redemption of all mankind. Thus, a wedge was driven into the communal cohesiveness of Judaism.

Dieter Zeller is probably correct in assuming that the main thrust of

Paul's conception of salvation history (Rom 9–11; also 1 Cor 15:20–28) was the dynamism of God's word, in particular the redemptive power of the Gospel:

> Christians in Rome had to be made aware that all human beings need the Gospel for their salvation.[209]

Paul includes the temporarily reluctant Jews in that dynamism (Rom 9—11). Precisely because he feels himself at one with his fellow Jews in regard to the Hebrew Scriptures (cf. e.g., Gen 12:1–3; Is 19:23–25; Joel 3:5), he argues with great forcefulness against arbitrariness, party slogans and presuming on holy traditions.

Other New Testament passages disclose similar awareness of Christianity's role in salvation history (see, e.g., the parables of the wicked vine growers, Mark 12:1–12; the royal wedding feast, Matt 22:1–14; the cry of the rabble, Matt 27:24f; and the words of Jesus to the weeping women of Jerusalem, Luke 23:27–31).

2. The Rabbinic Blessing Against Heretics

a. Research Problems

#176 It is generally assumed that around 90 to 100 CE, a synod under the leadership of Gamaliel II took place in Jabneh. The synod participants are said to have been mainly adherents of Hillel's interpretation of the Law, and the following items are presumed to have been on the agenda: the Canon (its extent, the writing of a standardized text with consonants), problems of prayer discipline, arrangements for worship serivces for a time without Temple, questions of doctrine and custom, and the excommunication of Jewish Christians. The latter point is said to be evident in the so-called blessing against heretics (*birkhat ha-minim*). The chief Jewish prayer became the Prayer of the Eighteen Benedictions (Tefillah, Shemoneh Esreh) by the addition of the blessing against heretics as the twelfth *berakhah*. This opinion was popularized particularly by Ismar Elbogen.[210]

While the synod of Jabneh is more or less undisputed, the benediction against heretics is not. Was it really composed at this time? Was it directed against the Jewish Christians? Was it declared an obligatory formula then? Joseph Heinemann points to the many and variable preceding formulas: e.g., the so-called cursing psalms (Pss 21; 89), Sir 36:1–12, and PssSol 17 and 18. Heinemann does not consider this benediction to be an addition but an extension and change in tone of an already existing one which was directed against separatists and sinners.[211]

An examination of rabbinic traditions on this score could help to determine whether and to what extent the benediction against heretics constituted excommunication of the Jewish Christians.

b. Rabbinic Traditions on the Blessing Against Heretics

#177 The following passage contains a story the tradition of which spans the periods of the second to fourth century CE:

> Our Rabbis taught: Simeon ha-Pakuli arranged the eighteen benedictions in order before Rabban Gamaliel in Jabneh. Said Rabban Gamaliel to the Sages: Can anyone among you frame a benediction to the Minim? Samuel the Lesser arose and composed it. The next year he forgot it and he tried for two or three hours to recall it, and they did not remove him (from the lectern). Why did they not remove him seeing that Rab Judah has said in the name of Rab: If a reader made a mistake in any of the other benedictions they do not remove him, but if in the benediction of the Minim, he is removed because we suspect him of being a Min?— Samuel the Lesser is different, because he composed it. But is there not a fear that he may have recanted?—Abaje said: we have a tradition that a good man does not become bad. But does he not? Is it not written, "But when the righteous turneth away from his righteousness and committeth iniquity"? (Ez 18:24). Such a man was originally wicked, but one who was originally righteous does not do so. But is that so? Have we not learned: Believe not in thyself until the day of thy death? For lo, Johanan the High Priest officiated as High Priest for eighty years and in the end he became a Min? (TB *Ber* 28b–29a).

This text does not say the benediction against heretics was composed in Jabneh. It only says that it was established and arranged, that is, it was given definite linguistic form and a set place, as the twelfth *berakhah* of Shemoneh Esreh. Even more striking is the behavior of Samuel the Lesser (Shlomo the Little). He was a highly respected scholar whose unassuming bearing, eagerness for study, and love of neighbor are praised. The *shekhinah* is said to have rested upon him, which was testified to by a voice from heaven:

> There is one here who is worthy that the shekhinah rest upon him. But his generation is not worthy of it! All the scholars directed their gaze at Shlomo the Little (TB *San* 11a).

Shlomo the Little was probably asked to update the benediction against heretics because he was expected to find a well-balanced formulation acceptable to all. But why did he forget it and did no longer remember it after one year? The Talmudic interpretation is probably the result of embarrassment. It is possible that Samuel intended to forget his formulation because after the institution of this benediction against heretics he changed his opinion: He was no longer convinced of the necessity for defensive prayers (as a daily prayer of obligation) against apostates, and he no longer believed that the danger of heresy and that of the Roman invading power were of the same magnitude. It could also be that by his attitude Samuel came under suspicion of sympathizing with heresy (cf. TB *Ber* 33b; TJ *Ber* 5:4). That would explain the behavior of his colleagues who did not permit him to leave the reader's pulpit. They wanted to know his true opinion of heresy. In that case, Samuel would be a witness to the fact that not all rabbinic scholars believed in the measures against those who deviate that inevitably would lead to a collision course.

#178 Several versions and paraphrases of the blessing against heretics are known to us. Commentators mainly refer to the so-called Palestinian recension, a text discovered by Solomon Schechter in the Cairo Genizah at the end of the nineteenth century. That text reads:

> For the *meshummadim* (apostates, traitors, or even: baptized ones?) let there be no hope. Uproot the kingdom of wickedness (*malkut zadon*) speedily in our days. Let the Nazarenes and the *minim* (heretics, degenerates) perish as in a moment. Let them be obliterated from the book of life. Let them not be inscribed with the righteous. Blessed are you, O Lord, who humbles the arrogant.[212]

This is the only text expressly naming the Jewish Christians. They are called an evil equal to heretics (gnostics, libertines, atheists) and the occupying and persecuting Roman authorities. On the (unproved) assumption that this is the oldest or even the original form of this blessing, conclusions were sometimes drawn that went much too far. Jewish Christians were said to have been considered national, religious traitors who for that reason were placed in the same category as the Roman occupation forces.[213]

#179 Approximately at the time of the Palestinian recension, the Babylonian version of the blessing against heretics was composed. Since the third century CE, it must have been familiar to Babylonian Jews:

> For the *meshummadim* let there be no hope. Let all heretics *(minim)* and traitors *(mosrim)* perish as in a moment. Uproot and destroy the

kingdom of wickedness speedily in our days. Blessed are you, O Lord, who breaks the enemy and humbles the arrogant.[214]

The kinship of this text with the Geniza version is evident, but Jewish Christians are not mentioned because they played no role in Babylonia. It is also interesting that not the Palestinian version but this Babylonian one was adopted by the traditional Jewish prayer books (cf. Seder Amram Gaon). For that reason, the latter is of greater significance.

#180 A paraphrase of the blessing against heretics has been transmitted from the time of the Mishnah (220 CE or slightly later):

> Wrongdoers of Israel . . . and wrongdoers of the Gentiles . . . go down to Gehinnom and are punished there for twelve months. After twelve months their body is consumed and their soul is burnt and the wind scatters them under the soles of the feet of the righteous, as it says, "And ye shall tread down the wicked, and they shall be as ashes under the soles of your feet" (cf. Mal 3:21), but as for the minim and the informers and the scoffers, who rejected the Torah and denied the resurrection of the dead, and those who abandoned the ways of the community, and those who spread terror in the land of the living and who sinned and made the masses sin . . . these will go down to Gehinnom and be punished there for all generations. . . . Gehinnom will be consumed but they will not be consumed (TB *R.H.* 17a; cf. Tos *San* 13:4).

In this version, the spectrum of offenders is greatly expanded. A clear distinction is made between sinners generally and persons antagonistic to communal life. They are threatened with eternal hellfire. Enumerated are, e.g., separatist Pharisees (those who wish to stand apart from the community, *porsin*), seducers, denouncers, religious doubters, etc. They are worse than sinful pagans. Again, Jewish Christians are not mentioned even though the text probably originated in the same Palestinian environment.

#181 In our time, the blessing against heretics is merely a generalized formulation within the Prayer of Eighteen Benedictions. The version of the Authorized Daily Prayer Book reads:

> And for slanderers let there be no hope, and let all wickedness perish as in a moment; let all thine enemies be speedily cut off, and the dominion of arrogance do thou uproot and crush, cast down and humble speedily in our days. Blessed art thou, O Lord, who breakest the enemies and humblest the arrogant (ed. Singer, London and New York, 1935, p. 48).

Thus the original prayer against heretics and heresy has become a call to help the errant's return and keep away outrage. It is comforting to an oppressed and imperiled group to have confidence in God to hold back, transform, or annihilate the powers inimical to man.

#182 No excommunication of Jewish Christians by all of the rabbis ever took place. According to the various versions of the blessing against heretics, they were not even perceived everywhere as particularly dangerous apostates. Neither, therefore, was the separation between Judaism and Jewish Christians irrevocable. In the beginning, the majority of Jews did not even focus attention on this situation and certainly did not rate it as an established, general evil. Even less final was the separation between Judaism and Gentile Christians. The principal reason is that non-Jews could hardly be subjects of Jewish law. Rabbinic *halakhot,* prayers, and judicial rules normally related only to Jews: good ones, bad ones, half-good and apostatizing ones, reverters, atheists, blasphemers, etc. Non-Jews are relevant for *halakhic* decisions only in relation to Jews as persecutors, seducers, etc. Since heretics, grumblers, apostates, and traitors among Jews were the true concern of the rabbis, they were secondarily, as it were, more dangerous than hostile non-Jews (cf. Mish *San* 11:4, the obstinate old man, and similarly Mish *San* 7:4, the blasphemer and idolater, both of whom are Jews). Judaism considered Jewish heretics a greater evil than non-Jewish sinners, a fact proved by the blessing against heretics as well as other texts.

3. Patristic Positions on Jewish-Christian Separation

#183 Jewish-Christian separation was of concern to the Church Fathers mainly for apologetic reasons.[215] Justin Martyr mentions the blessing against heretics several times in his *Dialogue with Trypho,* which was written between 155 and 161 CE. He writes to the Jews:

> . . . for you have murdered the Just One, and his prophets before him; now you spurn those who hope in him, and in him who sent him, namely, Almighty God, the Creator of all things; to the utmost of your power you dishonor and curse in your synagogues all those who believe in Christ (16:4).

Bishop Epiphanius (315–403) writes that the Jews bear hatred for Christians and that

> three times a day, when they pray in their synagogues, they curse the believers in Christ and anathematize them by saying that God should reject the Nazarenes (*Haereses* 24:9).

St. Jerome (330–410) mentions the topic several times in his *Commentary on Isaiah*. On Is 2:18, he writes that the Jews curse Christians, calling them "Nazarenes" (*sub nomine Nazaraeorum anathematizant vocabulum Christianorum*). On Is 49:7, he says "they revile Christ under the name 'Nazarene' " (*Christo sub nomine Nazaraeorum maledicunt*). And on Is 54:5,

> they curse the Redeemer day and night and overwhelm Christians with pejoratives three times a day, under the name "Nazarene," as already mentioned.

#184 We might infer indirectly from the above quotations that the Palestinian (Geniza) version of the blessing against heretics was widely known because only there do we find the word "Nazarene." Yet we must be cautious, for it is quite probable that the Church Fathers depended on Justin Martyr for their formulations. In all likelihood, Justin himself did not hear the blessing against heretics personally but was familiar with it from hearsay, namely by information he received from converts among the Hellenistic Jews. Tryphon, a literary fiction, speaks like them.

Apart from the fact that the Church Fathers' conjectures on the blessing against heretics must be seen in the context of reciprocal polemics, they also testify to the fact that Christians of the early Church identified with Christ. An insinuated abuse of Christ was perceived as directed against them, slander of Christians as directed against Christ (particularly evident in Justin and Jerome on Is 49:7 and 54:5). That attitude—not the individual accusations and the tone sounded by the Church Fathers—bears a hint of something transcending time.

#185 Beyond those harsh antisemitic statements by the Church Fathers, we must not forget that there is no papal bull officially excommunicating Jewry. From the Christian point of view, then, the separation between Christians and Jews is by no means total or irrevocable. It was previously mentioned (#182) that this also applies to Judaism, and such a state of affairs contains some seeds for hope.

On the other hand, we must not forget that the true abyss between Synagogue and Church is much deeper than implied by official and semi-official statements. The source is not to be sought in bans or excommunications but in centuries of divergent ways of life and deadly enmity. The tragedy of this estrangement inspires many Jews and Christians of our time to conceive bold suggestions and visions of unity. Conventional theologians and traditionalists among the faithful often do not understand and tend to ridicule such attempts. There is flippant talk of sectarian Christian enthusiasm for Judaism and Israel. Similar reactions are apparent among Jews. But an increasing number of individual Jews take upon their shoulders, so to speak, the great suffering of the whole Jewish people; at the same time, they are dismayed at the lack of comprehension among Jews about the Jewish mission to the nations. A Christian caught in the middle feels called upon to extricate such outsiders and bearers of hope and strength from their isolation. To theologians, this is a challenge to develop and preach Christologies of continuity with the Hebrew Scriptures and Judaism. Such bridge-Christologies would come to meet great Jewish and Christian seekers after unity and universal roots in faith.[215a] There are no clear, definitive dividing lines on either side, and any effort at mutual understanding conforms to the spirit of Judaism and Christianity.

II
CHRISTIAN ANTI-JUDAISM

1. Problems, Criticism, and Postulates of Holocaust Theology
#186

> The glow of the Auschwitz crematorium is the beacon that lights, that guides all my thoughts. Oh, my Jewish brothers, and you as well, my Christian brothers, do you not think that it mingles with another glow, that of the Cross?[216]

Those words were written by Jules Isaac during his isolated, underground existence in the years 1943–1945. He was one of the great visionaries of Christian-Jewish understanding after the Second World War. His concern was not to denounce the Nazi murderers of Jews and the ideologues behind them, but to lay the foundations for human co-existence, in the spirit of true Judaism and true Christianity. It is characteristic for him to link the crucified Christ with the scientific, collective annihilation of Jews in German concentration camps (cf. #160). Jules Isaac (along with Nelly Sachs and others) is one of the earliest representatives of Holocaust theology.

    #187 Holocaust theology has representatives among Jews and Christians who, with perspicacity and profound involvement, critically examine the foundations and historical developments of Christianity and certain aspects of Judaism. Auschwitz, that memorial to the mass annihilation of Jews which in part at least must be attributed to Christian failure, stands as a symbol for the Holocaust. The state of Israel symbolizes the unexpected rescue of Jews in spite of the ovens. The topics of Holocaust theology are derived from the experiences and ideas of survivors (e.g., Elie Wiesel) and from Christian theology of Israel since 1945. Starting points are offered also by a historio-critical exegesis of the New Testament and non-theological critiques of the Church. Some Holocaust theologians are fiercely and aggressively critical of the New Testament and anti-Jewish Christianity. In the main, however, all of them are concerned with building new foundations for Christian-Jewish, nay universal, solidarity.[217]

#188 It is due in great measure to Holocaust theologians that the effects of the Christian message on National Socialist antisemitism are keenly discussed. The following are the burning questions: What is the relationship between pre-Christian and Christian antisemitism? Does the New Testament contain antisemitic passages? When did Christian antisemitic ideology become fused with pre-Christian antisemitism? To what extent did Christian dogma and preaching of the Gospel encourage modern post-Christian antisemitism? What should be done to end the evil history of antisemitism?

#189 According to Rosemary Ruether,

> anti-Judaism developed theologically in Christianity as the left hand of Christology. That is to say, anti-Judaism was the negative side of the Christian claim that Jesus was the Christ.[218]

The author develops this thesis in the following words:

> We must recognize Christian antisemitism as a uniquely new factor in the picture of antique antisemitism. Its source lies in the theological dispute between Christianity and Judaism over the messiahship of Jesus, and so it strikes at the heart of the Christian Gospel.[219]

Ruether also thinks that the anti-Judaism amalgamated with the Christian message expresses the most compact, darkest aspect of Church triumphalism and is the direct cause of cultural as well as National Socialist antisemitism. She writes:

> Modern antisemitism is both a continuation and a transformation of the medieval theological and economic scapegoating of the Jews. But while the medieval tradition took its religious rationale from the Jewish refusal to accept Jesus as the Christ and enter the Church, modern antisemitism

builds on the medieval image of the Jew as a dangerous disease and demonic power.[220]

Franklin Littell holds:

> Theological antisemitism begins with the transfer of the base of the early
> Church from Jewish membership to a large Gentile majority. This hap-
> pened fairly quickly. Paul's mission to the Gentiles opened the way to a
> wholesale harvest of the thousands of Gentile fellow travelers who at-
> tended the synagogues of the Diaspora.... These "God-fearers"
> flooded into the young Christian churches.... Theological antisemi-
> tism began with the Gentile converts of many tribes, with their natural
> resentment of the priority of Israel, their resistance to the authority of
> events in Jewish history, their pride in their own ethnic values, lan-
> guages, cultures.[221]

Together with other theologians, Littell finds anti-Judaism ingrained
in Christianity and, possibly, the greatest catastrophe for Judaism as well
as Christianity. Defection from Christianity, so pervasive during the time
of National Socialism in Germany and after, is closely connected, he main-
tains, with ideological and human Christian failure vis-à-vis the Jews:

> That slide into damnation started ... with Christian lies about the Jew-
> ish people, with abandonment of the essential Jewishness of Christianity,
> with murder of those who could be identified as signal representatives of
> a counterculture the world hated and most of the baptized betrayed with
> enthusiasm. The baptized Gentiles' apostasy is the most significant reli-
> gious factor in the present crisis of Christendom. It did not end with the
> Holocaust. It will not be cured until the churches face with utterly ruth-
> less self-appraisal the meaning of that mass apostasy and trace it to its
> source.[222]

The critical emphasis of Holocaust theology is variously directed
against the Church as a whole, against the New Testament, against the
Church Fathers, against papal policy with regard to Jews, and against
Church leaders of the nineteenth and twentieth centuries. Yet in the background there always looms the problem of the New Testament and the role
it plays. Is it antisemitic or not? To be fair to Holocaust theologians, to
Christianity, and to Judaism, we must clarify the concept of antisemitism
before entering on a discussion of the New Testament. Some Holocaust
theologians—fired by prophetic élan—are lumping certain ideas together

instead of submitting them to sober analysis (though we must beware of associating such profound scholars as Franklin Littell with these short-comings).

2. Remarks on Content and Extent of Antisemitism, Anti-Judaism, Hatred of Jews, Animosity toward Jews

#190 Antisemitism, anti-Judaism, hatred of Jews and animosity toward them are usually held to be synonymous. Antisemitism could imply animosity toward Semites, yet it applies only to Jews. The other terms could mean any expression of animosity and opposition to Jews and Judaism. Hatred of Jews for any reason would then be different in quality from hatred of non-Jews. Anyone attacking the political stance of the state of Israel would also be an unqualified antisemite. Such definitions would dilate the meaning of the terms beyond control.

Still another demarcation is required: The separation of Judaism and Christianity since the second century CE (#168–185) does not in itself constitute antisemitism or anti-Christianity. We do not deny that antago-nistic feelings were partially to blame for the development and continuance of that separation. Neither do we deny that certain formulations indicating that separation could easily be perverted to antisemitic or anti-Christian purposes. We are grateful that, in the course of time, some expressions were mitigated (#181). Beyond all the ugly circumstances of the Jewish-Christian divorce, this separation also expresses the privileges of adherents to either religion to live and experience their faith more or less without molestation. This human right, unfortunately, was the object of great struggles with many tears and deprivation. But as long as people on both sides honestly endeavor to build bridges, in the interest of the unity of re-vealed religion, of the people of revelation, and of humanity, the division itself is not only an evil.[223]

#191 Antisemitism is an ideology specifically directed against Jews and Judaism. It

> comprises the full scale of rejection, from instinctive aversion not neces-sarily harmful to Jews, to hatred which makes the planned extermina-tion of Jews its immutable goal.[224]

Antisemitism is collective hatred of Jews, on principle and in practice, wholesale hostility toward Jews *qua* Jews. An antisemitic person can no longer clearly perceive and interpret the identity of Jews. He becomes de-

void of the faculty to differentiate between Jewry as a whole and individual
Jews, between Jews of yesterday and those of today:

> For that which differentiates antisemitism from other group prejudices
> . . . is that group prejudice is normally related to something contempo-
> rary, something which actually happened, even if it be wrongly or dis-
> tortedly interpreted; whereas antisemitism has almost no relationship to
> the actual world, and rests on a figment of the imagination, perpetually
> bolstered up by other figments.[225]

Antisemitism can be diagnosed when the following three conditions prevail: (a) ideologues tell horror stories about Jews, (b) already ingrained
ideologies prevent the man in the street from perceiving the truth about
Jews and Judaism, (c) anti-Jewish actions (arson, pogroms) take place, in-
cited by ideologues and ideologies.

3. Remarks on Possible Anti-Judaism in the New Testament

#192 Assuming that anti-Judaism as described above is *a priori* ha-
tred of Jews, it could be at most marginal and indirect in the New Testament. Not only were Jesus and Paul Jews, but the New Testament
hagiographers as well. Not one of them considered himself an apostate, not
one was ashamed of his Jewishness. All of them wished to represent genuine Judaism, pleasing to God (#129–133, 135–137). Antisemitism could
enter only from the outside; it could be created only by Jewish dissidents
or non-Jews.

#193 Based on these presuppositions, the following half-verse might
be called antisemitic: "They (the Jews) are displeasing to God, and are
hostile to all men" (1 Thess 2:15b). Behind it probably lurks the anti-Jewish pagan slogan, "They (the Jews) are displeasing to the gods and hostile
to all men." Hekataios of Abdera (300 BCE) and the Egyptian historian
Manethon—who in the third century BCE wrote a history of Egypt in
Greek and whose work appears in extensive excerpts in the *Antiquitates* by
Josephus Flavius—alluded to the Jews as being odious to the gods and
hostile to man. We find similar ideas in the writings of Pliny the Elder
(*Naturalis Historia* 13, 4, 46) and Tacitus (*Historia* V:3–5), while the Book
of Esther refers to them twice (Est 3:8, 13).

Probably it was not Paul himself but a later Gentile Christian glossator who added 1 Thess 2:15b to the First Letter to the Thessalonians. The
Pauline train of thought would not be disturbed but rather clarified if this
half-verse were omitted. There is some excuse for this antisemitic slip of

the pen by the non-Jewish glossator because he wrote under the anguish of persecution. If Paul himself was the author, one of those expressions common among non-Jews crept into his writing automatically and involuntarily. It would then indicate not Paul's antisemitism but his excessive agitation which may easily lead to inattentiveness. Paul certainly did not harbor Jewish self-hatred.

#194 The apostle Paul was probably the only New Testament writer who recognized the beginnings of Gentile Christian antisemitism. He exerted all his theological sagacity to keep it in check. Non-Jewish Christians in Rome were possibly infected by the prevailing pagan, pre-Christian antisemitism. For this reason, Paul wrote the grandiose chapters 9–11 of his Letter to the Romans. He points out that the Jews as a whole—though not all their representatives—despite their rejection of Christ continue to be Israel and ultimately will be redeemed. He warns Gentile Christians against anti-Jewish ideologies: "Not you support the root, but the root supports you" (11:18). "Do not be conceited but fear" (11:20b), "lest you should be wise in your own conceits" (11:25b). According to Paul, then, non-Jewish Christians must not think arrogantly of Israel's "obduracy."[226]

#195 Many authors, dismayed at the anti-Jewish past of the Church (#186–189), insist that the New Testament contains quite a number of antisemitic passages. They usually refer to Matt 22:1–14 (parable of the wedding feast), Matt 23 (indictment of the Pharisees), Matt 27:24f (clamoring masses before Pilate), and Luke 23:27–31 (Jesus and the mourning women). First place among such quotations is often accorded John 8:44, where Christ says to the "Jews": "You are children of the devil who is your father and you prefer to do what your father wants."

Under the influence of dualistic antithetic Johannine thinking, Christian exegesis tended to apply the words "the Jews" rather too universally. If we were to pay greater attention to the historical New Testament context, we would legitimately identify the Jews in John 8 as the upper class of Judean priests. In T Dan 5:6, "children of the devil" is not an antisemitic but inner-Jewish invective. In that text of Jesus' time a Jewish apocalypticist preaches to the Jews that the devil is their leader (*archon*). The Jewish-Hellenistic fictional tale of *Joseph et Aséneth* (#70) calls the devil the father of the Egyptian gods (12:8f). Fatherhood or leadership of the devil was an established polemical formula among Jews of the time and did not indicate basic hostility against Jews or non-Jews.

John 8:44 must not be isolated from such contemporary statements. We already discussed (#55, 111, 121ff) the inner-Jewish character of New Testament preaching and polemics. If that were not sufficient proof, the harsh words of the Old Testament prophets against the people of God should be considered. If one wishes by any means to subsume the New Testament under anti-Jewish literature, then the Hebrew Scriptures should be called even more antisemitic, which of course is absurd.

Study of the non-canonical Jewish literature of the time of Jesus—in particular, early midrashim and targumim (#82f, 94–102)—leads to the realization that the New Testament is written in the style of Jewish Palestinians (not of the Hellenistic Jewish fringe groups), even those parts where a critical, polemical stand against Jewish groups and individuals is taken.[227] The people of God of all periods and all sorts must be aroused and stirred, even with harsh words, by the prophets, leaders and representatives, over and over again. The purpose is to keep them from becoming unfaithful to their mission.

4. Remarks on Christian Anti-Judaism

#196 Christian or, if you wish, ecclesiastical anti-Judaism probably existed among non-Jewish Christians already in late New Testament times. Right from the beginning, it was a mark of religious chauvinism and anti-historical interpretation of revealed texts received from the Jews. Once the words of Christ, of Paul, and of all the hagiographers were no longer read in their Jewish historical context but in a fundamentalistic, rigid, "right-minded" manner, that is, ideologically, they became an alibi for antisemitism. In separating the words of revelation from their Jewish matrix, they became anti-Jewish germ-carriers. The words of Christ and of Paul which were not intended to be anti-Jewish became in the mind, on the lips, at the pen of many Christian homilists an anti-Jewish self-justification for Christian positions and weaknesses.

Yet, that negatively infected Christian message was not only the work of narrow-minded, malicious non-Jewish Christians. It also resulted from an encounter between the Christian teaching and pre-Christian pagan antisemitism. Strong anti-Jewish propaganda was current in pre-Christian Alexandria and Rome, and non-Jewish Christians already before their conversion lived in the obfuscated atmosphere of pagan antisemitism. The first disaster of Jewish-Christian history was the fact that it was modeled on pagan forms of antisemitism. Christians breathing such germs disseminated them and multiplied their effect, without recognizing or combating the harm done by their mixed ideology. (It seems that Paul was the only exception; cf. #194.) From that time on, antisemitism among non-Jewish Christians was a sinister potential for the perversion of Christian faith.

Antisemitism is a grave temptation to Christian faith, and Christians of all periods succumbed to it in droves.[228]

#197 Holocaust theology is not always characterized by balanced judgment and exactitude of method. Among theologians quoted here and others, some authors distort historical contexts and refashion the grief of Jews, innocently herded into the gas ovens, into rhetoric against the Church and Judaism. This is partly understandable as an expression of indignation at, and impatience with, a callous lack of interest among many ecclesiastic and non-ecclesiastic individuals. On the other hand, a believing Christian should not find it so very difficult to interpret the sacrifice of the Jews during the Nazi terror. His thoughts should be turned toward Christ to whom these Jewish masses became alike, in sorrow and death. Auschwitz is the most monumental sign of our time for the intimate bond and unity between the Jewish martyrs—who stand for all Jews—and the crucified Christ, even though the Jews in question could not be aware of it.

Despite all separation, diverging routes, and misunderstanding, the Holocaust stands as a milestone for believing Christians of the inviolable oneness of Judaism and Christianity, based on the crucified Christ. They must feel the call to align their life with the mind of Christ and those who died in his spirit. Yet, Auschwitz is not an isolated event; we must call among the victims and belonging to Christ those millions of others sacrificed under the Nazi terror: Russians, Poles, Serbs, Germans, Italians. Finally, believing Christians will extend the arc to include all witnesses to faith of all times. All of them eminently belong to the people of Christ, among whom they, too, hope to be counted.[229]

#198 Without the slightest doubt, many Church Fathers, Popes and other Christian representatives acted wickedly toward the Jews. John Chrysostom, for example, proved a spiteful Jew-hater in his sermons. The Church cannot evade responsibility by maintaining that only certain unworthy individuals were antisemitic while, basically, she never was infected. She canonized John Chrysostom and John Capistrano, both of them antisemites, though they were not canonized for that reason. Both saints were obviously not aware of the un-Christian line of their anti-Jewish provocations. There are others respects in which the Church became guilty. She did not sufficiently oppose the very dangerous joining of power and religion within her own sphere and among secular dictators. In the twilight of religion and power politics, theological and later cultural and racist antisemitism flourished relatively undisturbed.[230] The Church was also rather blind toward the danger of anti-Jewish words in preaching the

Gospel. During the Middle Ages, many murders were perpetrated in which "Christ-killer" served as slogan and alibi. The Church, then, has attended poorly to her office as guardian and protector of humankind, though we today would think it could not have been too difficult for her to recognize that pogroms and lynch justice are contrary to the will of God.[231]

#199 On the other hand, Church Fathers, Popes and theologians must not be placed on the same level, as is done by some people, with Hitler, Eichmann and other monstrous criminals of the twentieth century. First of all we must point to the normative power of the factual events. Anyone today, after Auschwitz, who still speaks and acts antisemitically— probably under disguise because antisemitism is no longer "good form" in our day and in most parts of the world—must be much more strongly condemned than, for example, the Church Father Augustine or some bishop of pre-Nazi times. Most of them could not predict fully the evil consequences of their anti-Jewish sermons.

I find it a very hopeful sign that in modern Holocaust discussions it is the traditional Jews who warn their Christian partners not to think too strongly in terms of scapegoating. We must take into consideration, according to them, that the Christianity of late antiquity, the Middle Ages, and our time did not wish to totally destroy the Jews, and that good Christians of all periods helped persecuted Jews with shelter and protection. That, indeed, is a far cry from Nazi criminality.[232]

#200 Franklin Littell who was mentioned previously (#189) is primarily concerned with the catastrophe that antisemitism spells for Christendom. Mass defections of Christians during the twentieth century are linked closely to Christian antisemitism, which caused an "erosion of Christian fundamentals," a "collapse of historical consciousness," "Christian accommodation to pagan thought," a "docetic heresy (which) is the typical heresy of Greek thought."[233]

We agree with this opinion. The Church's struggle for identity and credibility is eminently tied to her theological attitude toward Judaism and its history. Our questions about God and about our faith must be probed in the shadow of the grim fate and the continued existence of the Jews.

#201 Christians must not assent to any form of anti-Judaism. Attempts to justify it run counter to unambiguous, central precepts, prohibitions, and norms which may be summed up in the commandment to love one's neighbor. The obligation of fair-mindedness and regard for human rights, and the rejection of derision, slander, and proscription, for whatever reason, of fellow humans are contained in that commandment. Basic Christian principles, primarily the dogma of universal salvation through

Jesus Christ, do not allow any scope for antisemitism. We cannot harmonize ideas of the definitive rejection or condemnation of Jews and Judaism with the universal redemptive will of Christ. Christian belief in the intimate connection between the Tanakh and the New Testament contradicts theological bias against Jews; that belief is grounded in the faithfulness, dependability, and mercy of God toward the descendants of Abraham in the flesh and in the spirit.

6.
Jews and Christians in Our Time

#202 Christian-Jewish history consists not only of hatred and persecution but also of mutual faith, hope, and responsibility for one another, in the midst of hostility and in spite of separation. In the past, much valuable material within Judaism has been kept from affecting Christianity, while many precious Christian ideas were submerged within the Church, without being noticed by Jews. Although their life in isolation from one another can be explained historically and sociologically and may even have had its positive aspects, such a relationship between Jews and Christians must not continue. Christians as well as Jews are called by revelation to make themselves available to all mankind. That means that they are intended for, and must walk toward, one another. Their ways of life and of salvation must not be separate and unrelated.

In order to prepare the way for a more humane and dynamic co-existence, a Christian theologian of Judaism should become familiar with the most basic Jewish statements of identity and experiences of faith and evaluate them in a Christian context. He may then be able to indicate new perspectives for today and tomorrow.

I
JEWISH STATEMENTS OF IDENTITY

1. Israel
#203 "Israel" is the briefest, most universal, and most frequent term employed by Jews to designate the individual, the religious community, and the socio-political context.

When "Israel" is used existentially, as a personal mark so to speak, reference is often made to that profound tale of Jacob/Israel's night struggle with a heavenly being (Gen 32:22–29). To be Jewish, then, implies a struggle with God and man, similar to that of Jacob, and to win the upper hand—though in pain and humiliation (cf. Gen 32:29). From this biblical account a faithful Jew derives his obligation to love freedom and readily to take on responsibility without, however, abandoning his passionate wrestling relationship as partner of the God of Jacob/Israel. Thus, striving by prayer and action, a Jew is truly "Israel."

The Marxist Vitezslav Gardavski finds the nucleus of the Tanakh in Gen 32:22–29 and considers it a suitable point of reference for actualizing the Bible for atheists and Christians:

> It seems to me that this scene contains the key to understanding the Old Testament: it relates how man became a subject. . . . Man "is chosen" when he makes a decision, opts for freedom, and confirms this choice by his actions.[234]

Gardavski's view is somewhat reductivist, but Jewish tradition of freedom, responsibility and involvement with God also considers Jacob's struggle at the river Jabbok as a means to express Jewish (and not only Jewish) existential identity, similar to the *akedah* of Abraham and Isaac (cf. #94–100). In the Jewish tradition, "Israel" mostly refers to the religious community, the covenanted people of the Lord. As a praying congregation, as a social structure, and as a community with a mission, the people of God is "Israel." Emphasizing the fact that only the people of the Jews represent Israel, they are also convinced that Jews here and now cannot fully live up to the greatness of Israel and the claims made upon it (#17–20).

"Israel" also means a state and denotes a geographical area. The modern state of the Jews in the biblical land of the Israelite fathers bears the name of Israel. It indicates that every Jew is, at least potentially, a citizen of that state. The name also signifies that Israel does not only apply to the religious component but includes all spheres of human life. In the course of history, Judaism always endeavored to have the name of "Israel" appear in as many contexts as possible.[235]

#204 As the manifold use of "Israel" indicates, Jews always felt strongly impelled to express the unity of the full scope of life. For a short time only, for instance among liberal Jews of the nineteenth century, did the opinion prevail that Judaism was merely a religious community. Much

more predominant was the conviction that Judaism is a religious and social (ethnic and national) entity. In the course of history, various definitions of Judaism have been put forward, stressing sometimes the religious,
sometimes the social component. We will now examine these definitions.

2. Judaism as Social Structure

#205 According to *halakhah* (e.g. Mish *Kid* 4:7), one is a Jew who
has a Jewish mother or has converted to Judaism and does not adhere to
another religion. This minimal definition is indisputably derived from revelation (e.g., Ez 44:22) but can also be applied in civil law, though not
without considerable difficulties. An individual's religious attitude is not
necessarily of consequence. In the case of mixed marriages, change of religion, and unclear family relationships, this *halakhah* may lead to personal,
inter-religious, and even humane and international legal complications, as
has become evident in the state of Israel.

#206 Because of the above and other laws relevant to society, the
temptation lies at hand to view Judaism as mere "behaviorism" or a way of
life. It could be defined as an ethnic group whose members are not to enter
into community with non-Jews for marriage, meals, or cultic reasons. Several Jewish authors interpret Judaism in that way. According to Heinrich
Graetz (1817–1891) after a phrase by Ernst Rénan (1823–1892), Judaism
is "a minimum of religion."[236] Judaism should be defined mainly in historical and legal categories. Graetz came to this characterization of Judaism
through his historical view, his apologetic glances at Christendom, and the
doubtful light into which the "mythological" concept of religion had been
cast in his time. To Graetz, biblical law and rabbinic interpretation were
the evident, immutable foundations upholding Judaism over the course of
time.

#207 From the eighteenth to the early twentieth century—the time
of Enlightenment, Emancipation and German Idealism—Judaism was often called a religion of reason and logic that dispenses with myth and dogma. The traditional argument derived from *Abot* 2:2: "Study of Torah
along with worldly occupation (cultural, intellectual, or for the public
good) is seemly."

Study of Torah was interpreted mainly as rational, judicial guidance
for a meaningful and creative way of life (*derekh eretz*).[237] At times this
involved thoughts of assimilation to Christianity and European civilization. Such one-sided views are no longer acceptable in our time, since
esoteric-mystical and dogmatic traditions in Judaism have become so
clearly evident (cf. #39, 158–160). At the same time, socio-cultural fea-

tures must necessarily be included. Judaism has always been partly offensive, partly fascinating, to other peoples whose intellectual life it served to stimulate. Yet, such traits do not fully encompass Judaism which has certain characteristics that clearly transcend society.

3. Judaism as Religious Reality

#208 Rabbi Leo Baeck (1873–1956) was one of many who fought against a definition of Judaism as a religion of law, in the sense of a revealed logical and general directive for life. He wrote:

> Only out of the experience of the eternal mystery, of infinity, of the beyond, can the experience of the law emerge. One cannot be without the other. Behind the law, imperative and commanding, is the mystery, surrounding God the Eternal. Through the Law, since God has given it and man fulfills it in his sphere, man can approach the Eternal One. But the true discovery of the Law, and thus of God's nearness, is only possible to man if he discovers the mystery at the same time. We cannot experience God himself; but this people first made the discovery that we are able to experience the eternal mystery that surrounds God and the eternal Law rising out of the mystery. Through both of them man is led into the Kingdom of God, so that he may "walk in all his ways" and "cleave unto" the Eternal, his God (Deut 11:22).[238]

In order to rescue his hard-pressed brethren from the accusation that they were simply learning by rote and thereby fulfilled the Law—representing a rational alternative to Christianity which accentuates the mysterious—he was one of those who proposed the term "ethical monotheism" as a short definition for Judaism.[239]

Baeck's formulation was highly esteemed because it successfully parried the polemical term "nomocracy" (government based on a legal code) so often advanced by Christian New Testament scholars and historians of religion. Many Jewish scholars repeated after Baeck that Judaism is not a community governed by and subjugated to law; it is not nomocratic, they said, but "theonomic," under the will of God. However, Baeck's definition is too one-sided in its emphasis on the religious component.

#209 A short time before Leo Baeck, Franz Rosenzweig (1886–1929) showed the social and religious character of Judaism in a more balanced manner. His ideas, moreover, were greatly influenced by Jewish-Christian discussions:

> Judaism and Christianity have a peculiar position in common: even after having become a religion, they find in themselves the impulse to over-

come the fixity of a religious institution, and to return to the open field of reality. All historical religions are "founded." Only Judaism and Christianity are not founded religions. Originally they were something quite "unreligious," the one a fact, the other an event. They were surrounded by all kinds of religion, but they themselves would have been dumbfounded to be taken for religions.[240]

Rosenzweig must be credited for not having succumbed to Jewish apologetic that Christianity was a mere religion while Judaism was more than that. He was also mindful of the fact that the label "religion," though applicable to both, must be used in a restricted, different, clearly separable manner in Judaism and Christianity.

4. Judaism as Committed Historical Reality

#210 Judaism is not fully circumscribed by its dialectic relationship between religion and the mundane. It lives in and by its history. Over and above any dialectic or system, Judaism is the content of a narrative which begins in early biblical times and contains politics and religion, catastrophes and triumphs, hiddenness and revelation of God, discussions among men filled with the spirit and fearful as well as sanguine groups. The story is still not completed, its end not yet in sight. That end, however, will not mean destruction but universal salvation related to God. Jewish communities of all·times are instructed not to forget the past nor to push aside any Jewish experience, to view the present with a critical eye and to walk confidently, in spite of dark clouds, toward the future. As long as they obey this mandate, they constitute Jewry.

#211 Meaning and liturgical arrangement of the sabbath exemplify the extent to which history is existentially and institutionally inherent in Judaism. Many Jewish religious teachers consider the sabbath representative of the heart of Judaism. This interpretation is derived from old traditions according to which the final redemption of Israel will come about when the sabbath is kept holy by all members of the people of God, in a perfect manner (TJ *Ta'an* 1:1). Three features of the sabbath point in this direction, *kedushah* (holiness), *menuhah venofash* (rest and peace of mind), *onag* (joy) (TB *Shab* 118a–b). In the rabbinic view, if one fulfills the sabbath not merely as a duty but provides for holiness, recreational rest and joy, he causes God and his kingdom to be present, as they were in the revelation of the past and will be again to the fullest extent in the *eschaton*. The sabbath becomes that redemptive day when the small group of those celebrating together becomes aware of and gathers together, as it were, the promises of God, and the kingdom of God is present.[241] Similar ideas apply to the Passover festival (cf. #96).

#212 One of the reasons that from the very beginning modern Zionism found so many adherents among the Jewish masses was probably that its theoreticians represented Judaism as the historical people *par excellence*. The proto-Zionist Moses Hess (1812–1875) wrote in politically visionary diction:

> The Jewish people has been until the French Revolution the only people of the world which had at the same time a national and supernational religion. Through Judaism the history of mankind has become a sacred history, I mean a consistently organic process of development which, beginning with family love, is never quite finished till all humanity will become one family whose members will become just as bound solidarily through the sacred spirit of the creative genius of history as the different organs of a living body are so by means of a just as sacred, creative power of nature.[242]

5. Summary of Statements on Jewish Identity

#213 Jewry is "Israel," even if its members cannot do full justice to this noble signification. It is a social, religious entity linked to its history; it cannot relinquish any of these characteristics. A brief definition comprising all of the above might be that Jews are a "precursor people" (*vor-laeufig*). Precursor in this context takes on two different meanings. It indicates that Jews precede, run ahead of, pave the way for (other nations and communities), that they are a model, so to speak. Precursor also indicates a temporary, interim, not fully rounded, incomplete manner of existence, faith, and action. Jews set up standards for their own people and for many non-Jews in matters of society, religion, revelation and post-biblical history. Such standards contain seeds for the present and the future, applicable to all humanity. Judaism does not own anything to perfection, in full completeness, but everything is available as a beginning, provisionally. Whatever is there and has been laid as foundation is waiting to be transformed and to be merged with greater unities.

II
JEWISH EXPERIENCE OF FAITH

#214 It has often been said that Judaism lacks a system of dogmas and ethics, and it is difficult for non-Jews—even for Jews—to find their way among Jewish writings. No serious scholar in our day will continue to defend the Enlightenment thesis that Judaism is completely anti-dogmatic, that it is concerned with nothing but fulfillment of the Law, without any theological qualifications. Arguing about Judaism in the Christian dogmatic tradition, however, one soon comes up against equivocal, flexible Jewish theological concepts and their equally variable content. We hear that Jews talk about essential points of the Torah (*gufe Torah*), foundation stones (*yesodim*), roots (*sorasim*), and basic tenets (*ikkarim*). But it is difficult to discover the relationship between these technical theological terms, or where and how Judaism distinguishes between important and subordinate matters.[243]

1. Tenets to Preserve Peace among Jews

#215 Jewish tenets and practices of belief are mainly the result of challenges and disputations of the past. They represent compromises rather than firm principles, antitheses rather than balanced guidelines. The most pointed discussions used to take place between radical messianists and those who felt responsible for a peaceful and traditional community structure. The Bible and tradition contain many passages that could serve to justify holy wars, messianic revolts, destruction of transgressors, etc. In early Jewish, rabbinic, and later times the temptation to reach for the sword was often quite strong in periods of distress because such a reaction to aggression was considered as willed by God, even a preliminary step toward final redemption. Such military outbreaks added an abundance of suffering and tragedy to Jewish history.[244] Certain tenets of faith, then, must be seen primarily as defense against disrupters of peace within the Jewish communities.

#216 After the defeat of the messianic revolutionaries and the destruction of the Temple in 70 CE, the early rabbis found that their foremost task was to contain revolutionary messianism which endangered the people. Three men were dominant in that respect: R. Yohanan ben Zakkai (died about 80 CE), R. Yehoshua ben Hananya (died about 120 CE), and R. Yohanan of Tiberias (died about 279 CE).

#217 The following saying by R. Yohanan ben Zakkai has been transmitted:

> If there were a plant in your hand and they should say to you: "Look, the messiah is here!" Go and plant your plant and after that go forth to receive him. If the young men say to you: Let us go and build the Temple, do not listen to them; but if the old men say to you: Come and let us tear down the Temple, do as they say. For the building up of young men

is a tearing down and the tearing down of old men is a building up (*ARN* II:31).

R. Yohanan ben Zakkai considered more important the fulfillment of the biblical, creative task of planting a seedling than to greet the messiah. He wanted to provide for the continued existence of decimated Jewry, in the face of renewed risky messianic ventures which demanded active cooperation from the people. Reconstruction of the destroyed Temple was represented as a messianic deed of highest importance, and R. Yohanan had to try to prevent it if he wished to stem the dangerous messianic flood. The continued existence of the people and their living in relative peace were his most serious concerns; religious enthusiasm and messianic risks had to recede into the background (cf. *MekhY* on Ex 20:21–23).

#218 Soon after 110 CE, the Jews were again shaken by messianic fever. Groups of diaspora Jews prepared to reconstruct the Temple in Jerusalem, but their plans were thwarted. Thereupon they became rebellious and it became necessary to find a peacemaker. He was found in the person of R. Yehoshua ben Hananya, the "expert in Torah." An historical reminiscence of that event (of about 117 CE) is probably contained in the following rabbinic quotation:[245]

> So he (R. Joshua b. Hanania) went and harangued them: A wild lion killed (an animal) and a bone stuck in his throat. Thereupon he proclaimed: "I will reward anyone who removes it." An Egyptian heron, which has a long beak, came and pulled it out and demanded his reward. "Go," he replied, "you will be able to boast that you entered the lion's mouth in peace and came out in peace." Even so, let us be satisfied that we entered into dealings with this people in peace and have emerged in peace (*BerR* 64:10 on Gn 26:19).

At the root of the messianic passion to rebuild the Temple and stir up a revolt lay the gloomy expectation that they would all be "gobbled up" by the Romans. It was the people's dream to bring about the fall of the Roman Empire indirectly by such messianic preparations. According to chapters 2 and 7 of the Book of Daniel, the messianic time would cause the ruin of wicked secular powers. R. Yohanan ben Hananya, on the other hand, realized that far more important than any promises for the future was the peaceful survival of God's people. He was at one with R. Yohanan ben Zakkai in teaching that peace and security for the people should be primary pastoral concerns.

#219 Under the leadership of R. Yohanan of Tiberias, lively theo-
logical work went on in that part of Galilee. R. Abba bar Kahana, one of
his disciples, explained in the following words the will of God on peace
and messianic rebellion:

> The Holy One, blessed be he, intimated to him (R. Kahana) that he who
> attemps to resist the wave is swept away by it, but he who bends before
> it is not swept away by it (*BerR* 44:15 on Gen 15:10).

The meaning of this picture becomes clear in the context. The people
of God is likened to a swimmer in heavy seas; the onrushing wave is the
Roman world power threatening it. Survival is possible only by adapting to
the swell of the sea. Anyone opposing this power, challenging, insulting,
attacking it, for instance by messianic activities, will not harm the Roman
oppressors but bring injury to the Jews; he thereby becomes an accessory
to the misery and even death of God's people. Following this train of
thought, the Jewish theologians of Tiberias tried to mitigate messianism by
projecting it into the far-off future and a world beyond.[246]

2. Tenets Expressing Awe of the Transcendent

#220 Jews have always shown great reserve in categorizing powers
and spheres that lie beyond the experiential world. This does not imply
that great efforts were not expanded for systematization of the transcen-
dent and to search for links with the heavenly spheres. On the contrary,
within mystic-esoteric groups such attempts had been made from earliest
times (cf. #39f, 85, 103, 147f). What we wish to emphasize here is that
Jewish officials and prominent intellectual figures always tended to ward
off mystic-esoteric trends, providing thereby an additional reason for the
openness and flexibility of Jewish tenets of faith.

#221 Teaching about the Holy Spirit is a typical example of such
fluidity. It says in the Talmud:

> Our rabbis taught: Since the death of the last prophets, Haggai, Zechari-
> ah, and Malachai, the Holy Spirit (of prophetic inspiration) departed
> from Israel; yet they were still able to avail themselves of the Bath-Kol
> (divine voice). Once when the rabbis were met in the upper chamber of
> Gurya's house at Jericho, a Bath-Kol was heard from Heaven, saying:
> "There is one amongst you who is worthy that the Shechinah should
> rest on him as it did on Moses our teacher, but his generation does not
> merit it." The sages present set their eyes on Hillel the elder. And when

he died, they lamented and said: "Alas, the pious man, the humble man, the disciple of Ezra (is no more)" (TB *San* 11a).

The Holy Spirit is here synonymous with the *shekhinah,* the way of God's being and acting in the world (cf. #144–146). Parallel passages (e.g., Tos *Sot* 13:2–4; TB *Sot* 48b) indicate that the rabbis generally accepted that such terms could be interchanged.[247] Some parts of the Palestinian Targum tradition, evident in Codex Neophyti 1 (cf. #83, 96–99), use alternatively YHWH, word of God, glory of God, and glory of the *shekhinah* of God (cf. CN 1 on Gen 1:1, 3, 7f, 17, 26f; 3:10, 24). We have there undeniable documentation of the Jewish reserve with regard to expression in precise terms of the ways of God's acting, his life and attributes. Even the tradition of religious philosophy during the Middle Ages and in modern time has avoided analogical proofs of God's existence, limiting arguments almost exclusively to the *via negativa.*[248]

#222 Similarly variable is Jewish teaching on the angels, devils and demons, concepts that are employed even more elastically, at times quite vaguely and contradictorily. Angels are sometimes faithful messengers of God, sometimes intermediate beings trying to disrupt the relationship between God and man. Demons can be dangerous, frightening creatures as well as droll goblins. Angels, demons, natural monsters, and evil women are at times not much unlike one another. Even the devil goes under various names and has varying powers. It is quite justifiable to ask if early and rabbinic Jews really believed in the devil and demons, or whether such beings should be considered no more than ornamentation. With the exception of Qumran, Jewish theology does not give much weight to such creatures, whose powers and functions remained ambiguous. Belief in angels is better substantiated in rabbinic literature than frightening ideas of the devil, who at times is considered as wholly unnecessary.[249]

#223 The same is true for Jewish teaching on the resurrection of the dead. Not only is the openness and flexibility characteristic, but we can trace in Jewish history how the place accorded the idea in popular consciousness has changed and its perception has varied from one era to another.

With the early Maccabean period a new epoch of faith began, when hope for resurrection motivated many Jews to remain true to their faith in the face of cruel persecutions by the Seleucid occupation powers and an unprecedented crisis within Judaism (cf. #23–31). Belief in resurrection of the dead gave added weight and new meaning to the biblical past and the hope for the future. The apocalyptic author of the Book of Daniel (cf.

#66–68) was the most eminent exponent of hope for resurrection. He proclaimed it as glad tidings of salvation to the stumbling and almost desperate people:

> At that time your people shall escape, everyone who is found written in the book. Many of those who sleep in the dust of the earth shall awake; some shall live forever, others shall be an everlasting horror and disgrace. But the wise shall shine brightly like the splendor of the firmament, and those who lead the many to justice shall be like the stars forever (Dan 12:1–3).

These words were an answer to those who, in a severe crisis of faith and identity, were asking: Where is the covenantal faith of the God of Israel? Where are his mighty deeds in history? He permits the faithful to be ridiculed, persecuted and killed. With impassioned pastoral intuition, the author of Daniel places the God of Israel at the center of his message as Creator and Savior from a hopeless situation (cf. Dan 3:17, 29; 4:32; 6:28). This God was to him, as in all biblical tradition, the Lord over life and death (cf. Deut 32:39; 1 Sam 2:6; Pss 9:14; 16:10; 56:14; Prov 23:14; Is 24–27; Hos 13:14). The author of Daniel was convinced that it was equally difficult or easy for YHWH to save those living in hopelessness and those already dead. The resurrection message was, then, one of hope for the lost, rejected, and forgotten ones on earth and in the grave. It was not directed to all the world but to the faint-hearted who struggled for trust in God.[249a]

The Book of Daniel did not proclaim a dogma of resurrection but was an encouraging word in a time of serious crisis, offering guidance to those who were able to hear it. Soon after, however, it was discussed whether the message was acceptable or even binding on the people of God and how its content was to be interpreted. The disputes between Pharisees and Sadducees at the time of Jesus are characteristic for the situation (cf. *Ant* 13:288–298; *Bellum* 2:162–166; Mark 12:18–27; Acts 23:6–8). The Mishnah (about 220 CE) finally contains a formulation demanding obedience:

> But the following do not have a share in the world-to-come: anyone who says that resurrection is not of Torah origin (Mish *San* 10:1; cf. TB *San* 90a).

But even this formulation did not end the disputes; almost every generation up to the present has attempted to balance the teaching on resurrection against the concrete suffering and prevailing tendencies within Judaism. At times, resurrection was competing against immortality of the soul and that, again, resulted in fluctuations of the weight and expression of instruction on that point. Such oscillations were caused not only by the absence within Judaism of binding authorities but even more so by the peculiarity to argue constantly, with God and with one another, about everything that was revealed and taught. In that way, faith was deepened and enriched.

3. Affinities Between Medieval Jewish Doctrines and Christian Dogmas

#224 Since Philo of Alexandria (cf. *De Opificio Mundi* 170–172), collections and summaries of significant Jewish doctrines were undertaken. Nearly all the great medieval masters of Judaism—Saadya ben Joseph Gaon (892–942), Yehuda Halevi (1080–1145), Abraham ibn Daud (ab. 1110–1180), Moses Maimonides (1135–1204), Simon Duran (1366–1444), Hasdai Crescas (1340–1410), Joseph Albo (ab. 1380–1445), Isaac Arama (1420–1494), Isaac Abarbanel (1437–1508), and others—formulated guiding principles and articles of faith. This tradition continues in our time. Louis Jacobs examined these doctrines, comparing them with one another and making them intelligible to the modern reader.[250]

The thirteen Principles of Faith (*ikkarim*) of Maimonides were of greatest influence and included in the synagogue service.[251] None of the medieval or modern doctrinal systems should be interpreted as directed exclusively or mainly against Christianity; all of them came into being because of Jewish needs. Parallels within Jewish and Christian historical events can nearly always be discovered,[252] in regard to not only the situation but the content of faith. All Christian faith principles, with the exception of Christology, originated within Judaism, even though the latter lacks a binding doctrinal authority. For that reason all Jewish systems of faith remained at their beginnings. Franz Rosenzweig is correct when he points out:

> It has often been said, and even more often been repeated, that there are no dogmas in Judaism. As little as this is true—a superficial glance at Jewish history or the Jewish prayerbook shows differently—there is yet something to it that is true. Judaism has dogmas but no dogmatics.[253]

III
PERSPECTIVES

1. Christianity and Judaism as Open Institutions

#225 Christianity is an institution which is open and relates to all men and all periods of history; it exists and is still growing and becoming.

The churches, not unlike Jewry, are a precursor people (cf. #123). A Christian who would understand and proclaim his Church as a mere system, as a static and closed institution, degrades and reduces it; he builds fences and trenches which could serve as bases of aggression against non-Christians.

We tried to describe in this volume in how many respects Christianity is open especially toward Judaism. The Church is linked to Judaism in an unique manner. The Christian churches are now becoming increasingly aware that they must refer themselves to Judaism in questions of origin and renewal. The Second Vatican Council officially recognized and clearly expounded this position in the Declaration *Nostra Aetate* (n. 4):

> As this Sacred Synod searches into the mystery of the Church, it remembers the bond that spiritually ties the people of the new covenant to Abraham's stock. Thus, the Church of Christ acknowledges that, according to God's saving design, the beginnings of her faith and her election are found already among the patriarchs, Moses and the prophets. She professes that all who believe in Christ—Abraham's sons according to faith—are included in the same patriarch's call, and likewise that the salvation of the Church is mysteriously foreshadowed by the chosen people's exodus from the land of bondage. The Church, therefore, cannot forget that she received the revelation of the Old Testament through the people with whom God in his inexpressible mercy concluded the ancient covenant. Nor can she forget that she draws sustenance from the root of that well-cultivated olive tree onto which has been grafted the wild shoot, the Gentiles. Indeed, the Church believes that by his cross Christ our peace reconciled Jews and Gentiles, making both one in himself (cf. Eph 2:14–16).[254]

There is a great deal in Christianity which is Jewish; it has Jewish characteristics, a Jewish note. Christianity cannot declare itself "free of Jews," as was done under the National Socialists in Germany, greatly harming thereby Jews and Christians alike. Christians must study Judaism and take it seriously in its own right and in its relationship to Christianity. Christians must listen, wait, and believe.

#226 Judaism, too, is an open community, a trait already conferred on it by the Tanakh (Gen 12:1–3; Is 7:9; 19:23–25; 44:24–45:8). Like Christianity, Judaism's openness is directed mainly toward the future. Believing Jews hope that someday all the nations will come to the God of Israel, and that universal law, justice, and peace will prevail. Already in the past, Judaism sent out signals to the effect that, despite Christian anti-Judaism, Christianity is not exclusively considered an offensive, inimical power (cf. #119, 134, 136, 152, 162f, 173f, 181f).

2. Dialectical and Dialogical Cooperation between Christians and Jews

#227 Except for certain *halakhic* statements of identity based on descent (cf. #205f), the Church can apply to herself—though always with the Christological signature—all Jewish expressions of self-awareness. Christ is the center of the Church, and through him she is rooted in Israel, "grafted onto" the people of God (Rom 9—11; Eph 1—2). This self-understanding of the Church is indisputable (cf. #136), yet she must not abuse her identity ideologically as an alibi to denigrate and supplant Jews and Judaism. The Church knows, or should know, that in the course of history certain of her statements of self-identity were proclaimed erroneously and in an anti-Jewish manner. Christians must beware: it is not in accordance with Christian faith for the Church or certain Christian communities to call themselves the people of God without any added qualifications. Explanations and distinctions should try to represent one Israel in twofold form, the communities of Christ's disciples and those of the Jews.[255]

The following Christian self-representations are encouraging with regard to Jewish legitimacy and independence: Believers in Christ are the "people of the new covenant" (cf. #225, *Nostra Aetate*) or they are the "people of Christ." Such definitions express Christian openness and modesty toward Judaism. Jewry is part of the people of God, though not automatically every individual Jew, since circumcision is no more a guarantee of election by the grace of God than is baptism (cf. Rom 9:4f). "People of God" should not be applied too frequently and exclusively to Christians.

#228 In the hotly debated question of mission to the Jews, an attitude of open-mindedness, consideration, and witness to one's faith must prevail. No one could justifiably prevent Christians from witnessing to Christ in the presence of Jews. Yet, it is in contradiction to Christian faith and the human rights of Jews if mission to the Jews is practiced as propaganda and ideology so as to sow unrest, discord and fear among them. Witnessing to Christ before Jews must not be accompanied with hostility or depreciation of them.

Judaism, too, has a mission to the world, but Jews do not attempt to convert everyone to Judaism. Their concern is a turning (*teshuvah*) of the nations to the God of Israel; their hope is that persecutors and oppressors will become partners and friends (cf. Is 49; Dan 3:26—32; 6:26—29; 9:4—19; the Kaddish prayer, etc.). Christian evangelization, in the last resort, does not aim at gaining converts for one particular Christian group, but at converting (*teshuvah*) individuals to the God of Israel, the Father of Jesus Christ, of Christendom and of Jewry. Witnessing to Christ before Jews means, therefore, struggling together with them for recognition of God and protection of his people.

#229 A Christian theologian of Judaism, finally, must not disregard the existence of the state of Israel, which is of existential significance not only to the citizens of that state but to Jews everywhere. Yet neither Christians nor Jews should glorify the state; we must not be prevented from raising our voice in criticism of Israel's policies, nor should Bible verses be drawn upon in a fundamentalistic way to defend the state of Israel. Neither romantic nor nostalgic, neither sacral nor eschatological nor theocratic ideas are appropriate. The existence of the state of Israel should not be substantiated historically and theologically by the fact that Jews always wished to live in the area and that some of them actually did. The yearning for Zion in itself is not sufficient justification for the fundamental Jewish right to the state of Israel. Lastly, the state came into being because ever more Jews, escaping from European antisemitism of the nineteenth and twentieth centuries and Hitler's gas chambers, found their way to the mandated territory of Palestine. The state became a necessity in order to protect Jews from murderous antisemitism, in a home appealing to them. It should be accepted out of feeling of fellowship, in the interest of Jews and non-Jews who have their home there.

Acceptance does not imply intervention with the government of Israel. We do not have any word of Christ that would theologically justify Christian interference with Jewish concerns of land and state. Together with Jews, Muslims, and representatives of the great powers, Christians are nevertheless called to work for peace in the Middle East as much as they possibly can. Constantly developing confrontations of privileges and claims make efforts for peace extremely urgent for the well-being of Jews, Arabs, and all other people. The last word between Jews and non-Jews, whether on the state of Israel, the people, or anyone's religion, must be one of reconciliation and acceptance of responsibility for one another.[256]

Notes

1. Jakob J. Petuchowski, in John M. Oesterreicher, *The Rediscovery of Judaism* (S. Orange, N.J.: Inst. of Judaeo-Christian Studies, 1971) 11.

2. Norbert Lohfink, "Methoden zur Schriftauslegung unter besonderer Beruecksichtigung der das Judentum betreffenden Schriftstellen," in Clemens Thoma, *Judentum und christlicher Glaube* (Klosterneuburg: 1965) 19–41, quote on p. 39.

3. Goesta Lindeskog, *Die Jesusfrage im neuzeitlichen Judentum*, ein Beitrag zur Geschichte der Leben-Jesu-Forschung (Uppsala: 1938; reprint Darmstadt, 1973) 373.

4. Franz Mussner, "Theologische Wiedergutmachung am Beispiel der Auslegung des Galaterbriefes," in *Freiburger Rundbrief* 26 (1974) 7f; cf. Hans H. Henrix, "Oekumenische Theologie und Judentum, Gedanken zur Nichtexistenz, Notwendigkeit und Zukunft eines Dialogs," in *Freiburger Rundbrief* 28 (1976) 16–27; Ernst L. Ehrlich, *Moeglichkeiten und Grenzen des christlich-juedischen Gespraechs* (Vienna, n.d.).

5. Cf. *Concilium* 1974, new series, vol. 8, no. 10; *Evangelische Theologie* 34 (1974) no. 3; *Journal of Ecumenical Studies* 12 (1975) no. 4; *Judaism* 27 (1978) no. 3; *Michigan Catholic,* Nov. 1975; *New Catholic World* 217 (1974) no. 1297.

6. *Christian Attitudes on Jews and Judaism* (London); *Christian News from Israel* (Jerusalem); *Christlich-Juedisches Forum* (Basle); *Encounter* (Paris); *Face to Face* (New York); *Freiburger Rundbrief* (Freiburg i. Br.); *Immanuel* (Jerusalem); *Judaica* (Zurich); *NICM Journal* (Newton Centre, Mass.); *Oikoumene* (Geneva); *Sens* (Paris). Relevant Series: *Judaica and Christiana,* Clemens Thoma and Simon Lauer, eds. (Berne: Lang); *Stimulus Books,* Studies in Judaism and Christianity, Helga Croner, ed. (New York: Paulist Press); *The Bridge,* John M. Oesterreicher, ed. (New York: various publishers).

7. Cf. Helga Croner, comp., *Stepping Stones to Further Jewish-Christian Relations: An Unabridged Collection of Christian Documents* (London, New York: Stimulus Books, 1977) which contains the important official and semi-official statements of the various churches on Judaism and Christian-Jewish relations.

8. It is difficult to decide which historical works and books on systematic theology should be subsumed under Christian theology of Judaism and Jewish theology of Christianity. Certain publications by the following authors should definitely be so described: Shalom Ben-Chorin, Martin Buber, Luc Deqeker, Willehad P. Eckert, Ernst L. Ehrlich, Robert Everett, Eva Fleischner, David Flusser, Hermann Goldschmidt, Helmut Gollwitzer, Kurt Hruby, Pinchas E. Lapide, Friedrich W. Marquardt, Michael B. McGarry, Reinhold Mayer, André Néher, John M. Oesterreicher, James Parkes, John T. Pawlikowski, Jakob J. Petuchowski, Rudolf Pfisterer, Rolf Rendtdorff, Cornelius A. Rijk, Hans Joachim Schoeps, Shemaryahu Talmon, Hans Thieme, R. J. Zvi Werblowski, Michael Wyschogrod.

9. Leo Pinsker, *Auto-Emancipation* (Jerusalem: Masada, 1935).

10. Louis Jacobs, *A Jewish Theology* (New York: Behrman, 1973) 1.

11. This is the central concern particularly of James Parkes; cf. *Judaism and Christianity* (Chicago: Univ. of Chicago Press, 1948); *The Foundations of Judaism and Christianity* (London: Vallentine-Mitchell, 1960); *Prelude to Dialogue* (New York: Schocken, 1969). Cf. also Eva Fleischner, *Judaism in German Christian Theology Since 1945* (Metuchen, N.J.: Scarecrow, 1975).

12. R. J. Zvi Werblowsky, "Tora als Gnade," in *Kairos* 15 (1973) 156–173.

13. Cf. Rosemary R. Ruether, "Anti-Semitism and Christian Theology," in Eva Fleischner, ed., *Auschwitz: Beginning of a New Era?* (New York: Ktav, 1977) 80. Only someone who does not understand the hermeneutical problems of the Old Testament could make such a statement. From the very beginning, the disciples of Christ considered it a legacy which by the Christ-event was given new relevance. The rabbinic scholars, from their point of view, also endeavored to reactualize their biblical heritage. Cf. Antonius H. Gunneweg, *Understanding the Old Testament* (Philadelphia: Westminster Press, 1978).

14. Siegfried Herrmann, *A History of Israel in Old Testament Times* (Philadelphia: Fortress Press, 1975) 326.

15. Martin Noth, *The History of Israel* (New York: Harper & Row, 1958) 447f.

16. Martin Buber, *Two Types of Faith* (New York: Harper & Row, 1961).

17. Moses Mendelssohn's "Jerusalem," in *Jerusalem and Other Jewish Writings* (New York: Schocken, 1969), was the main influence on later Jewish apologetic. Also important was Samson Raphael Hirsch's *The Nineteen Letters of Ben Uziel* (New York: Feldheim, 1969). Cf. also Pinchas Gruenewald, *Eine Juedische Offenbarungslehre: Samson Raphael Hirsch* (Bern: Herbert Lang, 1977). Hermann Cohen's most important work appeared posthumously, *Religion of Reason out of the Sources of Judaism,* Simon Kaplan, trans. (New York: Fred. Ungar, 1972).

18. Franz Rosenzweig, *Kleinere Schriften* (Berlin: Schocken, 1937) 34.

19. Leopold Zunz, *Zur Geschichte und Literatur* (New York: G. Olms, 1976, reprint).

20. E. g., Hermann L. Strack, Paul Billerbeck, eds., *Kommentar zum Neuen Testament aus Talmud und Midrasch,* 6 vols. (Munich: Beck, 1961); Wilhelm

Bousset, Hugo Gressman, eds., *Handbuch zum Neuen Testament* (Tuebingen:⁴ 1966) esp. 319–336; Eduard Meyer, *Urspruenge und Anfaenge des Christentums,* 2 vols. (Berlin: 1921–1923); Martin Noth (see note 15).

21. *Forschungen zur Judenfrage,* aus den Sitzungsberichten der Forschungsabteilung fuer Judenfragen des Reichsinstituts fuer Geschichte des neuen Deutschlands (Hamburg: 1936–1943). Cf. Fritz Werner, "Das Judentumsbild der Spaetjudentumsforschung im Dritten Reich," in *Kairos* 13 (1971) 161–194.

22. For a general picture of "Spaetjudentum" research, cf. Hermann Greive, *Theologie und Ideologie, Katholizismus und Judentum in Deutschland und Oesterreich, 1918–1935* (Heidelberg: Lambert Schneider, 1969); Johann Maier, "Kontinuitaet und Neuanfang," in *ibid.* and Josef Schreiner, eds., *Literatur und Religion des Fruehjudentums* (Wuerzburg: 1973) 1–18; Kurt Schubert, "Spaetjudentum," in *Lexikon fuer Theologie und Kirche* (Freiburg: Herder, ²1964); Clemens Thoma, "Spaetjudentum," in *Sacramentum Mundi,* 1969.

23. Cf. Josef Gutmann, ed., *The Synagogue, Studies in Archaeology and Architecture* (New York: Ktav, 1975).

24. Shemaryahu Talmon, "Particularity and Universality: A Jewish View," in *Jewish-Christian Dialogue* (Geneva: International Jewish Commission on Interreligious Consultations, and World Council of Churches, 1975) 36–42.

25. On the theological significance of the Samaritan schism, cf., e.g., Adrian Mikolasek, *Les Samaritains, Gardiens de la Loi contre les Prophètes* (Strasbourg: 1969), dissertation.

26. Cf. A. Cody, *A History of Old Testament Priesthood* (Rome: 1969); Clemens Thoma, "Religionsgeschichtliche und theologische Bedeutsamkeit der juedischen Hohenpriester von 175–37 v. Chr.," in *Bibel und Liturgie* 45 (1972) 4–22.

27. There is an immense literature on the confrontation with Hellenism during the time of the Maccabees and Hasmoneans. Commentaries on the Books of Daniel, Esther and 1 and 2 Maccabees must be counted among it. The most important Christian work in our time is Martin Hengel's *Judaism and Hellenism* (London, SCM, 1974). Of Jewish authors we mention Elias Bickerman, *The Maccabees: An Account of Their History from the Beginnings to the Fall of the House of the Hamoneans* (New York: Schocken, 1947); Victor Tcherikover, *Hellenistic Civilization and the Jews* (Philadelphia: JPS, 1959).

28. Cf. Elias Bickerman (see note 27); also Isaak Heinemann, "Wer veranlasste den Glaubenszwang der Makkabaeer?" in *Monatsschrift fuer Geschichte und Wissenschaft des Judentums* 82 (1938) 145–172.

29. Cf. P. Grimal, ed., *Hellenism and the Rise of Rome* (London: Weidenfeld and Nicolson, 1968) 200f.

30. On the whole problem of Jewish religious parties at the time of Jesus, cf., e.g., Guenther Baumbach, *Jesus von Nazareth im Lichte der juedischen Gruppenbildung* (Berlin: 1971); Martin Hengel (see note 27); Maier, Schreiner (see

note 22); Kurt Schubert, "Die juedischen Religionsparteien in neutestamentlicher Zeit," in *Stuttgarter Bibelstudien* 43 (1970).

31. Cf. Kurt Schubert, *Die Kultur der Juden, Israel im Altertum* (Frankfurt: 1970) esp. 145–158.

32. Isaak Heinemann, *Philons griechische und juedische Bildung* (Hildesheim: G. Olms, 1962, reprint) 574.

33. Cf. Martin Hengel (see note 27) 193f; also H. H. Ben-Sasson, ed., *History of the Jewish People* (Cambridge: Harvard University Press, 1977) I, 242f.

34. This supposition corresponds to historic reality if the Temple founded about 160 BCE by Onias IV in Leontopolis was actually considered the eschatological fulfillment of Is 19:19. In any case, the construction of a competing Temple in Jerusalem points toward the exclusivist awareness on the part of Leontopolis priests; cf. *Ant* 13, 62–72; *Bellum* 7, 431f.

35. The leading work on the Jewish insurgent movement is to this day Martin Hengel, *Die Zeloten,* Untersuchungen zur juedischen Freiheitsbewegung in der Zeit von Herodes I. bis 70 n. Chr. (Leiden: Brill, 1961; reprint with additions 1976).

36. Cf. Clemens Thoma, "Der Pharisaeismus," in Maier, Schreiner (see note 22) 254–272.

37. In Jewish apologetic literature since the Emancipation, it has been the prevailing tendency to ascribe to Judaism, in contrast to Christianity, juridical, sapiential and rational elements. Cf., e.g., Moses Mendelssohn, *Schriften zur Philosophie, Aesthetik und Apologetik* (Hildesheim: G. Olms, 1968, reprint); Max Wiener, *Juedische Religion im Zeitalter der Emanzipation* (Berlin: 1933). Cf. the critical discussion in Moshe Schwarcz, "Jewish Thought and General Culture" (Heb.) (Tel Aviv: 1976).

38. Gerhard von Rad, *Theologie des Alten Testaments* (Munich: Kaiser, 1964) 315 (the English edition, *Old Testament Theology.* New York: Harper and Row, 1965 does not contain this passage; cf. II, 301f, translator's note). Cf. Johann M. Schmidt, *Die juedische Apokalyptik,* die Geschichte ihrer Erforschung von den Anfaengen bis zu den Textfunden von Qumran (Neukirchen: Neukirchener Verlag, 1969) 312.

39. On the problem of religio-historical appreciation of apocalyptic, cf. *Journal for Theology and the Church* 6 (1969) 1–207, quote on p. 135; also Karlheinz Mueller, "Die Ansaetze der Apokalyptik," in Maier, Schreiner (see note 22) 31–42; quote on p. 31.

40. Important medieval Jewish apocalypses were edited by Yehuda Eben-Shmuel, *Midrashe Geulah* (Jerusalem: ²1968).

41. J. Lindblom, *Die Jesaja-Apokalypse* (Lund: 1938) cf. 102.

42. H. H. Rowley, *The Relevance of Apocalyptic* (New York: Harper and Row, n.d.) esp. 47–50, 112–122.

43. Josef Schreiner, *Alttestamentlich-Juedische Apokalyptik,* eine Einfuehrung (Munich: 1969) 73–110; *idem,* "Die apokalyptische Bewegung," in Maier, Schreiner (see note 22) 214–253.

44. Johann M. Schmidt (see note 38) 312f.

45. *Ibid.*, 308.

46. Walter Schmithals, *The Apocalyptic Movement: Introduction and Interpretation* (Nashville: Abingdon, 1975) 18.

47. Karlheinz Mueller suggests these terms in an article of great significance for apocalyptic scholarship (see note 39).

48. Cf. J. T. Milik, ed., *The Books of Enoch* (Oxford: Oxford University Press, 1976) 22–41.

49. On this problem cf. Johann Maier, *Geschichte der juedischen Religion von der Zeit Alexanders des Grossen bis zur Aufklaerung, mit einem Ausblick auf das 19./20. Jahrhundert* (Berlin: DeGruyter, 1972) 27, 37–42. A. Strobel, *Untersuchungen zum eschatologischen Verzoegerungsproblem* aufgrund der spaetjuedisch-urchristlichen Geschichte von Habakuk 2:2f (Leiden: Brill, 1961) has an interpretative history of this passage.

50. J. Vanderkam, "The Theophany of Enoch I, 3b–7:9," in *Vetus Testamentum* 23 (1973) 129–150.

51. Meinrad Limbeck, *Die Ordnung des Heils,* Untersuchungen zum Gesetzesverstaendnis des Fruehjudentums (Duesseldorf: 1971) 51.

52. Cf., e.g., Johann Maier, "Tempel und Tempelkult", in *ibid.,* Schreiner, (see note 22) 371–390.

53. Cf. esp. Peter von der Osten-Sacken, *Gott und Belial*, traditionsgeschichtliche Untersuchungen zum Dualismus in den Texten aus Qumran (Goettingen: 1969).

54. Hartmut Gese, "Anfang und Ende der Apokalyptik, dargestellt am Sacharjabuch," in *Zeitschrift fuer Theologie und Kirche* 70 (1973) 20–49, quote on p. 37; cf. also Benjamin Uffenheimer, "The Visions of Zechariah, from Prophecy to Apocalyptic" (Heb.) (Jerusalem: 1961).

55. Ernst Kaesemann, "Die Anfaenge christlicher Theologie," in *Zeitschrift fuer Theologie und Kirche* 57 (1960) 162–185; quote on p. 180.

56. Eduard Schweizer, "I Korinther 15, 20–28 als Zeugnis paulinischer Eschatologie und ihrer Verwandtschaft mit der Verkuendigung Jesu," in *Jesus und Paulus,* Festschrift W. G. Kuemmel (Goettingen: 1975) 301–314; quote on p. 314.

57. Cf. H. Desroche, "Messianismus," in *Religion in Geschichte und Gegenwart* IV, 1960, 895–900; Norman Cohn, *The Pursuit of the Millennium* (London: Paladin, 1970); Walter Nigg, *Das ewige Reich* (Zurich: Siebenstern, 1967).

58. From the wealth of secondary literature on the messiah problem, we mention the following which have particularly animated the discussion: Ferdinand Dexinger, "Die Entwicklung des juedisch-christlichen Messianismus," in *Bibel und Liturgie* 47 (1974) 5–31, 239–266; Hugo Gressmann, *Der Messias* (Goettingen: 1929); S. Mowinkel, *He That Cometh:* The Messianic Concept in the Old Testament and Later Judaism (New York: Abingdon Press, 1954); Josef Klausner, *The Messianic Idea in Israel:* From Its Beginning to the Completion of the Mishnah (New York: Macmillan, 1955); Kurt Hruby, "Die Messiaserwartung in der talmudischen Zeit, mit besonderer Beruecksichtigung des leidenden Messias," in *Judaica*

20 (1964) 6–22; Kurt Schubert, "Entwicklung der eschatologischen Naherwartung im Fruehjudentum," in *idem, Vom Messias zum Christus* (Vienna: 1964) 1–54; David Flusser, art. "Messiah," in *Encyclopaedia Judaica*; Shemaryahu Talmon, "Typen der Messiaserwartung um die Zeitenwende," in *Festschrift G. v. Rad,* H. W. Wolff, ed. (Munich: 1971) 571–588; Ulrich B. Mueller, *Messias und Menschensohn in juedischen Apokalypsen und in der Offenbarung des Johannes* (Guetersloh: 1972).

59. Josef Klausner (see note 58) 9.

60. Samson Raphael Hirsch, *Der Pentateuch, Numeri* (Frankfurt: 1920) 326.

61. David Flusser, art. "Messiah," in *Encyclopaedia Judaica* 11 (1971) 1407–1417; quote on 1410.

62. Cf. Ulrich B. Mueller (see note 58); also Johannes Theisohn, *Der auserwaehlte Richter,* Untersuchungen zum traditionsgeschichtlichen Ort der Menschensohngestalt der Bilderreden des Aethiopischen Henoch (Goettingen: 1975).

63. On recent discussions about the Son of Man, cf., e.g., Rudolf Pesch and Rudolf Schnackenburg, eds., *Jesus und der Menschensohn,* Festschrift for Anton Voegtle (Freiburg: 1975).

64. Johann Maier (see note 49) 69.

65. On the Sadducees, cf., e.g., Guenter Baumbach, "Der Sadduzaeische Konservativismus," in Maier, Schreiner (see note 22) 202–213; Hugo Mantel, "The Development of the Oral Law during the Second Temple Period", in *World History of the Jewish People* (Jerusalem: Masada, 1976) vol. 7, 41–64, 325–337.

66. Hugo Mantel, "The Sadducees and the Pharisees", in *World History* (see note 65) vol. 8, 99–123, 346–351; cf. also Clemens Thoma, "Der Pharisaeismus," in Maier, Schreiner (see note 22) 254–272.

67. Cf. esp. J. T. Milik (see note 48) 47–57.

68. Cf. Gustav Dalman, *The Words of Jesus* (Edinburgh: 1902); F. M. Abel, ed., "Les Livres des Maccabées," in *Etudes Bibliques* (1949); Hugo Mantel, *Studies in the History of the Sanhedrin* (Cambridge: Harvard University Press, 1961); Ben-Zion Lurie, ed., *Megillat Ta'anit* (Jerusalem: 1964).

69. Cf. Clemens Thoma, "Das juedische Volk-Gottes-Verstaendnis zur Zeit Jesu," in *idem, Judentum und Kirche: Volk Gottes* (Zurich: Benziger, 1974) 93–117.

70. Jacob Licht, *Megillot hasserakim mimmegillot midbar yehudah, serek habberakot* (Jerusalem: 1965) 16f.

71. Cf. Hans Bardtke, "Literaturbericht ueber Qumran, VI. Teil, I. Die Kriegsrolle 1QM," in *Theologische Rundschau,* Neue Folge 37 (1972) 97–120; Johannes Hempel, *Die Texte von Qumran in der heutigen Forschung* (Goettingen: 1962).

72. As far as it is possible to survey the immense Qumran literature, most scholars seem to be wary of placing the beginning of the Qumran sect before 140 BCE. Such a prominent scholar as Shemaryahu Talmon, on the other hand, earnestly pleads for a date as early 200–180 BCE; cf. "Motiv hammidbar bammikra ubassifrut Qumran," in *Memorial Volume for Josef Amorai* (Jerusalem: 1973) 73–107.

73. Cf. Johann Maier, *Die Texte vom Toten Meer* (Munich: 1960) vol. 2, 89–91.

74. *Ibid.*, 85: "Trito-Isaiah is the most voluminous and clearest document on the piety of the poor."

75. Cf. G. Klinzing, *Die Umdeutung des Kultus,* in der Qumrangemeinde und im Neuen Testament (Goettingen: 1971) 55; Johann Maier (see note 49) 53f.

76. Several *Spaetjudentum* scholars between World War I and II argue in this direction; e.g., H. Wilbrich, "Urkundenfaelschung in der hellenistisch-juedischen Literatur," in *Forschungen zur Religion und Literatur des Alten und Neuen Testaments* 38 (1924). Cf. Johann M. Schmidt (see note 38) for an evaluation of the anti-Jewish "Christian" outlook of that statement.

77. The work primarily in use is R. H. Charles, *The Apocrypha and Pseudepigrapha of the Old Testament* (Oxford: Oxford University Press, 1963).

78. Cf. Alfred Mertens, *Das Buch Daniel im Lichte der Texte vom Toten Meer* (Wuerzburg: 1971) 48.

79. Albert-Marie Dénis, *Introduction aux pseudépigraphes grecs de l'Ancien Testament* (Leiden: Brill, 1970).

80. Cf. *idem* and Yvonne Janssens, *Concordance latine du Liber Jubilaeorum sive Parva Genesis* (Louvain: 1973).

81. Other critical translations and interpretations are: A. Vaillant, *Le Livre des Sécrets d'Henoch, Texte Slave et Traduction Francaise* (Paris: 1952); Pierre Bogaert, *L'Apocalypse Syriaque de Baruch;* Matthias Delcor, *Le Testament d'Abraham;* Jean-Marc Rosenstiehl, ed. and trans. *L'Apocalypse d'Elie* (Paris: 1973); Hugo Odeberg, ed. and trans., *3 Enoch or the Hebrew Book of Enoch* (New York: Ktav, 1973, reprint).

82. Cf. J. T. Milik (see note 48).

83. Cf. J. P. M. van der Ploeg, A. S. van der Woude, eds., *Le Targum de Job de la Grotte XI de Qumran* (Leiden: Brill, 1971); Michael Sokoloff, *The Targum of Job from Qumran Cave XI* (Ramat-Gan: Bar Ilan University, 1974).

84. Cf. Norbert Brox, "Zum Problemstand in der Erforschung der altchristlichen Pseudepigraphie," in *Kairos* 15 (1973) 10–23; Martin Hengel, "Anonymitaet, Pseudepigraphie und 'Literarische Faelschung' in der juedisch-hellenistischen Literatur," in *Pseudepigrapha* (Geneva: Vandeuvres, 1972) I/VII, vol. 18 of the series, "Entretiens sur l'Antiquité Classique"; B. M. Metzger, "Literary Forgery and Canonical Pseudepigrapha," in *JBL* 91 (1972) 3–24; W. Speyer, *Die literarische Faelschung im heidnischen und christlichen Altertum,* ein Versuch ihrer Deutung (Munich: 1971).

85. Practically any Introduction to the New Testament argues this way.

86. The classical work is Emil Schuerer, *A History of the Jewish People in the Time of Jesus* (Edinburgh: Clark, 1885); cf. the revised edition of the first volume by Geza Vermès, Fergus Millar, eds. (Edinburgh: Clark, 1973). Similarly, Martin Hengel, *Hellenism* (see note 27); also Maier, Schreiner (see note 22).

87. This also applies to research concerning Jesus. Jewish authors as well as Christian scholars of Judaism who study the New Testament in early Jewish and

rabbinic contexts usually discern in it much more that is Jewish than do most Christian form-critical historians and tradition-history scholars. The specifically Christian elements do not then stand out so abruptly. Typical for this trend are, for example, Kurt Schubert, *Jesus im Lichte der Religionsgeschichte des Judentums* (Vienna: Herold Vlg., 1973); David Flusser, *Die rabbinischen Gleichnisse und der Gleichniserzaehler Jesus* (Bern: Herbert Lang, 1978).

88. Typical for the attitude of not allowing for any Christian interpolations is Marc Philonenko, *Les interpolations chrétiennes des Testaments des Douze Patriarches et les manuscrits de Qoumran* (Paris: 1960); cf., e.g., his almost complete negation of interpolations in Benj 9, 1–5; Lev 4, 1–4; 14, 1; 16, 3.

89. H. H. Rowley (see note 42) 36f.

90. Otto Ploeger, "Das Buch Daniel," in *Kommentar zum Alten Testament* (Guetersloh: 1965).

91. Significant passages are esp. in chapters 2, 7, and 12. On the whole book, cf. Ferdinand Dexinger, "Das Buch Daniel und seine Probleme," in *Stuttgarter Bibelstudien* 36 (1969).

92. An indication of such acceptance already in Qumran is contained in the designation of the author of the Book of Daniel as *nabi,* prophet. Cf. esp. Alfred Mertens (see note 78) *passim.*

93. Even in post-biblical times, Assidean literature continued to have considerable influence. Clear traditional links can be established to rabbinic, early medieval, *hekhalot* literature and to messianic-millenarian Jewish and Christian writings of the Middle Ages.

94. There are many such apocalyptic interspersions in the Books of Daniel and Enoch; cf. also, e.g., Test Dan 5, 1–8; Test Levi 4.

95. Cf. the Introduction to the critical text edition by Marc Philonenko, *Joseph et Aséneth* (Leiden: Brill, 1968) 1–123.

96. On Jewish determination since the time of the Maccabees to keep rigorously apart (amixia), which degenerated into anti-paganism, cf. Leonhardt Goppels, *Christentum und Judentum im ersten und zweiten Jahrhundert* (Guetersloh: Bertelsmann, 1954); also Martin Hengel, *Zeloten* (see note 35).

97. Cf. Matthias Delcor (see note 81) 127–131.

98. Cf. Martin Hengel, *Hellenism* (see note 27) 128–130; also Clemens Thoma, "Judentum und Hellenismus im Zeitalter Jesu," in *Bibel und Leben* 11 (1970) 151–159.

99. Cf. Willem C. van Unnik, "Eine merkwuerdige liturgische Aussage bei Josephus, Jos Ant 8, 111–113," in *Josephus Studien,* Festschrift Otto Michel, O. Betz *et al.,* eds. (Goettingen: Vandenhoek & Ruprecht, 1974) 362–369.

100. In early Jewish times apparently no limits were set against excessive speculation. Topics such as God, creation, the eschaton, etc., were very popular, causing originally well-defined notions to be shattered. Compare, e.g., the unambiguous "Israel as son of God" in Jub 1:24–26 and Philonic speculations on *logos* and the term mmr' (word) in Codex Neofiti 1. Not until early rabbinic times were precautions taken against dangerous argumentation (Mish *Hag* 2, 1).

101. Divergent opinions on the relationship between early Jewish writings and the New Testament are burdened with the respective Jewish and Christian traditions. We must also consider the different existential attitudes and practices of tradition and faith which represent a cardinal point in biblical hermeneutics. Cf. Antonius H. Gunneweg (see note 13) 121–145.

102. Recent research increasingly indicates that we must take into consideration a varied and highly developed theology at the time of Jesus in Judea, Samaria and Galilee. Probably already before 70 CE, a stronger theological influence was emanating from Palestine toward the diaspora, rather than vice versa.

103. Cf. Martin Hengel, "Zwischen Jesus und Paulus, die 'Hellenisten,' die 'Sieben' und Stephanus, Acts 6:1–16; 7:54–8:3," in *Zeitschrift fuer Theologie und Kirche* 72 (1975) 151–206, where this is described in connection with the conversion story of Stephanus.

104. Cf. Matthias Delcor (see note 81) 45, 171f. See Michael E. Stone, trans., *The Testament of Abraham* (Missoula: Scholars Press, 1972) 57.

105. Cf., e.g., Hans Bietenhard, *Caesarea, Origenes und die Juden* (Stuttgart: 1974).

106. Martin Hengel, "Zeloten und Sikarier," in *Josephus Studien* (see note 99) 175–196, quote on p. 175.

107. Emil Schuerer (see note 86) I, 57.

108. August Schlatter, *Die Theologie des Judentums nach dem Bericht des Josefus* (Guetersloh: 1932) Preface.

109. Even such great Jewish philosophers of religion as Hermann Cohen and Franz Rosenzweig warned of a Judaism that was too spiritualized and open, à la Philo. Cf. Franz Rosenzweig (see note 18) 341, 531; *idem, Briefe* (Berlin: Schocken, 1935) 591; also H. A. Wolfson, *Philo* (Cambridge: Harvard University Press, 1947); Yehoshua Amir, art. "Philo Judaeus," in *Encyclopaedia Judaica* 13 (1971) 409–415.

110. There is disagreement on the impact of the destruction of the Temple in 70 CE. G. Allon, "Studies in the Jewish History in the Times of the Second Temple" (Hebr.) (Tel Aviv: 1957), has an excellent evaluation.

111. Cf. Clemens Thoma, "Auswirkungen des juedischen Krieges gegen Rom auf das rabbinische Judentum," in *Biblische Zeitschrift* 12 (1968) 30–54, 186–210; *idem,* "Das Amt im Judentum," in *Theologische Realenzyklopaedie* 2 (1978) 504–509.

112. I. Epstein, ed. *The Babylonian Talmud* (London: Soncino, 1935–1948); C. G. Montefiore and H. Loewe, eds., *A Rabbinic Anthology* (New York: Schocken, 1974); Adin Steinsaltz, ed., *The Essential Talmud* (New York: Basic Books, 1976); M. Schwab, ed., *Le Talmud de Jérusalem* (Paris: Maisonneuve, 1932, reprint).

113. Cf. Will Durant, *The Age of Faith,* The Story of Civilization (New York: Simon and Schuster, 1950) IV 353.

114. Herbert Danby, trans., *The Mishnah* (Oxford: Oxford University Press, 1954); Philip Blackman, *Mishnayoth* (New York: Judaica, 1965); M. Mielziner, *In-*

troduction to the Talmud (New York: 1968); A. Sammter and D. Hoffman, eds., *Mishnayot: Die sechs Ordnungen der Mischna* (Basle: Goldschmidt, 1968, reprint).

115. H. Freedman and Maurice Simon, eds. *The Midrash* (London: Soncino, 1961); Wm. G. Braude, trans., *The Midrash on Psalms* (New Haven: Yale University Press, 1959); *idem, Pesikta Rabbati* (New Haven: Yale University Press, 1968); Melvin J. Glatt, ed., *Avot, The Ethics of the Fathers* (New York: Burning Bush Press, 1971); Nahum N. Glatzer, ed. *Hammer on the Rock: A Midrash Reader* (New York: Schocken, 1962); H. S. Horovitz, A. Rabin eds., *Mechilta d'Rabbi Ishmael* (Jerusalem: Bamberger and Wahrmann, 1960, reprint); Jacob Z. Lauterbach, trans., *Mekilta de'Rabbi Ishmael* (Philadelphia: JPS, 1976, reprint); B. Mandelbaum, *Pesikta de Rav Kahana* (Heb. & Eng.) (New York: JTSA, 1962); M. Friedman, *Pesikta Rabbati* (Tel Aviv, 1962, reprint). As secondary literature, cf. H. L. Strack *Introduction to the Talmud and Midrash* (Philadelphia: JPS, 1931); A. G. Wright, "The Literary Genre Midrash," in *CBQ* 28 (1966) 105–138, 417–457. Cf. also John T. Townsend, "Rabbinic Sources," in *The Study of Judaism, Bibliographical Essays* (New York: Ktav/Anti-Defamation League of B'nai B'rith, 1972) 35–80; and Y. H. Yerushalmi, ed., *Bibliographical Essays in Medieval Jewish Studies* (New York: Ktav, 1976) vol. II (The Study of Judaism) 333–392; for excellent surveys of rabbinic literature and its availability.

116. J. M. Van der Ploeg (see note 83); Michael Sokoloff (see note 83).

117. Alejandro Diez Macho, ed., *Neophyti 1, Targum Palestinense MS de la Bibliotheca Vaticana* (Madrid/Barcelona: 1968–1974).

118. Alexander Sperber, ed., *The Bible in Aramaic* (Leiden: Brill, 1959–1973); Paul Kahle, *Masoreten des Westens* (Stuttgart: 1930); Roger Le Déaut, ed., *Targum des Chroniques* (Rome: Analecta Biblica, 1971); etc.

119. Maier (see note 49); cf. Klaus Koch, "Messias und Suendenvergebung in Jes 53-Targum, ein Beitrag zu der Praxis der aramaeischen Bibeluebersetzung," *Journal of the Study of Judaism in the Persian Hellenistic and Roman Period* 3 (1972) 117–128.

120. Cf. Matthew Black, *An Aramaic Approach to the Gospels and Acts* (Oxford: Clarendon Press, 1946) 151; Gustav Dalman (see note 68).

121. S. Hurwitz, ed., *Machsor Vitry nach der Oxforder HS* (Berlin, 1889); J. Mueller, ed., *Masechet Sopherim* (Leipzig, 1878).

122. Cf. Johann Maier, "Bedeutung und Erforschung der Kairoer 'Geniza,'" in *Jahrbuch fuer Antike und Christentum* 13 (1970) 48–61.

123. Cf. Ludwig Blau, *Das altjuedische Zauberwesen* (Berlin: ^{2}1914); L. Goldschmidt, ed., *Sepher Yezirah* (Darmstadt: 1969, reprint); Yehuda Eben-Shmuel (see note 40); M. Margalioth, ed., *Sepher Ha-Rasim* (Jerusalem: 1966); Jens H. Niggemeyer, *Beschwoerungsformeln aus dem 'Buch der Geheimnisse'* (Hildesheim: 1975).

124. Joshua Trachtenberg, *The Devil and the Jews* (New Haven: Yale University Press, 1943) 175.

125. Julius Wellhausen, *Prolegomena zur Geschichte Israels* (1894) 250.

126. On Talmudic polemics against Jesus and criticism of Christianity, cf. Kurt Hruby, *Die Stellung der juedischen Gesetzeslehrer zur werdenden Kirche* (Zurich: 1971); Johann Maier, *Jesus im Talmud* (Darmstadt: 1977); Jacob Z. Lauterbach, *Rabbinic Essays* (Cincinnati: HUC Press, 1951) 473–570.

127. Julius Guttmann, *Philosophies of Judaism,* David W. Silverman, trans. (Garden City: Doubleday, 1966) 49.

128. *Ibid.,* 53.

129. Abraham Geiger, "Erbsuende und Versoehnungstod," in *Juedische Zeitschrift f. Wissenschaft und Leben* 10 (1872) 166–171, gives a good survey of these positions.

130. Martin Buber's interpretation of Hasidism was very important for this rediscovery and re-evaluation. Gershom Scholem's most significant book is *Major Trends in Jewish Mysticism* (Jerusalem: Schocken, 1941); he has also greatly added to scholarship in Judaica, history and theology.

131. Leaving aside specifically Christian nuances of spirituality, this paraphrase approximately corresponds to the exposition by Josef Sudbrack, "Spirituality," in *Sacramentum Mundi, Encyclopedia of Theology,* 1623–1639.

132. Klaus Berger, "Abraham im Fruehjudentum und im Neuen Testament," in *Theologische Realenzyklopaedie* (1977) I 372–382; Johann Maier (see note 49) 118–121; Rolf P. Schmidt, *Aqedat Jishaq* (Cologne: 1975), dissertation; *idem,* "Abraham im Judentum," in *Theologische Realenzyklopaedie* (1977) I 382–385; Robert J. Daly, "The Soteriological Significance of the Sacrifice of Isaac," in *CBQ* 39 (1977) 45–75.

133. Cf. J. van Goudoever, *Biblical Calendars* (Leiden: 1961) esp. 68, on Jub 18:17–19, and on other early Jewish references to the interrelation between Passover and remembrance of Abraham-Isaac.

134. The Aramaic text is in A. Diez Macho (see note 117) II 76–79. The text is also available in Roger Le Déaut, *La Nuit Pascale* (Rome, 1963) 64. This work also represents the first extensive treatise on the history of Targumic interpretation of Gen 22 and Ex 12:42, in connection with the discovery and edition of CN 1.

135. Cf., e.g., Herbert Haag, "Vom alten zum neuen Pascha," in *Stuttgarter Bibelstudien* 1971, esp. 114–117 with regard to Ex 12:14, 42 and Mish *Pes* 10:5.

136. Cf. Moshe David Gross, *Osar Haaggadah* (Jerusalem: 1961) I 333–338.

137. On the possible connection between the *akedah* and the New Testament account of Jesus' baptism, cf. Fritzleo Lentzen-Deis, "Die Taufe Jesu nach den Synoptikern," in *Frankfurter Theologische Studien* (1970).

138. Cf. esp. Roger Le Déaut (see note 134) 66–71 on the Old Testament-New Testament-Targum context of *zkr.*

139. Cf. David Flusser, "Das juedische Martyrium im Zeitalter des Zweiten Tempels und die Christologie," in *Freiburger Rundbrief* 25 (1973) 187–194.

140. Thus, e.g., Jacob Z. Lauterbach (see note 126).

141. Cf. esp. Nahum N. Glatzer, *Untersuchungen zur Geschichtslehre der Tannaiten* (Berlin: Schocken, 1933); Johann Maier (see note 49); R. Meyer, "Tra-

dition und Neuschoepfung im antiken Judentum, dargestellt an der Geschichte des Pharisaeismus," in *Saechsische Akademie der Wissenschaften* 110 (1965); Peter Schaefer, "Zur Geschichtsauffassung des rabbinischen Judentums," in *Journal for the Study of Judaism in the Persian, Hellenistic and Roman Period* 6 (1975) 167–188.

142. Travers R. Herford, *The Pharisees* (Boston: Beacon Press, 1962) 83.

143. Jacob J. Katz, *Exclusiveness and Tolerance* (New York: 1962) 46.

144. David Flusser, *Jesus,* Ronald Walls, trans. (New York: Herder, 1969) 44f.

145. Respective references are in Moshe David Gross (see note 136) II 528–532, 670–679; III 1297f. Significant passages are contained in *Avot* 1:3; TB *Ket* 96a; 11b; *Sot* 22a.

146. August Schlatter, *Wie sprach Josephus von Gott?* (Guetersloh: 1910) 13.

147. H. L. Strack, Paul Billerbeck (see note 20) II 241.

148. H. Schoenweiss, "Gebet," in *Begriffslexikon zum Neuen Testament* I 427.

149. Great credit is due Joseph Heinemann, *Prayer in the Talmud* (Berlin: De Gruyter, 1977), for the form-critical and tradition-history study of the oldest Jewish synagogue prayers. Cf. also Jakob J. Petuchowski, *Contributions to the Scientific Study of Jewish Liturgy* (New York: Ktav, 1970); Joseph Heinemann, Jakob J. Petuchowski, *Literature of the Synagogue* (New York: Behrman, 1975).

150. Cf. David Flusser, "Sanktus und Gloria" (see note 99) 129–152; Johann Maier, "Serienbildung und 'numinoser' Eindruckseffekt in den poetischen Stuecken der Hekhalot-Literatur," in *Semitics* 3 (1973) 36–66.

151. Cf. S. S. Cohon, "Authority in Judaism," in *HUCA* 11 (1936) 595–646.

152. Julius Wellhausen, *Einleitung in die drei ersten Evangelien* (Berlin: 1905) 113.

153. Joseph Klausner, *Jesus of Nazareth* (New York: Macmillan, 1925) 363.

154. Rudolf Bultmann, *Das Urchristentum im Rahmen der antiken Religionen* (Zurich: ³1963) 67.

155. Hans Conzelmann, *Grundriss der Theologie des Neuen Testamentes* (Munich: ²1967) 145.

156. Siegfried Schulz, "Der historische Jesus, Bilanz der Fragen und Loesungen," in *Jesus Christus in Historie und Theologie,* Georg Strecker, ed. (Tuebingen: 1975) 3–25; quote on p. 18.

157. Franz Mussner, "Christliche Indentitaet in der Sicht des Neuen Testaments," in *Internationale katholische Zeitschrift* 5 (1976) 421–431; quote on p. 422.

158. Johann Maier, "Twisting Paths of Reception: On Modern Jewish Research about Jesus," in *Herder Correspondence* 30 (1976) 313–319, critically discusses the attitude of Jewish scholars.

159. On modern Jewish Jesus literature, cf., e.g., D. R. Catchpole, *A Study in the Gospels and Jewish Historiography from 1770 to the Present Day* (Leiden: Brill, 1971); Ernst L. Ehrlich, "Die Evangelien in juedischer Sicht," in *Freiburger Rund-*

brief 22 (1970) 61–68; Erich Graesser, "Motive und Methoden der neueren Jesus-Literatur," in *Evangelische Theologie* 18 (1973) 3–45; Goesta Lindeskog (see note 3); Morris Goldstein, *Jesus in the Jewish Tradition* (New York: Macmillan, 1950); Thomas D. Walker, *Jewish Views of Jesus* (London: Allen & Unwin, 1930); as well as the Jesus books by, e.g., the following authors: Robert Aron, David Flusser, Jules Isaac, Joseph Klausner, Samuel Sandmel, Ernest R. Trattner, Paul Winter, and Solomon Zeitlin.

160. David Flusser (see note 144) 10.

161. Martin Buber (see note 16).

162. *Idem, Briefwechsel aus sieben Jahrzehnten* (Heidelberg: 1975) III 197–200.

163. David Flusser, "In memoriam Samuel Hugo Bergmann," in *Freiburger Rundbrief* 27 (1975) 3. Rabbinic illustrations of *emunah* as equal to faith (*fides quae* and *fides qua*) are, e.g., *MekY* on Ex 15:1; CN 1 on Gn 4:7f; *BerR* 26:14.

163a. David Flusser (see note 163).

164. Cf. Jacob Jervell, *Imago Dei,* Gn 1:26f im Spaetjudentum, in der Gnosis und in den paulinischen Briefen (Goettingen: 1960); *idem,* "Imagines und Imago Dei, aus der Genesis-Exegese des Josephus," in O. Betz *et al.,* eds. *Josephus Studien* 197–204.

165. Cf. Johann Maier (see note 49) 139–151; Jacob J. Petuchowski, in Michael Brocke, Jakob J. Petuchowski, eds., *Das Vaterunser, Gemeinsames im Beten von Juden und Christen* (Freiburg: Herder, 1974) 90–101 (not contained in English version of the book); Peter Schaefer, "Die sogenannte Synode von Jabne, zur Trennung von Juden und Christen im 1.–2. Jh.n.Chr.," in *Judaica* 31 (1975) 54–64, 116–124; Guenter Stemberg, "Die sogen. Synode von Jabne und das fruehe Christentum," in *Kairos* 19 (1977) 14–21.

166. David Flusser, "The Crucified One and the Jews," in *Immanuel* 7 (1977) 25–37; quote on p. 28.

166a. Cf. S. G. F. Brandon, *Jesus and the Zealots: A Study of the Political Factor in Primitive Christianity* (Manchester: University Press, 1967).

167. Ulrich Luck, "Das Weltverstaendnis in der juedischen Apokalyptik, dargestellt am aethiopischen Henoch und am 4. Esra," in *Zeitschrift fuer Theologie und Kirche* 73 (1976) 283–305.

168. Eduard Schweizer (see note 56) 303.

169. In a coarse way and without any differentiation, this was done by H. A. Zwergel, "Die Bedeutung von Leben und Tod Jesu von Nazaret in tiefenpsychologischer Sicht," in R. Pesch, H. A. Zwergl, *Kontinuitaet Jesu* (Freiburg: 1974). No less than five times, the author insists that Jesus dissociated himself from the pathological religious coercions of his time by not submitting to the authority of the God of the Torah (or Torah ritual).

170. The uneasiness experienced by some Jewish personalities that certain abuses incriminated by Jesus might lead to a national and religious catastrophe finds expression in some extra-New Testament writings of the time. Cf. many pas-

sages in Josephus' works, esp. *Ant* 20:180f; *Bellum* 1:12; 5:444; 6:25. Also cf. Talmudic references, e.g., TB *Pes* 57a; *Ar* 11b; *MekY* on Ex 19:1; *EkhaR* on Lam 1:1.

171. The literature on the trial, condemnation and crucifixion of Jesus is immense. Cf., e.g., Paul Winter, *On the Trial of Jesus* (Berlin: De Gruyter, 1974); Haim H. Cohn, "Reflections on the Trial and Death of Jesus," in *Israel Law Review* (1967) 279–332; Solomon Zeitlin, *Who Crucified Jesus?* (New York: Bloch, 1964); see also note 159.

172. Similarly, Ellis Rivkin, "The Parting of the Ways," in Lily Edelman, ed., *Face to Face, A Primer in Dialogue* (Washington, D.C.: Jewish Heritage/Anti-Defamation League of B'nai B'rith, 1967) 33–41. Cf. also David Daube, *Collaboration with Tyranny in Rabbinic Law* (London: Oxford University Press, 1965).

173. Cf. Rolf-Peter Schmidt, "Abraham im Judentum," in *Theologische Real-enzyklopaedie* I 382–385.

174. Cf. Ludwig Berg, *Das theologische Menschenbild*, Entwurf-Ethos (Cologne: 1969) 111; Michael Brocke, "Nachahmung Gottes im Judentum," in A. Falaturil *et al.*, eds., *Drei Wege zu dem einen Gott* (Freiburg: Herder, 1976) 75–102.

175. Bernard Dupuy is almost too close to such a view in "What Meaning Has the Fact That Jesus was Jewish for a Christian?" in *Concilium* (1974), new series, vol. 8, no. 10, 73–79.

176. David Flusser, in Franz v. Hammerstein, *Von Vorurteilen zum Verstaendnis*, Dokumente zum juedisch-christlichen Dialog (Frankfurt: 1976) 83.

177. Shalom Ben Chorin, *Bruder Jesus* (Munich: 1967) 12.

178. Relevant proofs are in Ephraim E. Urbach, *The Sages, Their Concepts and Beliefs* (Jerusalem: Hebrew University Press, 1975); Louis Jacobs (see note 10) 54f; Johann Maier (see note 49) 160f.

179. Proofs and explanations are in Louis Jacobs (see note 10) 85–89, 318f; cf. also Hans Joachim Schoeps, *Juedisch-christliches Religionsgespraech in 19 Jahrhunderten* (Frankfurt: 1949) 24. The term *shittuf* came into use by tosaphists of the early Middle Ages, following certain misinterpretations of TB *San* 63b.

180. Hermann Cohen (see note 17) 239.

181. Jacob Katz (see note 143) 162–164; Louis Jacobs (see note 10) 318f; cf. also Shalom Ben-Chorin, *Juedischer Glaube*, Strukturen einer Theologie anhand des Maimonidischen Credo (Tuebingen: Mohr 1975) 120–125; Franz Rosenzweig, *The Star of Redemption*, William W. Hallo, trans. (New York: Holt, Rinehart & Winston, 1971) 398ff.

182. Cf. Goesta Lindeskog (see note 3) 17, 79–84.

183. Thus Johannes Hoekendijk in 1973; cf. Eva Fleischner (see note 13) 133.

184. Cf. Hans Joachim Schoeps (see note 179) 33.

185. Cf. André Néher, *L'Essence du Prophétisme* (Paris: 1972) 95, 99, 106, 111, 124, 221. Néher is strongly influenced by Abraham J. Heschel. Cf. also Louis Jacobs (see note 10) 78–80.

186. Cf. Arnold M. Goldberg, *Untersuchungen ueber die Vorstellung von der Schekhinah in der fruehen rabbinischen Literatur* (Berlin: 1969); Peter Schaefer,

Die Vorstellung vom heiligen Geist in der rabbinischen Literatur (Munich: Koesel, 1972); *idem, Rivalitaet zwischen Engeln und Menschen* (Berlin: DeGruyter 1975).

187. Cf. Peter Schaefer, *Rivalitaet* (see note 186) 233.

188. Particularly according to the Lurianic Kabbalah which, in contrast to older versions (up to Moses Cordovero, 1522–1570), conceived of the emanation of divine power in the context of an historical and eschatological process. It is impossible to discuss Jewish mysticism in all its variations here. Cf. Gershom Scholem (see note 130); *idem, On the Kabbalah and Its Symbolism* (New York: Schocken, 1965); Renée de Tryon-Montalembert and Kurt Hruby, *La Cabbale et la Tradition Judaique* (Paris: 1974).

189. Cf. Louis Jacobs (see note 10) 53, 85, 103–110; Francois Secret, *Le Zôhar chez les Cabbalistes Chrétiens de la Renaissance* (Paris: 1958).

190. Martin Buber, *On Judaism,* Nahum N. Glatzer, ed. (New York: Schocken, 1967) 91.

191. Goesta Lindeskog (see note 3) 78–84, contains many Jewish opinions against the possibility of Incarnation.

192. Michael Wyschogrod, "Warum war und ist Karl Barths Theologie fuer einen juedischen Theologen von Interesse?" in *Evangelische Theologie* 34 (1974) 222–236; quote on p. 226.

193. Cf. F. J. Schierse, "Die neutestamentliche Trinitaetsoffenbarung," in *Mysterium Salutis* (1976) II 85–131.

194. Oscar Cullmann, *The Christology of the New Testament* (London: SCM, 1963) 293.

195. Cf. A. Rahlfs, *Septuaginta I* (Stuttgart: 1935) 471–489; M. de Jonge, "The Use of the Word 'Anointed' in the Time of Jesus," in *Novum Testamentum* 8 (1966) 132–148.

196. The Babylonian and Palestinian recensions of the Shemoneh Esreh are contained, e.g., in the so-called Giessen *Mischna,* G. Beer, O. Holtzmann, eds. (Giessen & Berlin: Toepelmann, 1912) I 11–27.

197. Cf. Eugen Rosenstock-Huessey and Franz Rosenzweig, *Judaism Despite Christianity* (New York: Schocken, 1971) 113.

198. Cf. note 186; also, Peter Kuhn, *Gottes Selbsterniedrigung in der Theologie der Rabbinen* (Munich: 1968).

199. Cf., e.g., Samuel Abraham Adler, "Aspaklaria," in *Encyclopedia of Jewish Thought* (Heb.) (Jerusalem: 1975) esp. 459–468.

200. Elie Wiesel, *Night* (New York: Hill & Wang, 1960) 71.

201. Juergen Moltmann, *The Experiment Hope,* M. Douglas Meeks, ed. and trans. (Philadelphia: Fortress Press, 1975) 75.

202. David Flusser, "To What Extent Is Jesus a Question for the Jews?" in *Concilium* (1974), new series vol. 5, no. 10, 68–73; quote on p. 71.

203. Franz Mussner (see note 157) 425.

204. There is an immense literature on medieval Judaism. Cf. Salo W. Baron, H. H. Ben-Sasson, Simon Dubnow, Heinrich Graetz. Also, Jacob Katz (see note

143); *idem, Tradition and Crisis* (Glencoe, Ill.: 1961). There is a good survey in Y. H. Yerushalmi, ed., *Bibliographical Essays in Medieval Jewish Studies* (New York: Ktav 1976) vol II.

205. On the development and extent of Jewish-Christian division, cf., e.g., Shlomo Pines, *The Jewish Christians in the Early Centuries of Christianity According to a New Source* (Jerusalem: 1966); Jakob J. Petuchowski (see note 165); S. Safrai, M. Stern, eds., *The Jewish People in the First Century* (Assen: Van Gorcum, 1974); James Parkes, *The Conflict of the Church and the Synagogue* (Philadelphia: JPS, 1961); Hans Joachim Schoeps, *The Jewish-Christian Argument: History of Theologies in Conflict* (New York: Holt, Rinehart & Winston, 1963).

206. What could be the meaning of re-Judaizing, since the founder of Christianity was a Jew? Ethelbert Stauffer, "Wie die christliche Kirche entstand," in *Christ und Welt* 17 (1964), made "re-Judaizing" almost a journalistic term. Cf. on the whole question Hans Joachim Schoeps, *Das Judenchristentum* (Bern: 1964).

207. Hans Joachim Schoeps, "Die Tempelzerstoerung des Jahres 70 in der juedischen Religionsgeschichte, Ursachen, Folgen, Ueberwindung," in *Coniectanea Neotestamentica* 6 (1942) 1–15; quote on p. 8. Cf. Ellis Rivkin, *The Shaping of Jewish History* (New York: Scribner, 1971) chapter II.

208. Cf. S. G. F. Brandon, *The Fall of Jerusalem and the Christian Church* (London: Allenson, 1957) esp. p. 52; Heinrich Kraft, "Die Offenbarung des Johannes," in *Handbuch zum Neuen Testament* (Tuebingen: 1974) 153.

209. Dieter Zeller, *Juden und Heiden in der Mission des Paulus,* Studien zum Roemerbrief (Stuttgart: 1973) 58, 62.

210. Ismar Elbogen, *Der Juedische Gottesdienst in seiner geschichtlichen Entwicklung* (Darmstadt: 1967, reprint) 36–38.

211. Joseph Heinemann (see note 149) 141f.

212. This text was published by Solomon Schechter in *JQR* 10 (1898) 654–659.

213. This is still maintained by Jakob J. Petuchowski (see note 165) 98f.

214. The Babylonian version is given by Gustav Dalman (see note 68) 303; also in the "Giessen Mischna" (cf. note 196) I 21, according to the Siddur Yemen I.

215. In addition to the works given in note 205, cf. M. Freimann, "Die Wortfuehrer des Judentums in den aeltesten Kontroversen zwischen Juden und Christen," in *Monatsschrift fuer Geschichte und Wissenschaft des Judentums* 56 (1912) 49–64, 164–180; Dirk van Damme, "Gottesvolk und Gottes Reich in der christlichen Antike," in Clemens Thoma (see note 69) 157–168; Nicholas De Lange, *Origen and the Jews* (Cambridge: Cambridge University Press, 1976).

215a. Michael B. McGarry, *Christology after Auschwitz* (New York: Paulist Press, 1977) contains a good survey of such Christological beginnings.

216. Jules Isaac, *Jesus and Israel,* S. Gran, trans. (New York: Holt, Rinehart & Winston, 1971) 463.

217. Cf. the following as characteristic for contemporary Holocaust theology: Eliezer Berkovits, *Faith after the Holocaust* (New York: Ktav, 1973); A. Roy Eck-

ardt, *Your People, My People* (New York: Quadrangle, 1974); Emil L. Fackenheim, *God's Presence in History* (New York: Harper & Row, 1972); Eva Fleischner, ed. (see note 13); Franklin H. Littell, *The Crucifixion of the Jews* (New York: Harper & Row, 1975); Richard L. Rubenstein, *After Auschwitz* (New York: Bobbs-Merrill, 1966); Rosemary R. Ruether, *Faith and Fratricide* (New York: Seabury Press, 1974); Hans O. Tiefel, "Holocaust Interpretations and Religious Assumptions," in *Judaism* 25 (1976) 135–149.

218. Rosemary R. Ruether, in Fleischner, ed. (see note 13) 79.

219. *Idem,* (see note 217) 28.

220. *Idem,* in Fleischner, ed. (see note 13) 89. The thesis that modern fascist as well as Russian and Arab antisemitism derives directly from Christian antisemitism is maintained also by those authors who examine liberal and Christian-socialist antisemitism of the nineteenth and twentieth centuries; e.g. Isaak Hellwing, *Der konfessionelle Antisemitismus im 19. Jahrhundert in Oesterreich* (Vienna: Herder: 1972).

221. Franklin H. Littell (see note 217) 25f.

222. *Ibid.,* 41.

223. Cf., e.g., Nicholas De Lange, Clemens Thoma, "Begriff des Antisemitismus, vorchristlicher Antisemitismus," in *Theologische Realenzyklopaedie* II, 1978.

224. Walter Holsten, "Antisemitismus," in *Religion in Geschichte und Gegenwart* ³I (1957) 456–459; quote on p. 456.

225. James Parkes, *Antisemitism* (London: Vallentine-Mitchell, 1969) 62.

226. Franz Mussner, "Ganz Israel wird gerettet werden (Rom 11:26)," in *Kairos* 18 (1976) 241–255; Markus Barth *et al., Paulus Apostat oder Apostel?* juedische und christliche Antworten (Regensburg: 1977); John M. Oesterreicher (see note 1) 46.

227. Cf., e.g., the Jewish Palestinian traditions on Gen 16 and 21, in Gal 4:22–5:1, and the Targum tradition as evident in CN 1. The Targumist uses a typology that began already with the Tanakh, of Abraham/Sarah, Sarah/Hagar, Isaac/Israel, to represent the people of Israel and to bring it into relief against the nations of the world. Paul does something similar in Gal 4. He contrasts the followers of Christ with non-Christians but relaxes and opens the typology more than the Targumist does. On the possibly anti-Jewish character of certain New Testament passages, cf. Willehad P. Eckert *et al.,* eds., *Antijudaismus im Neuen Testament?* (Munich: 1967).

228. On the history of antisemitism, cf. Edward H. Flannery, *The Anguish of the Jews* (New York: Macmillan, 1965); also Clemens Thoma (see note 223); Leon Poliakov, *History of Antisemitism* (New York: Vanguard, 1965).

229. John M. Oesterreicher, *Auschwitz, the Christian and the Council* (Montreal: Palm, 1965).

230. Cf. Irving Greenberg, in Eva Fleischner, ed. (see note 13) 7–56.

231. Cf. Gregory Baum, in *ibid.* 113–128.

232. Cf. the conciliatory statement by the Jewish historian Yosef H. Yerushalmi, in *ibid.* 97–107.

233. Franklin H. Littell (see note 217) 41, 48, 49, 50, 67.

234. Vitezlav Gardavski, *God Is Not Yet Dead* (London: Penguin, 1973) 42f.

235. Cf. Johann Maier, "Jude und Judentum, Bezeichnungen und Selbstbezeichnungen im Wandel der Zeiten," in *Lebendiges Zeugnis* 32 (1977) 52–63.

236. Heinrich Graetz, "The Significance of Judaism for the Present and Future," in *JQR* 1 (1889); cf. Louis Jacobs (see note 10) 3ff.

237. Moses Mendelssohn (1725–1805), Solomon Maimon (1754–1800), Naftali Herz Wessely (1725–1805), Abraham Geiger (1810–1874), and Hermann Cohen (1842–1918) were prominent personalities who represented this view, each in his own way. Though they were exponents of the Emancipation, they did not in the least sympathize with Jewish-Christian syncretism.

238. Leo Baeck, *This People Israel: The Meaning of Jewish Existence,* Albert H. Friedlander, trans. (Philadelphia: JPS, 1965) 22.

239. *Ibid.*

240. Nahum N. Glatzer, *Franz Rosenzweig, His Life and Thought* (New York: Schocken, 1953) 203.

241. Cf. Jean Halperin, ed., *Le Shabbat dans la Conscience Juive,* Données et Textes (Paris: 1975); Clemens Thoma, "Die gegenwaertige und kommende Herrschaft Gottes als fundamentales juedisches Anliegen im Zeitalter Jesu," in *idem, Zukunft in der Gegenwart* (Bern: Herbert Lang, 1976) 57–77, esp. 59–62.

242. Moses Hess, *Rome and Jerusalem,* Maurice J. Bloom, trans. (New York: Philosophical Library, 1958) 61f; on Moses Hess, cf. Edmund Silberner, *Moses Hess* (Leiden: 1966).

243. On the problematics of Jewish theological concepts and their content, cf. Hermann Cohen (see note 17) 107; Louis Jacobs, *Principles of the Jewish Faith* (New York: Basic Books, 1964); Solomon Schechter, *Studies in Judaism* (Philadelphia: JPS, 1945, reprint).

244. A. H. Silver, *A History of Messianic Speculation in Israel* (Boston: 1959); Gershom Scholem, *The Messianic Idea in Judaism* (New York: Schocken, 1971) 1–36; Clemens Thoma, "Glaubenspraxis aus Erfahrung," in *Lebendiges Zeugnis* 32 (1977) 98–108.

245. Cf. Peter Schaefer, "Die messianischen Hoffnungen des rabbinischen Judentums zwischen Naherwartung und religioesem Pragmatismus," in Clemens Thoma, *Zukunft* (see note 241) 95–126, esp. 100f.

246. On the Jewish Palestinian theology of the third century CE, cf. Nahum N. Glatzer, *Anfaenge des Judentums* (Guetersloh: Bertelsmann 1966) 89–95; *idem, Hillel the Elder: The Emergence of Classical Judaism* (New York: Schocken, 1956); *idem,* "The Attitude to Rome in the Amoraic Period," in *Proceedings of the Sixth World Congress of Jewish Studies* (Jerusalem: 1975) II 9–19.

247. Peter Schaefer, *Heiliger Geist* (see note 186) 94f. But cf. also Ephraim E. Urbach (see note 178) III 37f.

248. Cf. Hermann Greive, *Studien zum juedischen Neuplatonismus,* die Religionsphilosophie des Abraham ibn Esra (Berlin: De Gruyter, 1973); *idem,* "Die

Maimonidische Kontroverse und die Auseinandersetzungen in der lateinischen Scholastik," in *Miscellanea Medievalia* 10 (1976) 170–180; Maier (see note 49) 265–307.

249. Herbert Haag, *Teufelsglaube* (Tuebingen: Katzmann, 1974); Peter Schaefer, *Rivalitaet* (see note 186). Cf. Bernard J. Bamberger, *Fallen Angels* (Philadelphia: JPS, 1952).

249a. Among the abundant literature, cf. esp. B. Alfrink, "L'Idée de résurrection d'après Daniel 12:2.3," in *Biblica* 40 (1959) 335–371; Matthias Delcor, *Le Livre de Daniel* (Paris: 1971); Guenter Stemberger, "Das Problem der Auferstehung im Alten Testament," in *Kairos* 14 (1972) 272–290.

250. Louis Jacobs, *Theology* (see note 10), and *Principles* (see note 243).

251. The Thirteen Principles of Faith are belief in the existence of God, in God's unity, in God's corporeality, in God's eternity, that God alone is to be worshiped, in prophecy, in Moses as the greatest of the prophets, that the Torah was given by God to Moses, that the Torah is immutable, that God knows the thoughts and deeds of men, that God rewards and punishes, in the advent of the Messiah, in the resurrection of the dead; cf. Louis Jacobs, *Principles* (see note 243) 14.

252. Hermann Greive, "Kontroverse" (see note 248) 170.

253. Franz Rosenzweig (see note 18) 31.

254. Cf. Helga Croner (see note 7) 1.

255. John M. Oesterreicher, "Unter dem Bogen des einen Bundes, das Volk Gottes: seine Zweigestalt und Einheit," in Clemens Thoma (see note 69) 27–69, esp. 63–69. Cf. also Manfred Vogel, "Covenant and the Interreligious Encounter," in Helga Croner, Leon Klenicki, eds., *Issues in the Jewish-Christian Dialogue: Jewish Perspectives on Covenant, Mission and Witness* (New York: Paulist Press, 1979).

256. Cf. Henry Siegman, "Ten Years of Catholic-Jewish Relations: A Reassessment," Paper given at Jerusalem 1976 meeting with Vatican Commission for Religious Relations with Jews. Also, Friedrich W. Marquardt, *Die Juden und ihr Land* (Hamburg: 1975); Rolf Rendtorff, *Israel und sein Land* (Munich: 1975); John M. Oesterreicher, ed. *Brothers in Hope* (New York: Herder, 1970).

Bibliography

Books

Alfred Adam, *Antike Berichte ueber die Essener* (Berlin: 1972)

G. Allon, "Studies in the Jewish History in the Times of the Second Temple" (Heb.) (Tel Aviv: 1957)

Alexander Altmann, *Moses Mendelssohn* (Tuscaloosa: University of Alabama, 1973)

Michael Avi-Yonah, *Geschichte der Juden im Zeitalter des Talmud* (Berlin: 1962)

Leo Baeck, *This People Israel: The Meaning of Jewish Existence*, Albert H. Friedlander, trans. (Philadelphia: JPS, 1965)

Hans Urs von Balthasar, *Martin Buber and Christianity* (London: Harvill Press, 1961)

Bernard J. Bamberger, *Fallen Angels* (Philadelphia: JPS, 1952)

Salo W. Baron, *A Social and Religious History of the Jews* (New York: Columbia University Press, 1965)

Guenther Baumbach, *Jesus von Nazareth im Lichte der juedischen Gruppenbildung* (Berlin: 1977)

G. Beer, O. Holtzmann, eds., *Mischna* (Giessen and Berlin: Toepelmann, 1912)

Shalom Ben-Chorin, *Bruder Jesus* (Munich: 1967)

————, *Dialogische Theologie* (Trier: 1975)

————, *Juedischer Glaube, Strukturen einer Theologie anhand des Maimonidischen Credo* (Tuebingen: Mohr, 1975)

Haim H. Ben-Sasson, ed., *History of the Jewish People* (Cambridge: Harvard University Press, 1977)

Ludwig Berg, *Das theologische Menschenbild, Entwurf-Ethos* (Cologne: 1969)

Eliezer Berkovits, *Faith after the Holocaust* (New York: Ktav, 1973)

Otto Betz, Martin Hengel, eds., *Abraham unser Vater, Festschrift Otto Michel* (Leiden: Brill, 1963)

Elias Bickerman, *The Maccabees, An Account of their History from the Beginnings to the Fall of the House of the Hasmoneans* (New York: Schocken, 1947)

Hans Bietenhard, *Caesarea, Origenes und die Juden* (Stuttgart: 1974)

Thomas E. Bird, *Modern Theologians, Christians and Jews* (London: 1967)

Matthew Black, *An Aramaic Approach to the Gospels and Acts* (Oxford: Clarendon Press, 1946)

Philip Blackman, *Mishnayoth* (New York: Judaica, 1965)

Ludwig Blau, *Das altjuedische Zauberwesen* (Berlin: 1914)

Franz Boehm, Walter Dirks, eds., *Judentum-Schicksal, Wesen und Gegenwart* (Wiesbaden: 1965)

Pierre Bogaert, *L'Apocalypse Syriaque de Baruch* (Paris: Cerf, 1969)

S. G. F. Brandon, *Jesus and the Zealots: A Study of the Political Factor in Primitive Christianity* (Manchester: University Press, 1967)

———, *The Fall of Jerusalem and the Christian Church* (London: Allenson, 1957)

Henry W. Brann, *Schopenhauer und das Judentum* (Bonn: Bouvier, 1975)

William G. Braude, trans., *The Midrash on Psalms* (New Haven: Yale University Press, 1959)

———, *Pesikta Rabbati* (New Haven: Yale University Press, 1968)

Michael Brocke, Jakob J. Petuchowski, eds., *Das Vaterunser, Gemeinsames im Beten von Juden und Christen* (Freiburg: Herder, 1974)

Martin Buber, *Two Types of Faith* (New York: Harper & Row, 1961)

———, *Werke* (Munich: Koesel 1962–1963)

———, *On Judaism,* Nahum N. Glatzer, ed. (New York: Schocken, 1967)

———, *Briefwechsel aus sieben Jahrzehnten* (Heidelberg: Lambert Schneider, 1972–1975)

Rudolf Bultmann, *Das Urchristentum im Rahmen der antiken Religionen* (Zurich: 1963)

G. B. Caird, *Jesus and the Jewish Nation* (London: 1965)

D. R. Catchpole, *A Study in the Gospels and the Jewish Historiography from 1770 to the Present Day* (Leiden: Brill, 1971)

R. H. Charles, *The Apocrypha and Pseudepigrapha of the Old Testament* (Oxford: Oxford University Press, 1963)

A. Cody, *A History of Old Testament Priesthood* (Rome: 1969)

Hermann Cohen, *Religion of Reason out of the Sources of Judaism,* Simon Kaplan, trans. (New York: Fred. Ungar, 1972)

Helga Croner, comp., *Stepping Stones to Further Jewish-Christian Relations: An Unabridged Collection of Christian Documents* (London, New York: Stimulus Books, 1977)

Helga Croner, Leon Klenicki, eds., *Issues in the Jewish-Christian Dialogue: Jewish Perspectives on Covenant, Mission, and Witness,* A Stimulus Book (New York: Paulist Press, 1979)

Oscar Cullmann, *The Christology of the New Testament* (London: SCM, 1963)

Gustav Dalman, *The Words of Jesus* (Edinburgh: 1902)

Herbert Danby, trans. *The Mishnah* (Oxford: Oxford University Press, 1954)

David Dauber, *Collaboration with Tyranny in Rabbinic Law* (London: Oxford University Press, 1965)

Nicholas DeLange, *Origen and the Jews* (Cambridge: Cambridge University Press, 1976)

Matthias Delcor, ed., *Le Livre de Daniel* (Paris, 1971)

———, ed., *Le Testament d'Abraham* (Leiden: Brill, 1973)

Albert-Marie Dénis, *Introduction aux pseudépigraphes grecs de l'Ancien Testament* (Leiden: Brill, 1970)

Albert-Marie Dénis, Ivonne Janssens, *Concordance latine du Liber Jubilaeorum sive Parve Genesis* (Louvain: 1973)

Ferdinand Dexinger, *Henochs Zehnwochenapokalypse und offene Probleme der Apokalyptikforschung* (Leiden: Brill, 1977)

Yehuda Eben-Shmuel, *Midrashe Geulah* (Jerusalem: ²1968)

A. Roy Eckardt, *Your People, My People* (New York: Quadrangle, 1974)

Willehad P. Eckert, Ernst L. Ehrlich, eds., *Judenhass-Schuld der Christen?* (Essen: Hans Driever Vlg., 1964)

Willehad P. Eckert, Nathan Levinson, eds., *Antijudaismus im Neuen Testament?* (Munich: 1967)

———, *Juedisches Volk-Gelobtes Land* (Munich: Kaiser, 1970)

Lily Edelman, ed., *Face to Face, A Primer in Dialogue* (Washington, D.C.: Jewish Heritage, Anti-Defamation League of B'nai B'rith, 1967)

Ernst L. Ehrlich, Roland Gradwohl, eds., *Religioese Stroemungen im Judentum* (Zurich: 1973)

Ismar Elbogen, *Der juedische Gottesdienst in seiner geschichtlichen Entwicklung* (Darmstadt: 1967, reprint)

I. Epstein, ed., *The Babylonian Talmud* (London: Soncino Press, 1935–1948)

Emil L. Fackenheim, *Encounters between Judaism and Modern Philosophy* (New York: Basic Books, 1974)

———, *God's Presence in History* (New York: Harper and Row, 1972)

A. Falaturil, ed., *Drei Wege zu dem einen Gott* (Freiburg: Herder, 1976)

Edward H. Flannery, *The Anguish of the Jews* (New York: Macmillan, 1965)

Eva Fleischner, *Judaism in German Christian Theology Since 1945* (Metuchen, N.J.: Scarecrow Press, 1975)

———, ed., *Auschwitz: Beginning of a New Era?* (New York: Ktav, Cathedral Church of St. John the Divine, Anti-Defamation League of B'nai B'rith, 1977)

David Flusser, *Jesus,* Ronald Walls, trans. (New York: Herder, 1969)

———, *Judaism and Christianity* (Jerusalem: n.d.)

H. Freedman, Maurice Simon, eds., *Midrash Rabbah* (London: Soncino Press, 1961)

M. Friedman, ed., *Pesikta Rabbati* (Tel Aviv: 1962, reprint)

———, ed., *Seder Eliahu Rabba* and *Seder Eliahu Zuta (Tanna d'be Eliahu)* (Jerusalem: Wahrman, 1969, reprint)

Johannes Friedrich, Wolfgang Poehlmann, eds., *Rechtfertigung, Festschrift Ernst Kaesemann* (Tuebingen: 1976)

Vitezlav Gardavski, *God Is Not Yet Dead* (London: Penguin, 1973)

Robert R. Geis, *Gottes Minoritaet* (Munich: 1971)

Melvin J. Glatt, ed., *Avot, The Ethics of the Fathers* (New York: Burning Bush Press, 1971)

Nahum N. Glatzer, *Anfaenge des Judentums* (Guetersloh: Bertelsmann, 1966)

————, *Franz Rosenzweig, His Life and Thought* (New York: Schocken, 1953)

————, *The Judaic Tradition, texts edited and introduced* (Boston: Beacon Press, 1970)

————, ed., *Hammer on the Rock: A Midrash Reader* (New York: Schocken, 1962)

————, *Untersuchungen zur Geschichtslehre der Tannaiten* (Berlin: Schocken, 1933)

S. D. Goitein, *A Mediterranean Society: The Jewish Communities of the Arab World as Portrayed in the Documents of the Cairo Geniza* (Berkeley: 1967–1971)

Arnold M. Goldberg, *Untersuchungen ueber die Vorstellung von der Schekinah in der fruehen rabbinischen Literatur* (Berlin: 1969)

Hermann L. Goldschmidt, *Weil wir Brueder sind* (Stuttgart: Katholisches Bibelwerk, 1975)

————, *Freiheit fuer den Widerspruch* (Schaffhausen: 1976)

Hermann L. Goldschmidt, Meinrad Limbeck, eds., *Heilvoller Verrat? Judas im Neuen Testament* (Stuttgart: Katholisches Bibelwerk, 1976)

L. Goldschmidt, ed., *Sepher Yezirah* (Darmstadt: 1969, reprint)

Morris Goldstein, *Jesus in the Jewish Tradition* (New York: Macmillan, 1950)

Helmut Gollwitzer, Eleonore Sterling, eds., *Das Gespaltene Gottesvolk* (Stuttgart: 1966)

Leonhardt Goppelt, *Christentum und Judentum im ersten und zweiten Jahrhundert* (Guetersloh: Bertelsmann, 1954)

J. van Goudoever, *Biblical Calendars* (Leiden: Brill, 1961)

Hermann Greive, *Studien zum juedischen Neuplatonismus, die Religionsphilosophie des Abraham ibn Ezra* (Berlin: De Gruyter, 1973)

————, *Theologie und Ideologie, Katholizismus und Judentum in Deutschland und Oesterreich, 1918–1935* (Heidelberg: Lambert Schneider, 1969)

Hugo Gressmann, *Der Messias* (Goettingen: 1929)

P. Grimal, ed., *Hellenism and the Rise of Rome* (London: Weidenfeld & Nicholson, 1968)

Pinchas Grunewald, *Eine juedische Offenbarungslehre: Samson Raphael Hirsch* (Bern: Herbert Lang, 1977)

Antonius H. Gunneweg, *Understanding the Old Testament* (Philadelphia: Westminster Press, 1978)

Joseph Gutman, ed., *The Synagogue, Studies in Archaeology and Architecture* (New York: Ktav, 1975)

Julius Guttmann, *Philosophies of Judaism,* David W. Silverman, trans. (Garden City, N.Y.: Doubleday, 1966)

Herbert Haag, *Teufelsglaube* (Tuebingen: Katzmann, 1974)

Judah Halevi, *Book of Kuzari,* Hartwig Hirschfeld, trans. and annot. (London: M. L. Cailingold, 1931; repub. New York: Pardes, 1946)

Jean Halperin, Georges Levitte, eds., *Le Shabbat dans la conscience Juive* (Paris: 1975)

Franz von Hammerstein, ed., *Von Vorurteilen zum Verstaendnis, Dokumente zum juedisch-christlichen Dialog* (Frankfurt: 1976)

Franz von Hammerstein, Gerhart M. Riegner, eds., *Jewish-Christian Dialogue: Six Years of Christian-Jewish Consultations* (Geneva: International Jewish Committee on Interreligious Consultations, and World Council of Churches' Sub-Unit on Dialogue with the People of Living Faiths and Ideologies, 1975)

Wolf-Dieter Hauschild, *Der roemische Staat und die fruehe Kirche* (Guetersloh: 1974)

Isaak Heinemann, *Philons griechische und juedische Bildung* (Hildesheim: G. Olms, 1962, reprint)

Joseph Heinemann, *Prayer in the Talmud* (Berlin: De Gruyter, 1977)

Joseph Heinemann, Jakob J. Petuchowski, eds., *Literature of the Synagogue* (New York: Behrman House, 1975)

Isaac A. Hellwing, *Der konfessionelle Antisemitismus im 19. Jhrdt. in Oesterreich* (Vienna: Herder, 1972)

Martin Hengel, *Judaism and Hellenism* (London: SCM, 1974)

———, *Anonymitaet, Pseudepigraphie und 'literarische Faelschung' in der juedisch-hellenistischen Literatur* (Geneva: Vandeuvres, 1972)

———, *Die Zeloten* (Leiden: Brill, 1961; reprint 1976, with additions)

———, *Der Sohn Gottes, die Entstehung der Christologie und die juedisch-hellenis-tische Religionsgeschichte* (Tuebingen: Mohr, 1977)

———, ed., *Juden, Griechen und Barbaren* (Stuttgart: Katholisches Bibelwerk, 1976)

Franz Henrich, *Die geistige Gestalt des heutigen Judentums* (Munich: 1969)

Travers R. Herford, *The Pharisees* (Boston: Beacon Press, 1962)

Siegfried Herrmann, *A History of Israel in Old Testament Times* (Philadelphia: Fortress Press, 1975)

Anselm Hertz, ed., *Gottesreich und Menschenreich* (Regensburg: Pustet, 1971)

Abraham J. Heschel, *God in Search of Man* (Philadelphia: JPS, 1959)

Moses Hess, *Rome and Jerusalem,* Maurice J. Bloom, trans. (New York: Philosophical Library, 1958)

Samson Raphael Hirsch, *The Nineteen Letters of Ben Uziel* (New York: Feldheim, 1960)

H. S. Horovitz, A. Rabin, eds., *Mechilta d'Rabbi Ishmael* (Jerusalem: Bamberger & Wahrmann, 1960, reprint)

Kurt Hruby, *Die Stellung der juedischen Gesetzeslehrer zur werdenden Kirche* (Zurich: 1971)

Claire Huchet-Bishop, *How Catholics Look at Jews* (New York: Paulist Press, 1974)

S. Hurwitz, ed., *Machsor Vitry nach der Oxforder HS* (Berlin: 1889)

Jules Isaac, *Jesus and Israel,* S. Gran, trans. (New York: Holt, Rinehart & Winston, 1971)

Louis Jacobs, *A Jewish Theology* (New York: Behrman House, 1973)

————, *Principles of the Jewish Faith* (New York: Basic Books, 1964)

Enno Janssen, *Das Gottesvolk und seine Geschichte, Geschichtsbild und Selbstverstaendnis im palaestinensischen Schrifttum von Jesus Sirach bis Jehuda ha-Nasi* (Neukirchen: Neukirchener Vlg., 1971)

Joachim Jeremias, *Unknown Sayings of Jesus* (London: 1964)

Jacob Jervell, *Imago Dei* (Goettingen: 1960)

Paul Kahle, *Masoreten des Westens* (Stuttgart: 1930)

Jacob Katz, *Tradition and Crisis* (New York: Schocken, 1972)

————, *Exclusiveness and Tolerance* (New York: Schocken, 1962)

————, *Out of the Ghetto: The Social Background of Jewish Emancipation 1770–1870* (New York: Schocken, 1978)

———— ed., *The Role of Religion in Modern Jewish History* (New York: Ktav, 1975)

G. Kittel, ed., *Theological Dictionary of the New Testament* (Grand Rapids: 1964)

M. A. Knibb, ed., *The Ethiopic Book of Enoch: A New Edition in the Light of the Aramaic Dead Sea Fragments* (Oxford: Clarendon Press, 1978)

Josef Klausner, *Jesus of Nazareth* (New York: Macmillan, 1925)

————, *The Messianic Idea in Israel* (New York: Macmillan, 1955)

Charlotte Klein, *Anti-Judaism in Christian Theology,* Edward Quinn, trans. (Philadelphia: Fortress Press, 1978)

G. Klinzing, *Die Umdeutung des Kultes in der Qumrangemeinde und im Neuen Testament* (Goettingen: Vandenhoek & Ruprecht, 1971)

Arthur Koestler, *The Thirteenth Tribe* (New York: Popular Library, 1978)

S. Koleditzky, ed., *Sifra* or *Torat Kohanim* (on Leviticus) (Jerusalem: Hatchiya Press, 1960)

Hans Kueng, *On Being a Christian,* Edward Quinn, trans. (Garden City, N.Y.: Doubleday, 1976)

Hans Kueng, Pinchas Lapide, *Is Jesus a Bond or a Barrier? A Jewish-Christian Dialogue,* in Hans Kueng, *Signposts for the Future* (New York: Doubleday, 1977)

Peter Kuhn, *Gottes Selbsterniedrigung in der Theologie der Rabbinen* (Munich: 1968)

Norman Lamm, *Faith and Doubt: Studies in Traditional Jewish Thought* (New York: Ktav, 1971)

Pinchas Lapide, *Three Popes and the Jews* (New York: Hawthorn Books, 1967)

————, *Israelis, Jews and Jesus* (Garden City, N.Y.: Doubleday, 1979)

————, *Hebraeisch in den Kirchen* (Neukirchen: Neukirchener Vlg., 1975)

Jacob Z. Lauterbach, *Mekilta de'Rabbi Ishmael* (Philadelphia: JPS, 1949)

————, *Rabbinic Essays* (Cincinnati: Hebrew Union College Press, 1951)

Roger Le Déaut, ed., *Targum des Chroniques* (Roman: Analecta Biblica, 1971)

―――, *La Nuit Pascale* (Rome: 1963)

Jacob Licht, *Megillot hasserakin mimegillot midbar yehuda, serek hatterahot* (Jerusalem: 1965)

Jean Paul Lichtenberg, *From the First to the Last of the Just* (Jerusalem: 1971)

Meinrad Limbeck, *Die Ordnug des Heils, Untersuchungen zum Gesetzesverstaendnis des Fruehjudentums* (Duesseldorf: 1971)

J. Lindblom, *Die Jesaja-Apokalypse* (Lund: 1938)

Goesta Lindeskog, *Die Jesusfrage im neuzeitlichen Judentum* (Darmstadt: Wissenschaftliche Buchges., 1973, reprint)

Franklin H. Littell, *The Crucifixion of the Jews* (New York: Harper & Row, 1975)

Norbert Lohfink, *The Christian Meaning of the Old Testament* (Milwaukee: Bruce, 1969)

Ben-Zion Lurie, ed., *Megillat Ta'anit* (Jerusalem: 1964)

Michael B. McGarry, *Christology after Auschwitz* (New York: Paulist Press, 1977)

Alejandro Diez Macho, ed., *Neophyti 1, Targum Palestinense MS de la Bibliotheca Vaticana* (Madrid/Barcelona: 1968–1974)

Jonathan Magonet, *Returning: Exercises in Repentance* (London: 1975)

Johann Maier, *Jesus im Talmud* (Darmstadt: 1977)

―――, *Geschichte der juedischen Religion, von der Zeit Alexanders des Grossen bis zur Aufklaerung, mit einem Ausblick auf das 19./20. Jhrdt* (Berlin: De Gruyter, 1972)

―――, *Das Judentum, von der biblischen Zeit bis zur Moderne* (Munich: Kindler, 1977)

Johann Maier, Josef Schreiner, eds., *Literatur und Religion des Fruehjudentums* (Guetersloh: Guetersloher Vlg., 1972)

Moses Maimonides, *The Guide of the Perplexed*, Shlomo Pines, trans. (Chicago: Univ. of Chicago Press, 1962)

Hugo D. Mantel, *Society and Religion in the Second Temple Period* (Jerusalem: Masada, 1977)

M. Margalioth, ed., *Sepher Ha-Rasim* (Jerusalem: 1966)

Friedrich W. Marquardt, *Die Entdeckung des Judentums fuer die christliche Theologie, Israel im Denken Karl Barths* (Munich: Kaiser, 1967)

―――, *Die Juden und ihr Land* (Guetersloh: Guetersloher Vlg., 1978)

Moses Mendelssohn, *Jerusalem and Other Jewish Writings* (New York: Schocken, 1969)

Eduard Meyer, *Urspruenge und Anfaenge des Christentums* (Berlin: 1921)

Adrian Mikolasek, *Les Samaritains, Gardiens de la Loi contre les Prophètes* (Strasbourg, 1969, dissertation)

J. T. Milik, ed., *The Books of Enoch* (Oxford: Clarendon Press, 1976)

Juergen Moltmann, *The Experiment Hope*, M. Douglas Meeks, trans. (Philadelphia: Fortress Press, 1975)

Arthur D. Morse, *While Six Million Died* (New York: Random House, 1967)

Ulrich B. Mueller, *Messias und Menschensohn in juedischen Apokalypsen und in der Offenbarung des Johannes* (Guetersloh: Mohn, 1972)

Andre Néher, *L'Essence du Prophétisme* (Paris: 1972)

Jacob Neusner, *First Century Judaism in Crisis: Yohanan Ben Zakkai and the Renaissance of Torah* (Nashville, Tenn.: Abingdon Press, 1975)

————, ed., *Understanding Jewish Theology* (New York: Ktav, 1973)

George W. E. Nickelsburg, *Resurrection, Immortality and Eternal Life in Intertestamental Judaism* (Cambridge: Harvard University Press, 1972)

Walter Nigg, *Das ewige Reich* (Zurich: Siebenstern, 1967)

Jens H. Niggemeyer, *Beschwoerungsformeln aus dem 'Buch der Geheimnisse'* (Hildesheim: 1975)

Andreas Nissen, *Gott und der Naechste im antiken Judentum, Untersuchungen zum Doppelgebot der Liebe* (Tuebingen: Mohr, 1974)

Martin Noth, *The History of Israel* (New York: Harper & Row, 1958)

Simon Noveck, ed., *Great Jewish Personalities* (New York: Bloch, 1960)

Hugo Odeberg, ed. and trans., *3 Enoch or the Hebrew Book of Enoch* (New York: Ktav, 1973, reprint)

John M. Oesterreicher, *Racisme, Antisémitisme, Antichristianisme* (New York: Maison Francaise, 1943)

————, *Auschwitz, the Christian and the Council* (Montreal: Palm, 1965)

————, *The Rediscovery of Judaism: A Re-Examination of the Conciliar Statement on the Jews* (South Orange, N.J.: Institute of Judaeo-Christian Studies, 1971)

————, ed., *Brothers in Hope* (New York: Herder, 1970)

John M. Oesterreicher, Anne Sinai, eds., *Jerusalem* (New York: John Day, 1974)

Bernhard E. Olson, *Faith and Prejudice* (New Haven: Yale University Press, 1963)

Paul D. Opsahl, Marc Tanenbaum, eds., *Speaking of God Today: Jews and Lutherans in Conversation* (Philadelphia: Fortress Press, 1974)

Peter von der Osten-Sacken, *Gott und Belial* (Goettingen: Vandenhoeck & Ruprecht, 1969)

Aimé Pallière, *Unknown Sanctuary,* Louise Waterman Wise, trans. (New York: Bloch, 1971)

James Parkes, *Antisemitism* (London: Vallentine-Mitchell, 1969)

————, *Judaism and Christianity* (Chicago: University of Chicago Press, 1948)

————, *Prelude to Dialogue* (New York: Schocken, 1969)

————, *The Foundations of Judaism and Christianity* (London: Vallentine-Mitchell, 1960)

————, *The Conflict of the Church and the Synagogue* (Philadelphia: JPS, 1961)

Rudolf Pesch, Herbert A. Zwergl, eds., *Kontinuitaet in Jesus* (Freiburg: Herder, 1974)

Rudolf Pesch, Rudolf Schnackenburg, eds., *Jesus und der Menschensohn, Festschrift Anton Voegtle* (Freiburg: Herder, 1975)

Jakob J. Petuchowski, *Ever Since Sinai* (New York: Scribe, 1968)

————, *Contributions to the Scientific Study of Jewish Liturgy* (New York: Ktav, 1970)

————, *Understanding Jewish Prayer* (New York: Ktav, 1972)

Marc Philonenko, *Joseph et Aséneth* (Leiden: Brill, 1968)

————, *Les interpolations chrétiennes des Testaments des Douze Patriarches et les manuscrits de Qoumrain* (Paris: 1960)

Shlomo Pines, *The Jewish Christians in the Early Centuries of Christianity According to a new Source* (Jerusalem: 1966)

Leo Pinsker, *Auto-Emancipation* (Jerusalem: 1935)

J. P. M. van der Ploeg, A. S. van der Woude, eds., *Le Targum de Job de la Grotte XI de Qumran* (Leiden: Brill, 1971)

Léon Poliakov, *The History of Antisemitism,* Richard Howard, trans. (New York: Schocken, 1974)

Gerhard von Rad, *Theologie des Alten Testaments* (Munich: Kaiser, 1964)

————, *Old Testament Theology* (New York: Harper & Row, 1965)

A. Rahlfs, *Septuaginta I* (Stuttgart: 1935)

Eva G. Reichmann, *Groesse und Verhaengnis deutsch-juedischer Existenz* (Heidelberg: Lambert Schneider, 1974)

Rolf Rendtorff, *Israel und sein Land* (Munich: 1975)

K. H. Rengstorf, S. v. Kortzfleisch, eds., *Kirche und Synagogue* (Stuttgart: Klett Vlg., 1968)

Ellis Rivkin, *The Shaping of Jewish History* (New York: Scribner, 1971)

Pinchas Rosenblueth, *Martin Buber, sein Denken und Wirken* (Hannover: 1968)

Jean-Marc Rosenstiehl, ed. and trans., *L'Apocalypse d'Elie* (Paris: 1973)

Eugen Rosenstock-Huessey, Franz Rosenzweig, *Judaism Despite Christianity* (New York: Schocken, 1971)

Franz Rosenzweig, *Star of Redemption,* William Hallo, trans. (New York: Holt, Rinehart & Winston, 1971)

————, *Briefe* (Berlin: Schocken, 1935)

————, *Kleinere Schriften* (Berlin: Schocken, 1937)

H. H. Rowley, *The Relevance of Apocalyptic* (New York: Harper & Row, n.d.)

Richard L. Rubenstein, *After Auschwitz* (New York: Bobbs-Merrill, 1966)

Rosemary R. Ruether, *Faith and Fratricide* (New York: Seabury Press, 1974)

S. Safrai, M. Stern, eds., *The Jewish People in the First Century* (Assen: Van Gorcum, 1974)

A. Sammter, ed., *Mishnayot: Die sechs Ordnungen der Mischna* (Basle: Goldschmidt, 1968, reprint)

Samuel Sandmel, *The Several Israel* (New York: Ktav, 1971)

Solomon Schechter, *Studies in Judaism* (Philadelphia: JPS, 1945)

Arno Schilson, *Geschichte im Horizont der Vorsehung* (Mainz: Matthias Gruenewald, 1974)

August Schlatter, *Wie Sprach Josephus von Gott* (Guetersloh: 1930)

————, *Die Theologie des Judentums nach dem Bericht des Josephus* (Guetersloh: 1932)

Johann M. Schmidt, *Die juedische Apokalyptik* (Neukirchen: Neukirchener Vlg., 1969)

Walter Schmithals, *The Apocalyptic Movement: Introduction and Interpretation* (Nashville: Abingdon, 1975)

Joachim Schoeps, *Das Judenchristentum* (Bern: 1964)

———, *Juedisch-christliches Religionsgespraech in 19 Jahrhunderten* (Frankfurt: 1949)

———, *The Jewish-Christian Argument* (New York: Holt, Rinehart & Winston, 1963)

———, *Studien zur unbekannten Religions- und Geistesgeschichte* (Berlin: Musterschmidt, 1963)

———, *Ja, Nein, und Trotzdem* (Mainz: Hase & Koehler, 1974)

Gershom Scholem, *Major Trends in Jewish Mysticism* (Jerusalem: Schocken, 1941)

———, *On the Kabbalah and Its Symbolism* (New York: Schocken, 1965)

———, *The Messianic Idea in Judaism* (New York: Schocken, 1971)

———, *Ueber einige Grundbegriffe des Judentums* (Frankfurt: 1970)

———, *Walter Benjamin, die Geschichte einer Freundschaft* (Frankfurt: 1975)

Jacob Schoneveld, *The Bible in Israeli Education* (Assen: Gorcum, 1976)

Josef Schreiner, *Alttestamentlich-juedische Apokalyptik* (Munich: Koesel, 1969)

Kurt Schubert, *Vom Messias zum Christus* (Vienna: Herder, 1964)

———, *Die Kultur der Juden, Israel im Altertum* (Frankfurt: 1970)

———, *Jesus im Lichte der Religionsgeschichte des Judentums* (Vienna: Herold Vlg., 1973)

Emil Schuerer, *A History of the Jewish People in the Time of Jesus* (Edinburgh: Clark, 1885). Revised edition of the first volume by Geza Vermès, ed. (Edinburgh: Clark, 1973)

Christian Schuetz, *Verborgenheit Gottes, Martin Bubers Werk* (Einsiedeln: Benziger, 1975)

Moshe Schwarcz, *Jewish Thought and General Culture* (Heb.) (Tel Aviv: 1976)

Ottilie Schwarz, *Verheissung und Erfuellung* (Vienna: Herder, 1975)

Eliezer Schweid, *Judaism and the Solitary Jew* (Heb.) (Tel Aviv: 1975)

Francois Secret, *Le Zohar chez les Cabbalistes Chrétiens de la Renaissance* (Paris: 1958)

Edmund Silberner, *Moses Hess* (Leiden: Brill, 1966)

Daniel Jeremy Silver, *Maimonidean Criticism and the Maimonidean Controversy, 1180–1240* (Leiden: Brill, 1965)

Michael Sokoloff, *The Targum of Job from Qumran Cave XI* (Ramat-Gan: Bar Ilan Univ., 1974)

Alexander Sperber, ed., *The Bible in Aramaic* (Leiden: Brill, 1959–1973)

W. Speyer, *Die literarische Faelschung im heidnischen und christlichen Altertum* (Munich: 1971)

Adin Steinsaltz, ed., *The Essential Talmud* (New York: Basic Books, 1976, reprint)

Hermann L. Strack, *Introduction to the Talmud and Midrash* (Philadelphia: JPS, 1931)

————, *Jesus, die Haeretiker und die Christen* (Leipzig, 1910)

Hermann L. Strack, Paul Billerbeck, eds., *Kommentar zum Neuen Testament aus Talmud und Midrasch,* 6 vols. (Munich: Beck, 1961)

Georg Strecker, ed., *Jesus Christus in Historie und Theologie* (Tuebingen: 1975)

August Strobel, *Untersuchungen zum eschatologischen Verzoegerungsproblem auf-grund der spaetjuedisch-urchristlichen Geschichte von Habakuk 2:2f* (Leiden: Brill, 1961)

Walter Strolz, ed., *Juedische Hoffnungskraft und christlicher Glaube* (Freiburg: Herder, 1971)

Frank Ephraim Talmage, ed., *Disputation and Dialogue* (New York: Ktav, 1975)

Victor Tcherikower, *Hellenistic Civilization and the Jews* (Philadelphia: JPS, 1959)

Johannes Theisohn, *Der Auserwaehlte Richter, Untersuchungen zum traditionsge-schichtlichen Ort der Menschensohngestalt der Bilderreden des Aethiopischen Henoch* (Goettingen: 1975)

Clemens Thoma, *Auf den Truemmern des Tempels* (Vienna: Herder, 1968)

————, *Kirche aus Juden und Heiden* (Vienna: Herder, 1970)

————, ed., *Judentum und christlicher Glaube* (Klosterneuburg: Klosterneuburger Vlg., 1965)

————, ed., *Judentum und Kirche: Volk Gottes* (Zurich: 1974)

————, ed., *Zukunft in der Gegenwart,* Judaica et Christiana vol. I (Bern: Herbert Lang, 1976)

Rudolf Thomas, ed., *Petrus Abaelardus* (Stuttgart: Roehrscheid, 1970)

Joshua Trachtenberg, *The Devil and the Jews* (New Haven: Yale Univ. Press, 1943)

Renée de Tryon-Montalembert, Kurt Hruby, *La Cabbale et la Tradition Judaique* (Paris: 1974)

Benjamin Uffenheimer, *The Visions of Zechariah* (Heb.) (Jerusalem: 1961)

Ephraim Urbach, *The Sages, Their Concepts and Beliefs* (Jerusalem: Hebrew University Press, 1975)

André Vaillant, *Le Livre des Sécrets d'Henoch, Texte Slave et Traduction Francaise* (Paris: 1952)

Thomas D. Walker, *Jewish Views of Jesus* (London: Allen & Unwin, 1930)

Trude Weiss-Rosmarin, *Jewish Expressions on Jesus, an Anthology* (New York: Ktav, 1977)

Julius Wellhausen, *Prolegomena zur Geschichte Israels* (1894)

————, *Einleitung in die drei ersten Evangelien* (Berlin: 1905)

R. J. Zvi Werblowsky, *Joseph Karo, Lawyer and Mystic* (Philadelphia: Fortress Press, 1976)

Dietrich Wiederkehr, *Perspektiven der Eschatologie* (Einsiedeln: Benziger, 1974)

Max Wiener, *Juedische Religion im Zeitalter der Emanzipation* (Berlin: 1933)

Elie Wiesel, *Night* (New York: Hill & Wang, 1968)

————, *Souls on Fire* (New York: Random House, 1973)

————, *Ani Maamin* (New York: Random House, 1974)

Paul Winter, *On the Trial of Jesus* (Berlin: De Gruyter, 1961)

H. W. Wolff, ed., *Festschrift G. v. Rad* (Munich: 1971)

Yosef H. Yerushalmi, ed., *Bibliographical Essays in Medieval Jewish Studies* (New York: 1976)

Solomon Zeitlin, *Who Crucified Jesus?* (New York: Bloch, 1964)

Dieter Zeller, *Juden und Heiden in der Mission des Paulus* (Stuttgart: 1973)

Moritz Zobel, *Gottes Gesalbter, der Messias und die messianische Zeit in Talmud und Midrasch* (Berlin: 1938)

M. S. Zuckermandel, ed., *Tosefta,* with supplement by S. Lieberman (Jerusalem: Bamberger & Wahrmann, 1937)

Leopold Zunz, *Zur Geschichte und Literatur des Judentums* (New York: Olms, 1976, reprint)

Periodicals

Samuel Abraham Adler, "Aspaklaria," in *Encyclopedia of Jewish Thought* (Heb.) (Jerusalem: 1975) 459–468

Bernard Alfrink, "L'Idée de resurrection d'après Daniel 12:2.3," in *Biblica* 40 (1959) 335–371

Hans Bardtke, "Literaturbericht ueber Qumran, VI. Teil; die Kriegsrolle 1QM," in *Theologische Rundschau,* Neue Folge 37 (1972)

Shalom Ben-Chorin, "Hoffnungskraft und Glaube in Judentum und biblischer Prophetie," in *Evangelische Theologie* 33 (1973) 103–112

Eberhard Bethge, "Versuchung des Glaubens, zur Kritik des christlichen Antijudaismus," in *Freiburger Rundbrief* 28 (1976) 40–43

H. D. Betz, "Zum Problem des religionsgeschichtlichen Verstaendnisses der Apokalyptik," in *Zeitschrift fuer Theologie und Kirche* 63 (1966) 391–406

Michael Brocke, "On the Jewish Origin of the 'Improperia,'" in *Immanuel* 7 (1977) 44–51

———, "Von Juedischer Weise die Schrift auszulegen," in *Lebendiges Zeugnis* 32 (1977) 109–124

Peter Browe, "Die Judenmission im Mittelalter und die Paepste," in *Miscellanea historiae pontificiae* VI, 1973.

Norbert Brox, "Zum Problemstand in der Erforschung der altchristlichen Pseudepigraphie," in *Kairos* 15 (1973) 10–23

Haim H. Cohn, "Reflections on the Trial and Death of Jesus," in *Israel Law Review* (1967)

S. S. Cohon, "Authority in Judaism," in *Hebrew Union College Annual* 11 (1936) 595–646

Robert Daly, "The Soteriological Significance of the Sacrifice of Isaac," in *Catholic Biblical Quarterly* 39 (1977) 45–75

Nicholas De Lange, "Begriff des Antisemitismus, vorchristlicher Antisemitismus," in *Theologische Realenzyklopaedie* II, 1978

Luc Dequeker, "Der juedisch-christliche Dialog, eine Herausforderung fuer die

Theologie? Offene Fragen und Interpretationen," in *Freiburger Rundbrief* 28 (1976) 13–16

H. Desroche, "Messianismus," in *Religion in Geschichte und Gegenwart* IV, 1960

Ferdinand Dexinger, "Die Entwicklung des juedisch-christlichen Messianismus," in *Bibel und Liturgie* 47 (1974) 5–31, 239–266

Bernhard Dupuy, "What Meaning Has the Fact That Jesus Was Jewish for a Christian?" in *Concilium* (1974), new series, vol. 8, no. 10, 73–79

Alice and Roy Eckardt, "The Theological and Moral Implications of the Holocaust (II)," in *Christian Attitudes on Jews and Judaism* 52 (1977) 1–7; 53 (1977) 1–7

Rafael Edelmann, "Das Judentum," in *Handbuch der Religionsgeschichte* 1972 191–264

Ernst L. Ehrlich, "Die Evangelien in juedischer Sicht," in *Freiburger Rundbrief* 22 (1970) 61–68

Robert Everett, "Christian Theology after the Holocaust," in *Christian Attitudes on Jews and Judaism* 50 (1976) 10–12

David Flusser, "A New Sensitivity in Judaism and the Christian Message," in *Harvard Theological Review* 60 (1968) 107–127

———, Article "Messiah," in *Encyclopaedia Judaica* 11 (1971) 407–417

———, "Das juedische Martyrium im Zeitalter des Zweiten Tempels und die Christologie," in *Freiburger Rundbrief* 25 (1973)

———, "In memoriam Samuel Hugo Bergmann," in *Freiburger Rundbrief* 27 (1975) 3

———, "To What Extent Is Jesus a Question for the Jews?" in *Concilium* (1974), new series, vol. 8, no. 10, 68–73

M. Freimann, "Die Wortfuehrer des Judentums in den aeltesten Kontroversen zwischen Juden und Christen," in *Monatsschrift fuer Geschichte und Wissenschaft des Judentums* 56 (1912) 49–64

Hartmut Gese, "Anfang und Ende der Apokalyptik, dargestellt am Sacharjabuch," in *Zeitschrift fuer Theologie und Kirche* 70 (1973) 20–49

Abraham Geiger, "Erbsuende und Versoehnungstod," in *Juedische Zeitschrift f. Wissenschaft und Leben* 10 (1872) 166–171

Nahum N. Glatzer, "The Attitude to Rome in the Amoraic Period," in *Proceedings of the Sixth World Congress of Jewish Studies* (Jerusalem: 1975)

Heinrich Graetz, "The Significance of Judaism for the Present and Future," in *Jewish Quarterly Review* 1 (1889)

Hermann Greive, "Die maimonidische Kontroverse und die Auseinandersetzungen in der lateinischen Scholastik," in *Miscellanea Medievalia* 10 (1976) 170–180

———, "On Jewish Self-Identification, Religion and Political Orientation," in *Leo Baeck Institute Annual* (1975) 35–46

John J. Guenther, "The Epistle of Barnabas and the Final Rebuilding of the Temple," in *Journal of the Study of Judaism in the Persian, Hellenistic and Roman Period* 7 (1977) 143–151

Herbert Haag, "Vom alten zum neuen Pascha," in *Stuttgarter Bibelstudien* (1971) 114–117

Isaak Heinemann, "Wer veranlasste den Glaubenszwang der Makkabaeer," in *Monatszeitschrift fuer Geschichte und Wissenschaft des Judentums* 82 (1938) 145–172

Martin Hengel, "Zwischen Jesus und Paulus, die 'Hellenisten,' die 'Sieben' und Stephanus (Acts 6:1–16, 7:54–8:3)," in *Zeitschrift fuer Theologie und Kirche* 72 (1975) 151–206

Hans Hermann Henrix, "Oekumenische Theologie und Judentum; zur Nichtexistenz, Notwendigkeit und Zukunft eines Dialogs," in *Freiburger Rundbrief* 28 (1976) 16–27

Heinrich Herrfahrdt, Paul Reinhardt, "Judenfeindschaft," in *Evangelisches Staatslexikon* (1975), 1062–1067

Walter Holsten, "Antisemitismus," in *Religion in Geschichte und Gegenwart* 1957, 456–459

Kurt Hruby, "Die Messiaserwartung in der talmudischen Zeit, mit besondrer Beruecksichtigung des leidenden Messias," in *Judaica* 20 (1964) 6–22

M. de Jonge, "The Use of the Word 'Anointed' in the Time of Jesus," in *Novum Testamentum* 8 (1966) 132–148

Klaus Koch, "Messias und Suendenvergebung in Jes 53-Targum, ein Beitrag zu der Praxis der aramaeischen Bibeluebersetzung," in *Journal of the Study of Judaism in the Persian, Hellenistic and Roman Period* (1972), 117–148

Heinrich Kraft, "Die Offenbarung des Johannes," in *Handbuch zum Neuen Testament* (1974)

Pinchas E. Lapide, "Hebraeisch im Evangelium," in *Judaica* 33 (1977) 7–29

Fritzleo Lentzen-Deis, "Die Taufe Jesu nach den Synoptikern," in *Frankfurter Theologische Studien* (1970)

Ulrich Luck, "Das Weltverstaendnis in der juedischen Apokalyptik, dargestellt am aethiopischen Henoch und am 4. Esra," in *Zeitschrift fuer Theologie und Kirche* 73 (1976) 283–305

Johann Maier, "Jude und Judentum-Bezeichnungen und Selbstbezeichnungen im Wandel der Zeiten," in *Lebendiges Zeugnis* 32 (1977) 52–63

———, "Serienbildung und 'numinoser' Eindruckseffect in den poetischen Stuecken der Hekhalot-Literatur," in *Semitics* 3 (1973) 36–66

———, "Twisting Paths of Reception: On Modern Jewish Research about Jesus," in *Herder Correspondence* 30 (1976) 313–319

———, "Bedeutung und Erforschung der Kairoer Geniza," in *Jahrbuch fuer Antike und Christentum* 13 (1970) 48–61

Peter Maser, "Luthers Schriftauslegung in dem Traktat 'Von den Juden und ihren Luegen,' ein Beitrag zum 'christologischen Antisemitismus' des Reformators," in *Judaica* 29 (1973) 71–82

R. Meyer, "Tradition und Neuschoepfung im antiken Judentum dargestellt an der Geschichte des Pharisaismus," in *Saechsische Akademie der Wissenschaften* 110 (1965)

Charles Moeller, "Zum 10. Jahrestag von 'Nostra Aetate' no. 4,' " in *Freiburger Rundbrief* 28 (1976) 12

Franz Mussner, "Christliche Identitaet in der Sicht des Neuen Testaments," in *Internationale katholische Zeitschrift* 5 (1976) 421–430

————, "Ganz Israel wird gerettet werden (Rom 11:26)," in *Kairos* 18 (1976) 241–255

————, "Theologische Wiedergutmachung am Beispiel der Auslegung des Galaterbriefes," in *Freiburger Rundbrief* 26 (1974) 7–11

Jakob J. Petuchowski, "Anglikaner und Juden, Leitlinien fuer die Zukunft," in *Freiburger Rundbrief* 27 (1975) 17–20

Kurt Rudolph, "Das Problem einer Entwicklung in der Religionsgeschichte," in *Kairos* 13 (1971) 95–118

Rosemary R. Ruether, "The Future of Christian Theology about Judaism," in *Christian Attitudes on Jews and Judaism* 49 (1976) 1–5

Peter Schaefer, "Zur Geschichtsauffassung des rabbinischen Judentums," in *Journal for the Study of Judaism* 6 (1975) 167–188

————, "Die sogenannte Synode von Jabne, zur Trennung von Juden und Christen im 1.–2. Jh. n. Chr.," *Judaica* 31 (1975) 54–64, 116–124

Solomon Schechter, "The Palestinian Recension of the Heretics Blessing," in *Jewish Quarterly Review* 10 (1889) 654–659

Rolf-Peter Schmidt, "Abraham im Judentum," in *Theologische Realenzyklopaedie* 382–385

H. Schoenweiss, "Gebet," in *Begriffslexikon zum Neuen Testament* 427

Joachim Schoeps, "Die Tempelzerstoerung des Jahres 70 in der juedischen Religionsgeschichte, Ursachen, Folgen, Ueberwindung," in *Coniectanaea Neotestamentica* 6 (1942) 1–15

Gershom Scholem, "Walter Benjamin," in *Leo Baeck Institute Annual* (1965) 117–136

Kurt Schubert, "Das Judentum in der Umwelt des christlichen Mittelalters," in *Kairos* 17 (1975) 161–217

————, "Die juedischen Religionsparteien im Zeitalter Jesu," in *Stuttgarter Bibelstudien* 43 (1970)

Ursula Schubert, "Spaetantikes Judentum und fruehchristliche Kunst," in *Studia Judaica Austriaca* 1974

Morton Smith, "Zealots and Sicarii, Their Origins and Relations," in *Harvard Theological Review* 64 (1971) 1–19

Ethelbert Stauffer, "Wie die christliche Kirche entstand," in *Christ und Welt* 17 (1964)

Guenter Stemberg, "Die sogen. Synode von Jabne und das fruehe Christentum," in *Kairos* 19 (1977) 14–21

Carroll Stuhlmueller, "Apocalyptic," in *Jerome Biblical Commentary* 20:21–24

Josef Sudbrach, "Spirituality," in *Encyclopedia of Theology* 1623–1639

Uriel Tal, "Strukturen der Gemeinschaft und des Gemeinwesens im Judentum," in *Freiburger Rundbrief* 26 (1974) 45–49

————, "Structures of Fellowship and Community in Judaism," in *Conservative Judaism* 28 (1974) 3–12

Shemaryahu Talmon, "Interfaith Dialogue in Israel, Retrospect and Prospect," in *Immanuel,* Special Supplement, 1973, 9–20

Clemens Thoma, "Auswirkungen des juedischen Krieges gegen Rom auf das rabbinische Judentum," in *Biblische Zeitschrift* 12 (1968) 30–54, 186–210

————, "Das Amt im Judentum," in *Theologische Realenzyklopaedie* II, 504–509

————, "Das Neue Testament und die Juden—Aufgabe einer aktualisierenden Pastoral," in *Bibel und Liturgie* 48 (1975) 213–222

————, "Glaubenspraxis aus Erfahrung," in *Lebendiges Zeugnis* 32 (1977) 98–108

————, "Judentum und Hellenismus im Zeitalter Jesu," in *Bibel und Leben* 11 (1970) 151–159

————, "Le Lien entre peuple, terre et religion dans l'Ancien et le Nouveau Testament," in SIDIC 2 (1975) 4–16

————, "Religionsgeschichtliche und theologische Bedeutsamkeit der juedischen Hohenpriester von 175–37 v. Chr.," in *Bibel und Liturgie* 45 (1972) 4–22

————, "Spaetjudentum," in *Encyclopedia of Theology*

Hans O. Tiefel, "Holocaust Interpretations and Religious Assumptions," in *Judaism* 25 (1976) 135–149

J. Vanderkam, "The Theophany of Enoch I:3b–7:9," in *Vetus Testamentum* 23 (1973) 129–150

Manfred Vogel, "Some Reflections on the Jewish-Christian Dialogue in the Light of the Six Day War," *Annals of the American Academy of Political and Social Science* 387 (1970) 96–108

Hedwig Wahle, "Die christlich-juedische Zusammenarbeit in Europa," in *Lebendiges Zeugnis* 32 (1977) 30–43

R. J. Zvi Werblowski, "Judaism," in *History of Religions* II, 1–48

————, "Tora als Gnade," in *Kairos* 15 (1973) 156–173

Fritz Werner, "Das Judentumsbild der Spaetjudentumsforschumg im Dritten Reich," in *Kairos* 13 (1971) 161–194

Wolfgang Wiefel, "Paulus in juedischer Sicht," in *Judaica* 31 (1975) 109–115

A. G. Wright, "The Literary Genre Midrash," in *Catholic Biblical Quarterly* 28 (1966) 105–138, 417–457

Michael Wyschogrod, "Warum war und ist Karl Barths Theologie fuer einen juedischen Theologen von Interesse?" in *Evangelische Theologie* 34 (1974) 222–236

STIMULUS BOOKS are developed by Stimulus Foundation, a not-for-profit organization, and are published by Paulist Press. The Foundation wishes to further the publication of scholarly books on Jewish and Christian topics that are of importance to Judaism and Christianity.

Stimulus Foundation was established by an erstwhile refugee from Nazi Germany who intends to contribute with these publications to the improvement of communication between Jews and Christians.

Books for publication in this Series will be selected by a committee of the Foundation, and offers of manuscripts and works in progress should be addressed to:

Stimulus Foundation
785 West End Ave.
New York, N.Y. 10025